The Bird

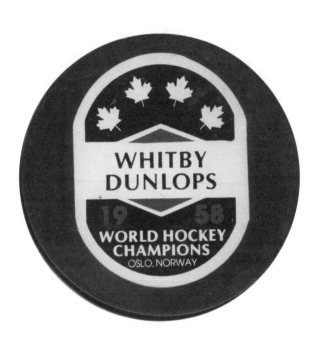

The Bird

The Life and Times of
Hockey Legend Wren Blair

by WREN BLAIR

with Ron Brown *and* Jill Blair

QUARRY
HERITAGE
BOOKS

This book is dedicated to my wife Elma, who encouraged me to throw my hat in the ring to go into hockey full time many years ago.

The publisher acknowledges the support of the Government of Canada, Department of Canadian Heritage, Book Publishing Industry Development Program.

ISBN 1-55082-294-2

Edited by Bob Hilderley
Design by Laura Brady

Printed in Canada

Published by Quarry Press Inc.
290 North Queen Street
Etobicoke, Ontario M9C 5K4

Contents

Preface

TO PERFORM WITH SUCCESS IN any environment for 50 years is considered a major achievement. To accomplish it in hockey is almost a miracle.

Wren Blair, known as "The Bird" in hockey circles, has spent 50 fruitful years in the sport he loves. He has coached, managed, and owned hockey teams in various leagues in North America. His name is linked with success in junior, senior, and professional loops. He has held executive positions with many hockey organizations and his involvement in the game has extended around the world.

With 50 years of stories to tell, it's a wonder that it took this long for someone to convince The Bird to put them down on paper. Wren writes from the bottom of his heart. His stories are neither manufactured nor manicured. He tells it like it was. He tells many fascinating anecdotes that any hockey aficionado will love to discover. Readers will be privy to stories concerning such hockey legends as Bobby Orr (who Wren signed to the Boston Bruins organization), Harry Sinden, Gump Worsley, and Bill Goldsworthy, among the more than 1100 players who have skated for Wren's teams over the years. All of these tales are told from the prospective of a dedicated and astute hockey man, with a ribald sense of humor.

There is, however, one story that does not appear within the pages of this book, an event I witnessed years ago. The year was 1960. The place: the Olympic Arena in Squaw Valley, California. The event: the gold medal game between Canada and the United States. The Bird had been appointed by the Canadian Amateur

Hockey Association as a consultant to Canada's team, the Kitchener-Waterloo Dutchmen, based on his success in winning the World Championship in 1958 with his famous Whitby Dunlop team.

The Bird watched in anguish as U.S. goalie Jack McCartan played the game of his life and the Americans stole a 2-1 victory to win the gold medal. When the horn sounded to end the game, I looked over to where Wren had been sitting. Now he was standing, with his back to the ice, smashing his camera against the boards.

I enjoyed reading the story of the life and times of this impassioned hockey legend and I'm sure all hockey fans will do so as well.

George Gross
Corporate Sports Editor,
The Toronto Sun

Introduction

Boisterous!
Highly excitable!
Stern, but fair!
Those adjectives aptly describe "The Bird."

MY FIRST MEETING WITH W.A. (Wren) Blair, alias "The Bird" — the supreme commander of the Kingston Frontenacs, as we used to call him — came in September of 1962. I had just resigned as the Sports Editor of the *Woodstock Sentinel-Review* to take a job as a sports writer with the *Kingston Whig-Standard*. During that winter, I covered a majority of the Kingston Frontenac games, an area in which I worked closely with Blair.

It was, to say the least, an enlightening experience. It was refreshing to find someone so intent on winning in minor professional hockey. He approached every game as a war and demanded the most out of every single player on his team. When the Boston Bruins sent players to Kingston for 'seasoning', as they did periodically throughout the season, Blair's standard line to the media in post-game sessions in his office was, "Another damn National Leaguer I have to straighten out." And on almost every occasion he did straighten them out, he did make them better players.

Ed Westfall, Pat "Whitey" Stapleton, Wayne Connelly, and goaltender Bruce Gamble were four of the players off that 1962-63 team who came down from the big time to play under Blair's excruciating glares. All of them finished the season in Kingston and went on to extensive National League careers, never again to play in the minors.

I can remember early in the season when he told Bruce Gamble that he was too fat, benched him, and ordered him to lose 20 pounds. Gamble's reply: "The extra weight keeps me warm." Blair eventually rescinded his 20-pound ultimatum when Gamble pared 10 pounds off his frame, and he starred the rest of the way.

"The Bird" also had a penchant for fining players, for mediocre performances, but, in the final analysis, always found a way to "repay" the fines to them.

I can recall one Saturday night at the Kingston Memorial Centre, when the Frontenacs lost 5-0 to the Hull-Ottawa Canadiens. Before the game ended, Blair, in disgust, had stormed off the Kingston bench and left the arena. When the players trudged into the dressing room after the defeat, they were greeted with a sign on the dressing room's chalkboard: "You call yourselves hockey players, that effort just cost you all $50."

The next afternoon, the team was back in Hull for a return match with the Canadiens. Blair refused to make the trip and turned the team over to assistant coach Harry Sinden. Even though Blair wasn't in attendance, his seething remarks from the night before were evident as the Frontenacs rallied for a win.

The Frontenacs played an interlocking schedule with the International Hockey League that year (home-and-away games) as there were four teams left in the EPHL – Kingston, Hull-Ottawa, Sudbury and St. Louis, which had moved to Missouri after starting the season in Syracuse.

The Frontenacs finished the season in first place in the regular season and gained a bye into the league final. Sudbury ended up eliminating Hull-Ottawa in the league semi-final, but was no match for the Frontenacs in the best-of-seven final. Kingston was in complete command in winning in five games, thus giving Blair another league championship and the first-ever professional title for the City of Kingston.

Although the Frontenacs left Kingston the following year for Minneapolis, and the formation of the Central Hockey League, my ties with Blair have never been broken. As I continued my newspaper career, I met him on various occasions over the next 25 years and finally the circuit came full cycle again when he returned to Kingston in the 1989-90 season as one of three new owners of the Kingston Frontenacs of the Ontario Hockey League.

My association with Wren Blair came full cycle in 1994. When I first met the colorful "Bird" in September 1962, the furthest thing from my mind was the fact that one day I would end up working for him. I left *The Whig-Standard* in July of 1994 after a 35-year newspaper career. A month later Wren left a message on my answering machine. It was simple and to the point: "Brownie, it's Wren, we're having a press conference at the Hockey Hall of Fame tonight and I'd like you to attend. I want to talk to you."

The press conference was to announce the signing of Gary Agnew as the new General Manager-Coach of the Kingston Frontenacs, a team Blair, Bob Attersley, and Don Anderson had saved from leaving the Limestone City four years earlier. The press conference ended and we adjourned to the back room of the Hall of Fame for a few drinks and a rehash of days gone by. An invitation followed to join Bob, Wren, and Agnew for breakfast the next morning at the LaSalle Motel.

And then the bomb dropped. It turned out that Shannon Homer, the marketing director of the Frontenacs, was resigning and right out of the blue Blair offered me the position on a part-time basis. Two weeks later, it was a full-time position. After more than three decades of writing about hockey, I was now going to sell it.

Over the next five years, we had our share of arguments, but in the final analysis I found Blair to be the same person I had first met some 30-odd years before . . . tough, but fair.

Even though he was approaching his 70th birthday, he still had that burning desire to win. I can still see him climbing the glass at the west end of the Kingston Memorial Centre during the final regular-season game of the 1994-95 season. He was on the ledge, pounding the glass and screaming at the referee over a non-penalty call on the Oshawa Generals Larry Courville, who had slashed David Ling, the Frontenacs' leading scorer, breaking his thumb, three minutes into the first period. During this tirade, Bob Kilger, the MP for Dundas-Stormont and father of Chad Kilger, came out of the stands and said: "Wren, come on, settle down, you're going to have a heart attack." "To hell, I am," said Blair, "but I am going to give him (the referee) one."

When the period ended, Blair disappeared. I proceeded to walk around the rink, and as I was heading for the media/scouts room, I came across Blair with a Kingston policeman. The officer had "The Bird" pinned against the wall. Blair had attempted to enter the referee's room to further voice his displeasure. The police officer didn't know who Blair was, but when he finally found out he released him.

I saw him during the next period and said, "You escaped, eh?"

"What the hell, do you mean, I escaped?"

"I saw that police officer had you against the wall outside the referee's room."

"You saw that, he hollered. Why didn't you help me out?'

" I figured it was none of my business. You got yourself into that jam, so you'd have to get out of it." He was livid at that time, but since then we've laughed about it over the years.

My association with Wren Blair was a true hockey education. His ideas on marketing were just as sharp as his wit, and during my tenure with him, we had more sellouts than half-empty buildings.

He was not only concerned with the product on the ice, but also with the reputation of the team off the ice and in the community. We talked daily, not only in the hockey season, but even more so, in the off-season. Season-ticket holders were of the utmost concern to him. Season-ticket holders are the lifeblood of the team, he'd say. Without them, we're dead in the water. In his early years in Kingston, he started the annual season-ticket holders' barbecue, where the fans had a chance to mingle with the players on the day prior to the opening of training camp. Each and every season-ticket holder was treated to a hot dog, hamburger, and coke as a gesture for their support of the hockey club. He also insisted that we look after the team's advertisers by setting aside two games a year where every single advertiser was given two complimentary tickets to a league game. I found him to be first and foremost a hockey man, but at the same time, a businessman, who looks after his clients both on and off the ice.

On draft day, the day when teams select their players for the years to come, he was always front and center. It didn't matter to him if a player indicated that he didn't want to play in Kingston, he would take him anyway. Over the years, players such as Chad Kilger, Brett Lindros, Curtis Cruickshank, and Mike Zigomanis, to name a few, had all indicated that they would not report to Kingston if they were drafted. And yet, on every occasion, Blair, the salesman, had them all signed and in a Kingston uniform when training camp opened.

I can recall, vividly, the day he drafted Zigomanis. "Ziggy" is from the Toronto area and had a strong desire to stay in Toronto for his junior career. Belleville Bulls drafted right ahead of Kingston that year and they had approached the Zigomanis family before making their selection in the second round. They wanted to know if he would report to Belleville if the Bulls drafted him. The answer was an emphatic no. With the next pick, Blair claimed him.

The Bulls were baffled. He wouldn't come to Belleville and Kingston is 50 miles further east. A month later, Zigomanis signed. "The Bird" had struck once again.

And today, just as he was in 1962-63, when we first met, Wren Blair is still boisterous, yet fair, highly excitable, and still striving for perfection from everyone he touches.

Ron Brown
Former Sports Editor,
Kingston Whig-Standard

First Impressions

I STOOD STARING OUT THE window of my suite in the Viking hotel overlooking the taxi circle below in Oslo, Norway. It was late Saturday night, March 8, 1958; the snow was drifting down softly. Tomorrow my great hockey team, the Whitby Dunlops, would skate out onto the ice against the mighty Soviet Union, to decide the 1958 World Hockey Championship. We were undefeated heading into this crucial game, while the Soviets had been tied in an earlier round-robin match by Czechoslovakia. I couldn't help but feel nervous. The world championship! A single game! Everything on the line for 60 minutes! What if Canada lost for the second straight time? I didn't want to think about that.

Neither Canada nor the United States had competed in the 1957 championships in protest of the uprisings in Hungary. When Canada last played in 1956 at the Olympics in Cortina, Italy, we had been represented by the Kitchener-Waterloo Dutchmen, who had lost in the final to the Soviet Union. Tomorrow we would face off at 7 p.m. in our attempt to win back the crown.

King Oluv of Norway had been in attendance for the entire series, which was played in a stadium built by the great Sonja Henie, the women's Olympic figure skating champion in 1936, who later became a movie star. We had breezed through our first eight games of this tournament, winning by such scores as 8-3 over the United States, 10-2 over Sweden, 12-0 over Norway. We had a powerful team, but we sensed in every game we played and every practice we had that the Soviets were watching us — just as we were watching them. We knew that we were in for a helluva battle. It was not going to be easy. In those days, the Soviet Union molded players from right across its vast empire into a mighty all-star team.

As I looked forward to tomorrow, I began to think back to where all this had all started. Ten months ago, in May 1957, I had traveled to Edmonton, Alberta, armed with a 16-page brief arguing why I thought the CAHA should select our Whitby Dunlops to represent Canada at the World Championship in Oslo. We were a unanimous selection. I began to wonder in amazement how a kid like me from the streets of Oshawa was now leading Canada's national team. It was a bit overwhelming. I was only 33 years of age.

As I stood there watching the snow come down, my mind began to drift back . . . back to the beginning, where I was born, the neighborhood I was raised in, my school days, the kids I chummed around with, the hockey players I had coached . . .

Basic Training for a Hockey Career

1

I WAS BORN IN LINDSAY, ONTARIO, on October 2, 1925. My parents, Alvin and Audrey, were both raised in the Haliburton area and had married in 1918 when my father was 20 and my mother was just 16. In 1924, they had asked my father's Uncle Tom, who owned a dairy in Lindsay, to let them know if a small dairy ever became available because they were interested in purchasing one. Later that year, Uncle Tom found a one-route dairy for sale in Lindsay called Model Dairy. Mom and Dad purchased the company and moved 60 miles south to the city, which in those days was tantamount to leaving the entire country, forever. It must have taken a lot of courage for my parents to pull up stakes and make the move. I was born in 1925, a year after they moved to Lindsay, their second child. My sister Merle was born earlier in Haliburton.

I believe the next three years really took their toll on my parents because in 1927 they put the dairy up for sale. My dad had to get up around three every morning, go to the area farmers and pick up their milk, bring it back to the house (dairy), where in the basement they had a pasteurizing machine to separate the milk, pasteurize it, bottle and cap it. After that was done, my father would leave the house and head out for his milk route to peddle the milk, not returning home until three in the afternoon. The ritual would then start all over again. He had to go to bed by seven or eight every night in order to get seven hours sleep.

This daily grind became back-breaking for mother, too, because she worked side-by-side with my father, as well as keeping a house, preparing meals and caring for me and my sister. Then Dad finally sold the dairy and the family moved south to Oshawa, where my Dad secured a job with Beaton's Dairy. He worked there for the rest of his life.

With help from some of the neighbors, my parents built a new home at 414 Park Road South during 1927 and early 1928. We lived in an area called College Hill where almost every boy and many of the girls played hockey. If you were to live respectably as a child on College Hill, you had to be a hockey player. We also played a great deal of soccer in the summer months. Many of the College Hill families had recently arrived in Canada from England, Ireland or Scotland and most of the fathers had played soccer. In fact, when we got older we used to have father and son games up on the hill.

I attended Westmount Public School in my elementary school years. We had our own outdoor rink at the school, and as soon as it got cold enough in late November we made ice and it lasted until the thaw in March. We used to help the teachers flood the rink with hot and cold water every other day. The girls had a hockey team back then. We also played a great deal of soccer at Westmount and had bitter rivalries with Centre Street School, Ritson Road South School, Simcoe Street South School, Simcoe Street North, and Harmony School.

I was a very good student —I was nearly always first or second in the standings — and I competed very hard against Melba Dodd, who was also a very good student. I used to hate it if she finished ahead of me in the exams because she would always rub my nose in it. But I can remember one year when I came eighth in my class standings on the first set of exams. My mother went nuts. God, there were 40 kids in the class! On the next two sets of exams I finished first, then first again.

Although these were the Depression years and we may have

lacked money, we never had a lack of friends. Everyone stuck together. We entertained ourselves playing sports, playing cards, and socializing in the neighborhood. Many of my friends then are still my friends now, such as Don Trotter, Sid Dixon, Big John Hurst, Little John Hurst, and Bill Hurst. Their sisters were my friends, too — Marg and Barbara Trotter, Vera Dixon, Margaret Hurst, Peggy and Irene Hurst. The Dodd family lived next door, and I was very close to Melba and Lola. The older boys in the Dodd family were Orval, Willard, and Gord , who later became one of my sponsors of the first hockey team I ever organized. Later in life, he became owner of a used car lot named Dodd Motor Sales. I was also a friend to Grant Dodd, who was six years younger than I was. Among other College Hill friends were "Beans" Smith, his sister Helen Smith, and his older brother "Scrooge" Smith, and Scotty Myles, a cousin of Gordie Myles, When I organized my first team, a juvenile softball team, many from this group played for me.

Gordie Myles also played for me on the Whitby Dunlops team. I practically raised him as a hockey player on Warnes' Pond before he played bantam and midget all-star hockey. I can still remember when we used to hitch-hike to Toronto to watch the Oshawa Generals play the Marlies and St. Mike's in Maple Leaf Gardens on Saturday afternoons.

I said to Gordie one day, "It won't be long before you're down there playing with the Generals."

"I'll never make the Generals," he shot back.

"Oh yes, you will." And two years later, at age 16, Gord Myles did make the Generals. He was later traded to Stratford and played for the Kroehlers, then moved on the next year to St. Catharines where he became a big star with the Teepees back in the days when Rex Stymers broadcast the games on radio and we could pick them up in Oshawa.

After my graduation from Westmount, I went on to OCVI

(Oshawa Collegiate and Vocational Institute) for two years, but I became very restless because of the war. In those days kids were quitting school and getting good jobs because of the war. I quit school when I was 16. My dad was very upset with me. "If you quit school, you are not going to lay around home," he declared. "You are going to get a job. Nobody in my family is going to lay around the house." The next week he found me a job at Beaton's Dairy. At 16 I had my own milk route. I was responsible for all the money on the route and I had to cash in to the exact cent every day. If you were short when you cashed in, you had to make up the difference yourself. You had to make your own change and I was seldom short, even though most of the time you were making change in the dark. I had to leave the dairy at around six in the morning, even in winter. The money and milk tickets were placed in the bottles that I picked up on the route, and in the winter they were usually frozen at the bottom of the bottle. We had little gas heaters in our wagons to thaw out the bottles in order to get the money out.

I worked at the dairy until I was about "17 $^{1}/_{2}$" – I had made up my mind that I was going to join the army. You could enlist at 17. My parents were adamant that I was not going to join, but I told them that if I didn't have their blessing, then I would simply run away from home. I had to get written permission from them in order to join. Finally, my mother persuaded my father to let me go. I think she was probably happy to get rid of me because I was a very opinionated, strong-willed kid. My father called my Uncle Bert in Haliburton to come down and take over the milk route from me. I had to give two weeks notice at the dairy, and during those two weeks Uncle Bert came with me on the route. After three or four days, he said to me, "Wren, I'm going back home. I'll never learn this route the way you do it. You know every call, whether they take a quart of homo or plain or whipping cream on Thursdays or eggs and butter on the weekend." Gradually, as we moved into the second week, he started to get the hang of it, and by the end of the week, he was ready to take it over.

On January 13, 1943, I traveled to Toronto and joined the Canadian army. I was about three months past my 17th birthday. I can still remember my medical. You had to get undressed, stand in a lineup totally naked, get your shots. . .and then get weighed. When I got on the scale, there was a guy with a clipboard taking down the weights. When I got on the scale, the guy running the scale looked at the weight and yelled over to his buddy with the clipboard, "Hey, Joe, the war'll be over soon now ... 117 pounds." I told the guy, "Go to hell, you smart ass." But that's how much I weighed in 1943 when I joined up.

I was stationed in Toronto at the Canadian National Exhibition Grounds for several months before being sent to Simcoe, Ontario for basic training at No. 25 Basic Training Centre. I was the youngest guy in the hut — and, of course, they soon began calling me "kid." "Crippy" Hoffman and his friend kept at the guys to get off my back. They soon became good friends of mine.

Shooting craps was a popular game back then, though we weren't allowed to gamble in the barracks at all or you could be charged for it. One day we were playing in the abolition room (the washroom), which connected two huts together, when a one-hook wonder walked into the room, a Lance-Corporal, and put all five of us on charge for gambling in the barracks. We were coming up for a 72-hour pass on the 24th of May holiday weekend when the charges were laid. We had to go before the Colonel the next day, and he confined us to barracks for the next four days, which meant our 72-hour pass was wiped out. I was devastated. I had plans to go to Oshawa for the weekend. I had several young girl friends I had planned to meet at a dance at the Avalon. The next day – Friday at noon – the whole camp emptied for the weekend except for the five of us. We had nothing to do except report to the guardhouse every hour and register in with the Regimental Police at the guardhouse. We did this all day Friday. The next day was a beautiful day, and I said, to hell with this, I'm getting out of here. I had no idea the severity of going over the wall when you were confined to barracks. I found out later, I could have been court martialed. I told the guys I was leaving and they said I had to be nuts. I went out over the back of the camp, through the rifle range . . . jumped the fence . . . got onto the highway and hitch-hiked home. I had lots of fun at the dances.

When I came back to the camp on Monday, all the guys were streaming through the gate. I went right along with them, but when I hit the gates, two big burly Regimental Police grabbed me and my feet never touched the ground until I landed in a cell in the guardhouse. I stayed in the guardhouse overnight and the next morning I had to go before the Colonel. They paraded me in and read off these charges, which had devastating sounds to them. "This is Private Blair, Regimental number B-138572 and he is charged with the following ..." Then they rattled off these charges, which must have taken five minutes.

I'll always remember the way the Colonel looked at me before he said, "How old are you Blair?"

I answered, "17, Sir."

"I think this might be a good time in life for you to learn a lesson. I am sentencing you to 28 days detention in the Canadian Army Detention Centre in Brampton, Ontario."

I'd heard about this place — it was called the "glass house" — the worst thing in history was to go to the glass house. My stomach turned right upside down. I couldn't believe it. I was a good kid, what were they doing? They immediately took me to an old-fashioned station wagon with no windows at the back, and two Lance Corporals drove me to Brampton. They got me out into a big vestibule area. I had no idea where this building was, but it must have been an office building at one time.

I stood there for a moment and looked around when all of sudden this big regimental guy appeared and yelled, "Turn your face to the wall, stupid!"

As the guys who had brought me there left, I said to the guy, "What are you talking about?"

"You turn to the wall right now and don't give me any lip or I'll hit you on the side of the head so hard you won't know what hit you."

There's an old saying that you'll never break the army, they'll break you. How true! I gave it a little bit of a run for a while but they won. I waited there with my face against the wall, and then they took me downstairs. The first thing they said was "strip" and I had to go through another medical. Then they plopped me in a barber's chair. Now I had already gone through the original "fritz" army haircut a few months earlier, and my hair was just starting to grow back in. I had beautiful wavy hair and it was just starting to get back to normal. They took the clippers and just shaved me bald. The hair fell on the floor. I couldn't believe it. They pulled me out of the chair and put some dungarees on me, the standard dress for prisoners in the glass house, and marched me down to a cell block.

My cell number was C22 in C Block. There was only a little small peep hole to see out of through a solid wooden door. The cell doors were all controlled by a single control at the end of the block. After they shoved me in there, I never saw or heard another person for the rest of the day. At dinner time, they brought me rice, a piece of cheese, and a couple of pieces of stale bread – no butter. The bunk was a piece of wood, no mattress, no pillow, only an army blanket to put down on the wood and one to cover yourself. That's where you stayed. There was nothing to read there, except the Bible. I read the Bible from cover to cover, noting the sexy parts. I was only 17 . . .

The next morning I woke up a 6 a.m. as the other inmates were running down to the abolition room. I couldn't figure out why everybody was hurrying. Pretty soon everyone was gone and I had just barely gotten my shaving cream on. Then a guard came in and said, "Let's go."

"Don't be stupid, I just got my shaving cream on." With some help from another guard, he dragged me down the hall again and they threw me into my cell. I didn't even get a chance to get the shaving cream off, let alone shave. I went to say something just as this big blond guy, who was really mean, stepped into my cell. I said, "Hey you can't come in here." He shut the door behind him.

"Listen you little jerk, you shut your mouth. If you ever say another word again to me I'm going to beat you to a pulp . . . and I would kind of love to do that to you." I was scared now. He continued to glare at me and then left.

A few minutes later they brought in what they called breakfast — heavy porridge with no milk, cream, water or sugar, two pieces of hard, dry toast, and black tea. The breakfast was exactly the same every day I was there. We had rice and jam for lunch and rice and cheese for dinner. Every day.

After breakfast, a guard yelled, "Outside in front of your cell." You then trooped down the hall and put on your woolen uniform with a full pack and steel helmet and went out to the parade ground. It was late May, hot as hell, and we were in full winter battle dress. A Scots Sergeant then called out, "Attention. Stand still and shut up. Now listen boys, my name is Sgt. Clark. I am going to drill you guys until you drop. If anybody drops, you keep going or I will hit you with this billy. You will march quick time and you will march double time. Now, right turn," he bellowed. "March, quick time. All right double time."

We did that all day, every day until five o'clock. We got a 10-minute break in the morning, which the drill sergeant announced by yelling, "Sit down and shut up." Sometimes the guys would try to whisper something to someone else and he would hear it. "Someone is talking. One more word and you will ALL run for 10 minutes straight." Pretty soon you didn't talk to anybody.

My sister Merle was married during the time I was in there. She wrote letters to everybody in the Canadian Army — the Commanding Officer of the Detention Centre, my Commanding Officer in Simcoe — to try and get me out for her wedding —- but there was no way. Although I was sentenced to 28 days, I got out in 24 days. Four days off for good behavior because after that big blond guy threatened me, I was no problem to anyone, anymore. I came out of there in the best shape of my entire life. I didn't have an ounce of fat on me. I was muscle-toned and everything was great.

When I was taken back to Simcoe and went before the Colonel, he said, "Blair, what do you think of the glass house?"

"Everything you told me about it was true, Sir."

"Now look, Blair, you're a smart kid, I can tell. And as a smart kid, you resent this kind of army discipline, badly. But you are not going to beat the army. If you elect to just shut up and do as we tell you — if we say sit, sit, turn right, turn right, turn left — and don't open your mouth, you could become a very good soldier. If you want to fight it, you are not going to like it and you are not going to win."

"Colonel, I think I have learned a very good lesson," I admitted, "which I guess in the end I thank you for."

I did become a very good soldier. I only made one mistake after that. We were having Bren gun drill out on the back range and the guy in charge was Cpl. Crawford, from Kirkland Lake, Ontario, I believe. He was a pain in the neck. We had to learn to disengage the Bren gun and put it back together in 30 seconds. While he was demonstrating, I made a remark that I could do it.

He glared at me and said, "Do you think you can beat me, Blair?"

"Maybe I could."

"Boys sit on the ground. Mr. Blair and I will have a competition to see if he can beat me." They all sat down, we had the competition and I beat him. His eyes were full of hatred when he finished.

When we went to the hut that night, "Crippy" said to me, "You've got to be the craziest guy I've ever met."

I said, "Why? I beat him!"

And "Crippy" said, "Yeah and do you think he's ever going to forget it?" He was right. He was on my back from that day forward until I finished Basic Training there and moved on to Camp Borden, for advanced training.

We moved to Advanced Training at Camp Borden after a short leave. This was pretty well the ritual for every young soldier during active duty days. Advanced training was roughly the same length as basic training – eight weeks. I was in the infantry in the Queen's Own Rifles and as such was stationed in an infantry unit in Camp Borden in A-10. Advanced training was a lot tougher than basic training, completed before you headed overseas. Of course, I knew that this was not going to be true for me because I was only 17, and according to Canadian army rules you were not allowed to go overseas until you were 19 years of age. We took extensive rifle training, marched for hours, and negotiated all sorts of obstacle courses.

About a week or so before the completion of advanced training, our commanding officer called our entire A-10 unit onto the parade square and told us that we would soon be going overseas. We would have four days of embarkation leave. As the Colonel started calling out the names, I wasn't paying too much attention until I heard the name: "Blair." I was thrilled because I wanted to accompany my Regiment overseas. I went home on leave to Oshawa and went to the dances. I was laying it on pretty good with all the young girls, saying that I would be leaving shortly for overseas and probably would never see them again . . . and on and on and on.

The day after I was back in camp, a Lance Corporal came into our hut and summoned me to see the Colonel. The Colonel sat there for a moment looking at me and finally said, "How old are you, Blair?"

I stuttered and stumbled around because I didn't want to say that I wasn't 19 yet. I finally said, "I think I'm just past 19, Sir."

"Don't give me that, Blair," he interrupted. "You were born in 1925, there's no way you're 19. You're not even 18 yet. Your name will be removed from the embarkation list and you will be transferred somewhere very shortly."

I was stunned, but I guess the worst thing was two weeks later when I was back to Oshawa and had to face all these same young ladies at the dances. It was an embarrassing weekend.

During my time at Borden, I began to have a great deal of difficulty on the rifle range. My vision was impaired to about 20-80 in my right eye because I had been struck in that eye by a hockey stick. I got into the rifle corps by sliding the shield across my eye during an eye examination so they didn't realize that I had a vision problem. One day on the rifle range, I was having difficulty shooting because I couldn't see out of my right eye so I was sliding my head across the rifle to lineup the target with my left eye when the gunnery sergeant bellowed at me, "What the hell are you doing?"

"I'm trying to line up the target, sir."

"You shoot like that," he said, "and you are going to blow your jaw right off. Why the hell don't you shoot properly?" I finally had to tell him that I couldn't really see well enough with my right eye. "How the hell did you get into the infantry if you can't see well enough out of your right eye?" I told him how I slid my head across during the eye examination so the doctor didn't suspect that I had a vision problem. "Well, I'm sending you back to the doctor for another eye test. And this time I'm going to tell him to watch you, so don't pull the same stunt again."

I went back for another eye test, and the doctor certainly didn't allow me to cheat again. He categorized me, so that there was no way I could remain in the infantry. A week after that I was transferred to the Medical Corps, then a week after that I was sent to Winnipeg, Manitoba to work in the hospital at the Fort Osborne Barracks. I was in Winnipeg for about nine months, all one winter. I had thought when I was young that it was cold many days during the winter, but I have never been any place (except Minnesota years later), where it has been as cold as it was in Winnipeg that year. Once it got into December it was below zero — well below zero — and that's Fahrenheit, every day throughout the winter until mid-April.

Still, I enjoyed Winnipeg because there was a lot of hockey played throughout the winter. I skated with a couple of Major Junior "A' Teams, first with the St. Boniface Seals and then with the St. James Canadiens, but I just wasn't good enough to make Major "A" Hockey. I played in the Army League for the balance of the winter and spent a lot of hours roller skating.

The following summer, I was transferred back to Toronto to Manning Depot. Eventually, I went to Sunnybrook Hospital to work in the office. The following year, in the spring of 1945, everybody could see that the war was soon going to be over. The Allied troops were romping across Germany. The Canadian government decided to begin discharging all troops still at home in Canada. In April 1945, I was discharged from the Canadian army.

I secured a job after my discharge in General Motors in Oshawa, assigned to the rods and tubing department. Everybody who started a job at General Motors at that time started in this department. We wound copper and various tubing for use inside a motor. My foreman was a gentleman named Jack Barkley, who was probably in his late 40s. He was like a father to all us young lads, a great guy to work for, and I was really happy in this job.

We all chummed around together, went to dances, and formed a pretty good softball team that played in the Oshawa Softball

League. I was somewhat of a novice pitcher in those days, but I hadn't pitched until we were in our third or fourth game. Our coach was Bill Trewin, not popular with his players, but he had been a tremendous softball player in Oshawa over the years. One night we were playing in Thornton Park and Trewin told me I was going to start. Our catcher, Sam McNabney, came from Northern Ontario to play hockey for the Oshawa Generals and he was staying in town because he had another year of junior eligibility. The umpire had not shown up, so Trewin said he would umpire.

Sam had crouched down ready to start and Trewin said, "Play Ball!" I wound up just as Sam moved out a bit to fix his mask, but Trewin was still crouched down in position. Well, I let the pitch fly and it hit Trewin right in the throat . . . and he went down like a ton of bricks. All the kids on the team were laughing and snickering, 'Good shot.' When Trewin got up, he glared at me and said, "Out." He meant out of the game. He put in another pitcher. Nothing really worked between Trewin and me after that.

A few years later, I ran softball teams in Oshawa, which eventually led me to start coaching and managing hockey teams. My first team was a Juvenile softball team stocked with the kids who grew up with me on College Hill. This outstanding team moved up together to Junior, and we stayed together for four or five years more, adding new kids from all over the city. Many of the players who played with the Oshawa Generals eventually played ball with me, players like Harry Sinden, Bill Berwick, and Jed Wilson. Spending time with these lads eventually led me to starting a hockey club in 1949. I formed a team out of Brooklin to play in the Ontario Rural Hockey Association. Not only did I organize and manage the team, I played myself. I think I was the waterboy and stick boy, too. I convinced one of my players, Grant Dodd, to talk to his older brother, Gord, who owned a used car lot, to sponsor the team. We played in Lindsay, Orono, Blackstock, Stouffville, and Newcastle. It was an exciting but also a very trying year. We won the championship that year, which got me thinking about entering the team in the Oshawa Mercantile League, a very strong league with players who had come back from the service or who had graduated from the Generals.

I convinced Gord Dodd that we should move up to a higher challenge. It was going to cost him more money, but by this time he had been bitten by the hockey bug and was quite prepared for the extra expense. In our first year, we went to the league final, but lost out. The next year, we won the league championship. Over the course of the summer, I began to look at the players in the Mercantile League and saw that there were enough good players to form an OHA Senior B team. Now we had to start paying players and we needed to negotiate a contract with the Oshawa arena. I talked with Bill Hanley, then secretary-manager of the OHA. "As a matter of fact," he advised me, "there is a meeting of the OHA Eastern Senior B League in Peterborough next Sunday and if you're interested, perhaps you should attend." My career as a hockey team owner, manager, and coach had begun.

PROFILE

Elma (Pearce) Blair

IN 1944, WHEN I WAS ON A weekend pass from the army, I went to a dance at the Avalon, where I met an old schoolmate of mine, Elsie McClimond, who was standing with a friend. As I was dancing with Elsie, I asked her about her friend. I was stag that night, as most of us were. "Her name is Elma Pearce and she works with me at the Bell."

When the record finished, I asked Elma to dance, and as it turned out, we danced every dance for the rest of the evening. Near the end of the evening, I asked Elma if I could walk her home. I had no car in those days and she lived away down on Simcoe Street South, which was quite a walk from the Avalon on King Street West. As we were going by Memorial Park, we noticed that the park was full of people, even though it was after midnight.

"I wonder what's going on?" Elma asked.

"I know what's going on. I bet the Oshawa Generals won the Memorial Cup tonight." The Generals were in the Memorial Cup finals that year playing against the Trail Smoke Eaters. I had been to the first three games of the series, which the Generals won easily, and I figured they would probably win in four straight, so I decided to go to the dance instead of the game. The Generals had just returned from Maple Leaf Gardens where they were playing the series. It was quite a celebration.

We started dating off and on until later that year. We had many things in common. Elma was from Coboconk, about 35 miles south of where I had spent many summers in Haliburton. In the spring of 1945, I asked Elma to marry me, and on June 30, 1945, we were married in her hometown of Coboconk in the Anglican Church.

We moved in with my mother and father for some time until we got a small apartment. In 1947 we started to build our own home on a lot on College Avenue, in the neighborhood where I had been raised. We bought the lot for $250 and built the house ourselves, with considerable help from my father, uncle, and several buddies. We poured our own foundation on a Saturday in June and pushed wheelbarrows up the ramp for 12 hours until I could hardly hold onto the wheelbarrow without spilling it. Eventually, we got it poured. Dad and Uncle Bert laid in the floor joists over the next few weeks. On July 1, Elma and I walked from our apartment all the way to College Hill and started laying that sub floor from corner to corner. We were both determined not to quit until we had completed it. It was a blistering hot day, and when we finally finished the moon was out. For the next few days, we could hardly move because of the sunburn and aching muscles. We moved in before the brick was laid with only tarpaper on the outer walls and without a basement floor or a furnace. We survived without heat until the middle of January when we got up one morning to discover that the water in the toilet bowl was frozen over.

"That's it," I told Elma, "we're getting a furnace."

I went down to McLaughlin Coal in Oshawa and bought a new furnace for $260. I put $75 down and charged the rest. When my Dad saw that furnace, he asked me how I had managed to pay for it. He was upset when I told him I had made a down payment and charged the rest. He had grown up in the Depression and didn't want to see me go into debt. We were able to pay off the furnace and finish the house without taking out a mortgage, thanks in a great part to my father. That gave us a great start in life.

Our son Danny was born in February 14, 1953, a Valentine's baby. Four years later, our daughter Jill was born. Following the World Championship victory of the Whitby Dunlops in 1958, I left my job at the Central Mortgage and Housing Corporation and went into hockey full time. Elma supported my decision all the way. "Why don't you throw your hat in the ring and go for it." In 1960, when I was assigned by the Boston organization to manage the Kingston Frontenacs, Elma and I had decided that she would not accompany me to Kingston in my first year in pro hockey until I had established myself. The following year, we rented a home in Kingston, where we lived for two more years until the Kingston team moved on to the Central Hockey League in Minneapolis. We then returned to Oshawa and built a new house, using all the equity we had in our first home and some money we had saved, on Juliana Drive in Oshawa. When I signed with the Minnesota North Stars in

1966 to become their first general manager, Elma and the children stayed at home during the first year, but then moved to Edina, Minnesota, a suburb of Minneapolis, where we built a new home in 1968. We remained in Minnesota until 1975, until Jill and Danny had both graduated from high school.

Soon the family dispersed. Danny went to work for the IHL team I had bought in Saginaw, Michigan, Jill returned to Oshawa to go to business college, and Elma and I moved to Pittsburgh when I purchased the Penguin franchise with two partners.

Today, our son Danny and his wife Libby live in Brampton, Ontario. They have given us three wonderful grandchildren, Brandon, Ryan, and Laura. Meanwhile Jill is married to Peter Krahule and lives in Whitby. She has also given us a beautiful grandaughter, Jennifer. For the past decade or so, Jill has been my administrative assistant and secretary. Elma and I are happily living back in my hometown of Oshawa again.

Through all these years, Elma has been the glue that held the family together and gave me the courage to venture forth from the streets of Oshawa to the bright lights of the NHL in Minnesota, Pittsburgh, and Los Angeles. I'm very grateful to my family for allowing me to be away from home so much over the past 50 years while I pursued my hockey dreams.

When I look back across the years, it seems somewhat ironic that on the first night that I ever met Elma Pearce, we stopped in Memorial Park to see the Oshawa Generals celebrate their Memorial Cup victory. Perhaps we were predestined to be a hockey family.

The Founding of the Oshawa Truckmen and the Whitby Dunlops

2

AS I SAT IN THE MEETING ROOM of the Empress Hotel in Peterborough during the meeting of the OHA Senior B League executives, I was much in awe of everybody in the room. The Convener of the league was Mr. Frank Buckland, a very dynamic guy with a hair-trigger temper who later became President of the Ontario Hockey Association. The alternate Convener was Lorne Cook of Kingston, who became a close friend of mine. The members of the league were Orillia, Peterborough, Belleville, Kingston, and Brockville.

The directors worked through their agenda and when they were finished, Mr. Buckland said, "We have a gentleman here from Oshawa, who is considering the possibility of entering a team in our league. Mr. Blair, would you like to stand up and introduce yourself and tell us your thoughts."

I stood up, introduced myself, and confessed, "I have some interest in what Mr. Buckland has said, but I have no idea how to proceed. How do you get in the league?"

"Well, you pay an entry fee of $10 and you're in the league," he explained. "You have to follow all the bylaws and so on."

I can remember taking out my wallet — and I had about $12 in it. I guess I was a gutsy guy in those days because I said, "Will you take cash?"

"Certainly." I walked to the front, gave him the $10 in cash, and he gave me a receipt. Mr. Buckland then announced, "We are now a six-team league and we will begin drawing up the schedule in the next few days."

As I was driving back to Oshawa I began thinking: What the hell am I doing? I don't have an arena contract. I don't have any players. I don't have a sponsor. When I got back, the first thing I decided to do was to try to get an arena contract. At the time, the Oshawa arena was owned by the Hambly family. Stu Hambly operated the Coca-Cola franchise and his older brother Ab was the operator of the arena. I phoned Ab shortly after I arrived back in Oshawa and arranged to go down to the arena and meet him. I told him that I had entered a team in the OHA Senior B League and needed to negotiate an arena contract for ice time. He said that the Generals have the preference on ice time, but on the nights that the Generals are not playing, if I wanted to pay him $125 a night rental, then the other nights were mine. I thought that was pretty neat . . . $125. I had no idea how tough that was going to be later on. He also said that you pay in advance and, if you miss one payment you're out, the whole thing is cancelled.

Now that I had an arena contract, we picked the dates to start our training camp in September. I secured the services of numerous players — Doug Williams, Jack Tisdale, Frank Hooper, Ronnie Nelson and several others who had played for the Generals. Most of these players were on teams in the Toronto Hockey League in Toronto, even though they lived in Oshawa. The first thing they asked when I approached them was, How much are you paying? In response, I asked, How much are you making now? They all said between $10 and $15. I immediately offered $5 more.

I started signing players left, right, and center. When many other guys heard about it, they started calling me. Les Colvin, who played goal for the Generals when they won the Memorial Cup in 1939-40, was now about 31. He said he'd love to play at home in

Oshawa. Then I heard that Ab Barnes, who used to play with the Oshawa Senior A team, was available. So I talked to him about becoming player-coach.

But as the days ticked off to the start of the season, I began to sweat . . . I still didn't have a sponsor. We had now hit the ice, and on a Friday, I took the afternoon off from my job at Oshawa Field Aviation, which was a service for time-expired parts on aircraft. We had to strip all the equipment off the aircraft that landed at the Oshawa airport and ship them back to the company to be redone. I worked in the stores department there. I traveled all over Oshawa that day. I went to Fittings Limited, which was a big company in Oshawa, and met with Walter Branch, the personnel director, whom I knew, but he said, "Wren, we can't take that on, our company is losing money." I went to Coulter Manufacturing, then I went down to Houdaille Hershey Corporation, who manufactured automobile bumpers, but they declined. It was getting near five o'clock in the afternoon and I was getting pretty discouraged. As I was driving past the old CNR station, I stopped at Bloor Street for a red light. On the northeast corner of Bloor and Simcoe was Smith Transport Offices. I thought to myself, there's a company that as far as I know has never had anything to do with supporting sports in Oshawa. I thought, I'm going in. As I walked into the office, it struck me, who am I going to ask for? If I ask for Mr. Smith, the receptionist is probably going to laugh me out of the office. But I didn't know what else to do.

I approached the woman at the reception desk and she asked: "Can I help you, sir?" I thought, well, here goes nothing.

"I would like to see Mr. Smith, please"

"Mr. S.P. Smith or Mr. Ted Smith?"

I thought, Oh my God, now I've got two of them. Well, S.P. sounded a little more like the top guy, so I said, "Oh, Mr. S.P. Smith, of course."

"Well, he's on the phone and will be for quite a while."

What I didn't know was that Mr. S.P. Smith had hundreds of phones on his desk, all connected to the various Smith Transport terminals across the country, and he talked with every terminal at the end of every day. After about half an hour, the receptionist left for the day, but a short while later, another man approached me. "My name is Mr. Bert Williams," he said "and I am one of Mr. Smith's assistants. If you want to continue to wait I will come and get you when he is free."

Finally, after about a 60-minute wait, Mr. Williams came out and took me into Mr. Smith's office. I don't think I had ever been in a bigger office in my entire life. After I got in the office, Mr. Smith continued for another 15 minutes on his various phones before he finally finished. He was really a big, good-looking guy, with wavy hair, in his mid-30s . . . he looked a bit like a football player. I later found out he was the son of the owner, the founder of Smith Transport. Finally, he put the phone down and then asked me: "Mr. Blair, what can I do for you?"

I couldn't help thinking to myself, if I ever get the floor he's not going to get it back for a while. "Well," I said, "Mr. Smith, there are a lot of good, young hockey players in Oshawa who played for the Generals, the Oshawa Junior A team, but once they finish junior, those players have no place to play anymore. I have entered a team in the Eastern Ontario Sr. B League to fill that void. I have all the players signed, a rink contract in place, but I have no sponsor." I carried on for another 10 or 15 minutes, naming some of the players, before I finally sat down.

He stared at me for a moment, and finally said, "You know, Mr. Blair, I can't think of anything less I'd rather do than sponsor a hockey club. However, I feel I'd be remiss if I first didn't go down and have a look at what the hell you're so enthused about. You mentioned they're on the ice. Do they practice tomorrow (a Saturday)?"

"Yes," I said, "we're on the ice from 12 to 2 p.m."

"Do you think, you could pick me up at 1 p.m.?"

"Of course."

The next day while we were on the ice, I blew the whistle and said I'm leaving here for about 10 minutes. I told the players, "When I come back here I will have someone with me, a prospective sponsor. We're going to scrimmage, but not an ordinary one, it'll be as if you are playing for the Stanley Cup. I want to impress this gentleman." I left and went to pick up S.P. or Sam as I called him later. We went back to the rink and I put on my skates. When we started the scrimmage, Sam came right down on the bench. He could hear the guys talking and yelling. Most men get caught up in that sort of atmosphere pretty quickly when you can actually smell the sweat from the guys in the heat of battle. Finally, we finished the scrimmage and I told the guys to go in the dressing room, shower and change. There were a couple of cases of beer in there so they wouldn't leave until I came back. I went onto the bench and talked with S.P. He asked me once again who was in the league. I could see him measuring up where they might have outlets for Smith Transport. So I rhymed off the teams once again: Orillia, Peterborough, Belleville, Kingston, Brockville, and now Oshawa.

He thought for a minute, and then said, "You've got a sponsor." He stuck out his hand, but I wouldn't shake it.

"Just a minute. For how much?"

"Well," he said, "we take the gate receipts down to our office, every week you come down to the office and Bert will have the salaries ready in brown envelopes. Isn't that the way they do it?"

"Oh! Oh, yeah, that's the way they do it." I never dreamed I'd ever get anybody to underwrite the operation.

"You come down early next week and we'll get this set up right."

After I took him back to his office, I returned to the rink, and then told somebody to go out and get a couple of more cases of beer because we really had something to celebrate. And with that, the Oshawa Smith Truckmen were born that day in the fall of 1952. We played a 48-game schedule and had a strong hockey club. I'm sure our proximity to Toronto helped because I was able to sign a couple of pretty good Toronto hockey players who commuted to play with us. We finished the regular season in first place that year and ended up meeting Kingston in the opening round of the playoffs. Kingston beat us out in six games . . . and I was devastated. But that's sports and Kingston also had an extremely good team.

When we had won the ORHA title in Brooklin, we moved up to the Mercantile League, where, in two years, we won the title there, and now we were in Senior B. As I readied myself over the summer, I was determined that we were going to win the championship next year. Every time I won a championship, I wanted to move up.

All that summer I worked vigorously to improve the hockey club in hopes that we could win the championship, then in mid-August when I got a call from S. P. Smith's secretary. She wanted me to come down to Mr. Smith's office and meet with him the next day. We sat in his office for a few moments before he said, "You know Wren, I have never had more fun than I had last year operating that hockey club with you. Unfortunately, my dad and my brothers don't share my enthusiasm for hockey. We lost a fair amount of money running the team last year and my brothers and father voted that we should drop our sponsorship for this year. However, I have a cheque for you in the amount of $2,500 and you can keep this cheque yourself or put it in the hockey club's bank account, or whatever you want. If I had more people here, working as hard as you do on that hockey club, Smith Transport would probably be farther ahead than it is."

I was really disappointed because it came so late in the summer that I had no idea, at this point, where I could turn for a new sponsor. Sam had been tremendous. He bought us all new equipment, the best quality available. He said we could keep it. He threw a tremendous banquet for the team at the end of the season and bought us all suede jackets. They were long blue overcoat jackets, the likes of which I had not seen before. He did everything first class.

"Oh, by the way, I also want to buy 12 season tickets because I intend to continue going to the games," Sam said. I asked him if we took the name Smith off the sweaters, could we continue to call the team the Oshawa Truckmen. "Wren, I don't see any problem with that. It's just that our company name, Smith, has to come off."

At that point, I decided that we could call the team the Oshawa Truckmen and the $2,500 would be placed in the hockey club's account. I now went out and sold eight corporation shares in the team to seven other fellows and myself. We each put in $250, which gave us another $2,000.

Our troubles were not over. Early in September, about 6 a.m., my phone rang. It was Stan Waylett, my trainer, and he said go to your front window and take a look.. I was groggy, still half-asleep, but I went to my front window and looked out. I couldn't really see anything. "Can you see all that smoke?" he asked. I said, yes, even though I didn't see it. "The rink's on fire, I'll see you down there."

I went back to my room and then realized what he said and said to my wife: Oh, my God, the rink's on fire! I pulled my clothes on over my pyjamas, threw on a jacket and went racing out the door to the arena, which was located on the banks of the Oshawa creek in those days. I leaped out of the car and went running across the parking lot toward the arena. As I got closer, a fireman grabbed me and said, "Wren, where do you think you're going?"

"I've got to get into the rink, all our equipment is in there.'

"The entire roof caved in about 3 this morning. There's nothing left in there."

I went around to the side of the rink where our dressing room was located. Stan was there and we peered through the window. "Just look at that, all that brand new equipment gone," he said. We could see pieces of skates, shoulder pads, burned gloves, everything all charred up.

I stood there for a few moments — it was now just about 7 a.m. — and finally said to Stan, "I'm heading to Bowmanville.'

"What are you going to Bowmanville for?"

"Do you know any other arena around here? There were no kids' rinks, no rink in Whitby."

I asked him if he wanted to come with me. "Hell, I'm supposed to go to work, but I'll take the day off to see this," he said.

Stan and I drove to Bowmanville, to the arena, which was just off the main street, and pulled into the parking lot. We didn't see anybody around, but we found one guy at the back of the arena, putting some stuff in the garbage. I asked him if he was associated with the arena and he said, "Yes, I guess I'm the caretaker and half-assed manager." I asked if the arena had a committee, a board of management, and he said yes. I asked who the chairman of the committee was and he told me, Mr. Bob Watt. He told me that he worked right in town at the Goodyear plant. I asked if it was possible for him to get in touch with him and we went into the arena and he got him on the phone. Bob and I talked on the phone and I asked him if he could come over to the arena and meet me.

By this time, the news of the arena fire was all over the area and I'm pretty sure he knew what was up. He came over to the arena and I said to him, "Bob, as you know the Oshawa arena burned down this morning and I need an arena badly in which to play our games. Do you think we could make a deal where we could play our home games in Bowmanville?"

"Sure." We already had our schedule so we worked out a deal — I think it was $100 per game — where we could play our 24 home games in Bowmanville. We worked out the dates and had the contract signed by 9 o'clock that morning.

Shortly after that, Stan and I went back to Oshawa and headed to Joe Bolahood's Sports Store, where we had bought all our equipment the year before. The store was jammed with people, all talking about the fire. As we were walking up and down the aisles, Joe spotted us and came over and said, "Well, kid, what are you going to do now?"

"Whaddya mean? We're finished! We have no arena, no equipment, no money! We're finished!"

"Don't say you're finished," and with that he took out a catalog and threw it on the counter and said, "Here, order your equipment."

'Joe, either you're nuts or I am. I told you I have no money." I had run ball clubs before and bought equipment from him in the past without any money, but we had always managed to pay.

"You'll get me the money, one way or another. Just order the equipment."

I stood there for a moment and then threw the catalog down and started walking out the store. He's staring at me and then I said to him, "If you're any kind of businessman, you should have that order from last year in your files somewhere."

"I'm sure I do."

"Well, then just repeat the bloody order." Just as I reached the door, I turned and said, "Oh, by the way, Joe, have that order here by next Thursday, because we're opening training camp that night in Bowmanville and if we don't have it by then I'll take my order somewhere else.

When I left the store, I heard him mutter, "You are too much," because he realized then I had already signed a contract in Bowmanville, even though when I came in the store I had told him we were finished.

We opened training camp the next Thursday with all of the new equipment except shin pads. I don't know if you have seen hockey players on the ice without shin pads, but with their spindly legs it's a sight to behold. The shin pads came in a couple of days later. We finished our training camp and opened the season on time. In the 1953 season, television came on the scene big time in Ontario and Canada. People wouldn't even go out of the house to watch a hockey game next door, let alone nine miles away in Bowmanville. As a result, we didn't draw very well all year. It was a very difficult year. I had told the players that we were going to start a Fire Fund where we would play as many exhibition games as we could in order to raise money and pay for the equipment. When we played exhibition games, there was no pay for the players and all the money would go to Joe Bolahood. We played exhibition games in Markham, Orillia, Minden, Fenelon Falls, Lindsay, Orono, and God knows where else.

At one point, during the season, Harry Sinden came to me and said, "How many more games are we going to have to play before this equipment is paid for." I told him, don't you worry about that. I'll tell you when we're finished. We are going to pay off Joe. Eventually the season wore on and we were getting into debt. The money that Sam had given us and the money that I had raised from the seven other corporate investors and myself was all gone — and we were getting deeper into debt. Gradually, the debt went up and the bank threatened to cut off our line of credit. Finally, the bank called me and said if you are prepared to put your house up as security, we'll loan you up to $10,000. I said, Okay, and without telling my wife, I put my house on the line.

By the end of the season we were over $10,000 in debt and I was a basket case because it looked as if our house was going to go down the tube. We started the playoffs, and again we met Kingston. The first game of the playoffs was in Bowmanville, and I thought maybe we'd draw more people, but I don't think we had more than 15 extra fans for the opening game. To make matters worse, we lost the opening game and our home-ice advantage. Things looked even bleaker. We traveled to Kingston for the second game of the series on a Wednesday night. Kingston had a new arena and they were packing the place. We played that night and won 4-2 to get back our home-ice advantage. After the game, while the players were dressing, I walked around the arena to Jim McCormick's office. McCormick was the manager of the Memorial Centre at that time.

I went into his office and said, "Jimmy, how many people did you have here tonight?"

"I don't know," he answered, then asked one of the girls in the office for a box office statement. He looked at the statement that said 4,300.

"How much money did you take in?" Prices then for games were $2 to $2.50.

"$8,900."

I had never heard of a gate being that big before and certainly not in senior or amateur hockey, at those prices. I looked at Jimmy for a moment and then said, "What would you think if we moved the rest of our games to Kingston?" It was late in the year and he didn't have much else going on in the building except the playoff games.

"That'd be okay with me."

"If we did, what kind of a deal, financially, could we work out."

"The same as the home club."

"And what's that," I asked?

"Twelve per cent rental," he said.

Our next home game was Friday, so I asked if Friday night was open, and if dates were open for the rest of our home games if the series was to go seven games.

"Yes," he said, "I can clear anything."

"Fine," I said, "we're moving here. You can start the advertising right now."

After that, I called Bob Watt at home. He had listened to the game on radio, so he knew that we had won. "Way to go," he said, when he came on the phone. "Now, we can get those buggers on Friday night."

"Well, Bob, that's what I'm calling you about. There's not going to be a game in Bowmanville on Friday night. We're playing in Kingston."

"Why, has there been a change in the schedule?" he queried.

"No," I said.

"Well, what's going on?"

"We're moving the rest of our home games in this series to Kingston."

"You can't do that, you've got a contract here."

"Bob, I haven't got the contract with me, but if my memory serves me right, that contract was for 24 home games in the regular schedule. There was no mention of playoffs."

"Just a minute." I guess he had a copy of the contract at home and went to check it. He came back on the phone a couple of minutes later and said, "You bastard, you do that and I'll never speak to you again." The way things were going, I had wanted a contract as short as possible to ease my financial liabilities. Bob was mad then and I felt bad about it.

Finally, I said, "Bob, we'll play there on Friday night on one condition."

"What's that," he said?

"I personally owe over $10,000 to the bank. You take half of that responsibility off my back and we'll play in Bowmanville Friday night."

"I'm not going to do that," he said and hung up.

We played in Kingston on Friday night. It was our home game. We won and went up 2-1 in the series. I went around to the office after the game to pick up our check. They had 4,900 people at the game and the gate was $9,000. When we took the 12 per cent off for the rink, we still cleared $7,500. I took the check to the bank the next day and plunked the $7,500 down against my debt, which reduced it to about $2,800. We played again on Saturday night, which was their home game, and they won to tie the series 2-2. We were back there again on Monday for our home game. We had another sell-out crowd, and with that cheque I had paid off my debt at the bank. We even had a little money in the bank. The series went back and forth until there was a seventh game, which we won — and got half the gate. I used some of that money to pay off Joe Bolahood for our equipment.

We were now matched against the Stouffville Clippers for our next series, and I asked Jim McCormick how he thought we would draw if we continued to play in Kingston. "I don't think you'll draw near as well as you did against Kingston, but you have built up a pretty good following and should average 2,500 to 3,000," he said. I didn't know anywhere else we could play where we would draw that well, so I said okay and we arranged the series dates. I talked with Tim O'Neill, the Stouffville manager, because I had to give him a little extra money for travel. Again we put them out in the seventh game as well and averaged 3,500 a game. Now, it was on to the all-Ontario final against the Simcoe Gunners.

I asked Jimmy if we could draw a crowd in Kingston for this series.

"Well," he said, "I don't think so, it's getting late in the year, the golf courses are open, I don't know how well you'd draw." I reluctantly agreed and thanked Jimmy. I later wrote him a nice letter, because he literally saved my life financially at that time. After my meeting with McCormick, I phoned the manager of the Simcoe team and told him that we didn't have a home ice surface and was wondering if there was enough ice time available in Simcoe so that we could play the entire series there.

"Sure, I think so." I could see him counting the silverware right then and under his breath saying, "Are you dopey or what? You want to play the whole series in our backyard!" He then gave me the name and phone number of the Simcoe arena manager so I could make the arrangements for our dates along with the financial aspects. I made the deal with the Simcoe arena and we played the entire series in Simcoe. We won the series and the Ontario Senior B championship in the 1953-54 season in six games.

I don't think that any team had ever won an ultimate championship, up until then or after that, by playing all their playoff games on the road. It was especially exciting for us to get back to the Oshawa-Whitby area around 3a.m. and celebrate our championship by getting the fire trucks out. Some of the players on that team were the playing coach Ernie Dickens, who had played in the NHL with Chicago and Toronto, Harry Sinden, Bill Berwick, Jack Tisdale, Gerry Scott, Les Colvin, Red Peters, Frank (Sonny) Hooper, Jack Naylor, Jed Wilson, Geoff Boniface, Paul Jago, and Gord Boniface, among others.

The next season we moved the team to Whitby. There was a new arena being built in Whitby at this time and I visited Don Wilson and Norm Irwin to find out if I could move my hockey club from Bowmanville/Oshawa to Whitby for the 1954-55 season. Don owned Whitby Motors, a Pontiac-Buick dealership. His good friend was Norm Irwin, who had married Kay McLaughlin, the daughter of George McLaughlin, the brother of R.S. McLaughlin. Norm and Kay owned a beautiful home outside of Whitby called Stone Haven and the beautiful Red Wing orchards. Norm and Don had become great friends.

I sensed right away that they heard about my escapades from the previous season where I had pulled my team out of the Bowmanville Arena and played all our playoff games on the road. I figured the best way to tackle this was to be open about what had happened the year before. "I'm sure you have heard what happened last year, but I want you to understand that I had no contract for the playoffs, I was personally deep in debt and the only way out for me was to move the games out of Bowmanville," I explained.

"If you move over here, there are a couple of things we would want," Norm said. "First of all, we want your assurances that it will be called a Whitby team, with no Oshawa connotations; and secondly, we have to agree on an arena contract in which there will be stipulations for the playoffs."

"I can't blame you for that," I laughed.

A couple of days later we got together and drew up a contract for us to move to Whitby. At that time I had been stumbling around for more than a year now without a sponsor so I refused to call the team anything but the Whitby Seniors. I wasn't going to put any name on the team until I got a sponsor. Bunny Morganson, who wrote for the *Toronto Telegram*, used to call the team the Whitby "Wrens" in his columns.

We started the season and it was very difficult financially. At our first game in Whitby, I don't think we had 200 fans in the arena that seated 1,100. I was puzzled. Nobody knows about us in Whitby. In the *Oshawa Times Gazette*, there were two pages of Whitby news, but George Campbell, the Oshawa sports editor, would never mention us in his columns. The Oshawa Generals had folded after the fire and their players had been drafted around the league. It meant that we were the only meaningful hockey club in the area, but we still couldn't get Campbell to write about us. We were hurting.

I went to the box office manager, Art Moore, and said, "Art, keep 300 tickets for sale and give me the other 700." I didn't want to give any complimentary tickets away in Whitby or even Oshawa, so I headed for Ajax to the Dowty Plant and met with the personnel director and told him we were going to honor the employees of Dowty at our next home game. I told him a little about the hockey club and that we would like to have the president and vice-president drop the puck. We would have a little cocktail party for your officials upstairs in the arena. He thought it was a marvelous idea. I told him that the only thing I wanted him to do was to assure me that he would distribute these tickets, two to each employee, and emphasize to them that it was important that they attend the game.

The next week when we played I don't even think we sold the 300 tickets that were left at the box office, but the arena was almost filled. I've always learned that the greatest thing in hockey is that a crowd draws a crowd. You have to keep your arena full because that impresses them. If somebody from Whitby went to our game and then stopped in at the Royal Hotel for a beer after the game and a buddy said to him, "Hey where have you been?" And, he says, "Oh, I was at the hockey game." "Anybody there," his buddy asks. "No, not really," he says. You know he's not about to start coming to the games. But, if you take the other scenario and he says, "Yeah, it was almost sold out," then the buddy thinks, what the hell am I missing, I've got to start going.

So for the next seven or eight games, I honored companies all through the Pickering-Ajax area. I started telling Art (the box office manager), okay, Art, you keep 400 and I'll take 600; then you take 500 and I'll take 500; and so on. Gradually, our attendance started to pick up and pretty soon we were selling out and continued to sell out all the time that we were in Whitby.

Along about this time the Dunlop Rubber Company had moved into Whitby to build a new plant. By this time, I got to know Mayor Harry Jermyn fairly well. One day I went up to meet Harry at the town office and I said to the Mayor, "Harry, we need a sponsor desperately and I've been thinking that since the Dunlop Rubber Company and the Senior hockey team arrived in this town at the same time, don't you think we should become partners of some sort?"

Harry was a great philosopher, a former school teacher. He thought for a moment and agreed with my thinking.

"I suppose you know the heavy hitters with Dunlop," I asked the Mayor.

"Oh yes, I'm very familiar with John Anderson, the chairman of the board. He's about 72 and an Englishman as all the Dunlop people are."

So I asked Harry if he could get in touch with Mr. Anderson and explain our plight. About a week later, I got a letter with the Dunlop letterhead on the envelope. Inside was a letter for me and a check for $100. I deemed that Mr. Anderson had made a mistake and must have thought we were a kid's team, so I wrote him a letter saying that our team was comprised of all men, that they were paid to play, and you might compare us to a Division II team in English soccer. Therefore, I am returning your cheque for $100 because I think the Dunlop Rubber Company might need it more than we do. A few days later, I got a call from the Mayor and he asked: "What did you tell Mr. Anderson, he's really hot?" I told him what I'd written. The Mayor told me that when he talked with Mr. Anderson about my response, he asked, "Who is this cheeky fellow, Blair? Listen to the letter he sent me. I then asked the Mayor if he could talk to the guy and explain things to him. The next game we played was against the Kingston Goodyears, so now you've got Goodyear against Dunlop. To give credit to Dunlop, they decided to send 22 of their top executives from Toronto to that game. Whitby decided to throw a little banquet and cocktail party for them and they could sit at one end of the arena, upstairs in a glassed in area. We had dinner and I left to go down and get the team ready for the game. We played two periods and the game was tied 2-2. The rink was going nuts and I rushed upstairs to see how the English executives from Dunlop were doing. They were all worked up and they had gathered up 22 ten-dollar bills and gave them to me. "Give these to your chaps," they said. "We cannot let these Goodyears beat us. Do you understand, Mr. Blair? That would be very embarrassing for us." I told them I wasn't sure this would help, but I would certainly give them to the players. I went back to the dressing room and threw the ten-dollar bills all over the room and told the players, "Leave them there. If you win, you can pick up one each after the game."

We had a torrid third period, where we outscored Kingston 2-1 and won the game 4-3. After the game, the players were scrambling all over the room for the money — $10 was a pretty good dollar in those days. I went up to see the Dunlop boys after the game and they were all very excited about what they had seen and would write a report. A few days later, I got a call from a gentleman named Mr. Bill Hannah. "Mr. Blair, my name is William Hannah and I am an executive with the Dunlop Rubber Company. Mr. Anderson has asked me to contact you and ask you what you would like from Dunlop?"

I told him that I would like to see the team dressed in Dunlop colors. If Dunlop would buy our uniforms and then give us $2,500 in cash to put the name Whitby Dunlops on our team's sweaters, that would make us partners. He said, "Oh boy, I don't know if we can do that." I said that I understood, but I wouldn't take anything less. A few days later, I got another call from Mr. Hannah and he said everything was a go, but that Mr. Anderson wanted him to work with me in supervising the colors and design of the uniforms and that all of the money was to be spent on hockey operations. Bill and I went to work immediately and got the uniforms designed and ordered in black and gold with a touch of red. We were off and running.

In the playoffs that year, the Whitby Dunlops were beaten by Cornwall, which had just returned to Senior B ranks after playing Senior A the year before in Quebec. Now I had to retool and see if we could win another Senior B championship.

PROFILE

Bob Attersley

WHEN I WAS DELIVERING milk for Beaton's Dairy in Oshawa, the first part of my route took me down Burke Street, where Bob Attersley lived. Bob was about eight years of age at that time. I got to know him seven or eight years later when he was playing juvenile softball in Oshawa. I was running another team in that same juvenile league, called Veterans Taxi, while Bob was playing on a team called Fabric Town. He was playing Junior "B" hockey, and a year later, at 16 years of age, he made the Oshawa Generals in the OHA Major Junior A Hockey League.

In the 1952-53 Season, I had started an OHA Senior "B" team, playing out of the old Oshawa Arena, and so I began to see Bob a lot around the rink. Bob won the "Red Tilson Award" as the most valuable player in the Ontario Major Junior "A" Hockey League that year, an outstanding achievement. Some of Bob's teammates during his three years with the Generals were Lou Jankowski and Alex Delvecchio who went on to play in the NHL. When the Oshawa Arena burned to the ground in September 1953, the Generals decided to disband. The league decided to place all the names of the Generals players in a hat and each team would draw. The Guelph Biltmores drew Attersley. Some of Bob's teammates in Guelph that year were Eddie Shack, Ron Howell, Billy McCreary, and Billy Graham. Shack was 15 years of age at that time and went on to play with New York and Toronto in the NHL. Ron Howell also played briefly in the NHL, but he became much better known as a football player for the Hamilton Tiger-Cats. Billy Graham also became a famous player in the CFL.

Bob belonged to the Boston Bruins of the NHL, and when he finished his junior career in Guelph, he was invited in 1954 by the

Bruins to their training camp in Hershey, Pennsylvania. After attending camp and not receiving the financial deal he wanted, Bob returned to Oshawa and signed with the Whitby Dunlops. Bob was our number one centerman for the Whitby club for the next six years.

Like most of the players on the "Dunnies," Bob appreciated humor and created a lot of laughs, often at my expense. A rumor spread that Bob could hypnotize people. On a bus trip one night, some of the players challenged Bob to hypnotize them. Bob selected Don McBeth as a willing participant and began to talk in a low monotone. "Mac, close your eyes. You feel your eyes getting heavier and heavier." Gradually Bob's voice began to rise as he said, "You try to open your eyes, but you can't." All of us on the team had gathered around, some on their knees backwards on both sides of the aisle. Tommy O'Connor was sitting across the aisle from Mac. I looked at Tommy and he, too, was falling under Bob's spell. Bob then said, "Mac, I am going to snap my fingers in a moment, and when I do, you will wake up from a deep sleep, and then I will put you under again, but deeper." Bob snapped his fingers and both Mac and Tommy woke up. He asked them how they felt and then hypnotized them again. "You are in a deep, deep sleep. You try to open your eyes but you can't. Go ahead, try and open your eyes, but you can't." Both Mac and Tommy appeared to be totally out. "Okay guys, we're going for a little trip." Mac and Tommy were told they were rowing a boat together on a beautiful lake. Both Mac and Tommy start using their arms as you would to row a rowboat. All of a sudden Bob says, "Hey guys, look at those beautiful girls in bikinis in that boat beside you." They both start waving like crazy, and all of a sudden Tommy stands up a bit, as though to be more noticed by the girls. Bob quickly said, "Sit down Tommy, you are going to upset the boat." Tommy quickly sat right down again, but was still waving and grinning at these girls.

By this time, all our guys are roaring with laughter on the bus. "Okay guys," Bob continued, "I'm going to snap my fingers and you will wake up." He snapped his fingers and Mac and Tommy both woke up. They looked around at all of us kind of strangely. "How do you feel guys?" Bob asked. "Great!" they exclaimed. "Do you remember when you were asleep that you saw these nice girls out on the lake?" Bob asked. "Don't give us that crap Bob, we just drifted off to sleep for a minute," Mac replied.

On another road trip, I began to hear rumblings that Bob should try and put me under. We were staying at a hotel in Cornwall, and the guys started bugging Bob to try hypnotizing me. I didn't want to be a spoilsport, so I agreed. Everyone came to my room. Bob lowered the lights, sat me in one chair and sat himself in another chair facing me. All the guys gathered around. He asked me to close my eyes and started droning, "Your eyes are getting heavier and heavier. You are really tired. Your eyes are getting heavier." After awhile he started to raise his voice again and stood right over me. "You try to open your eyes, but no matter how hard you try, you can't open them." He keeps saying this for almost a minute. Now I could hear the other guys saying, "Hey Bob, I think you've got him." At that moment, with him staring right down at me and the guys quietly in awe, I opened my eyes and said, "Who the hell can't open their eyes," and stood up.

In June of 1960, the Whitby Dunlops ceased operations, and when I took over the Kingston Frontenacs, I added Bob Attersley to our line-up. He also did some emergency duty for our Clinton Comets team one year when we were devastated by injuries, but he soon retired – all too soon – from professional hockey. Back home, Bob was elected to the Whitby Town Council in 1964. Years later in 1980, Bob became Mayor of Whitby and served for 11 years, the longest term in the history of the Town of Whitby. Bob was also a member of the Durham Regional Police Board from 1981 to 1983 and served as the chairman.

During these years I would often visit Bob in the Mayor's office to chat about our old hockey days. One of these conversations in 1989 led us to buy the OHL Major Junior A team in Kingston along with Don Anderson, another old friend. We had some fun and some pain operating the Frontenacs for a decade or so until we sold our interest in the hockey club to the Springer Family of Kingston on a five-year buy-out plan.

Over the years, Bob built a very successful company in Atterlsey Tire, another in Redfern Auto Parts, and dealt in real estate as well. Although he has sold most of his business interests, he is still the President of Attersley Tire, where he maintains an office that serves as our meeting place almost every week. For most of the years that Bob played for me, we roomed together. We've spent a great deal of our lives together. Bob and his wife Joan and their children remain very important to everyone in our family.

One day somebody asked me, "Did your fame really start when you signed Bobby Orr?"

"No," I replied, "my fame, if that's what you want to call it, really started with two Bob's. First when I signed Bobby Attersley to the Whitby Dunlops and, of course, again when I signed Bobby Orr to the Boston Bruins junior team, the Oshawa Generals.

3

Senior A Hockey and the Allan Cup Championship

WITH THE DUNLOP RUBBER Company sponsorship, I was determined to rebuild our team and go after our second OHA Senior B championship. Even though we had lost in the playoffs the previous year, we had a pretty good team and most of the players were returning. That was the year the Toronto Lynhursts represented Canada in the world championship, and before they left for that tournament, we had beaten them soundly in an exhibition game.

To start the new season, we played two exhibition games – one in Whitby and one in Orillia – against the Cleveland Barons of the American Hockey League. Jim Hendy, always a hero of mine, was the general manager of the Barons, one of the most popular and powerful teams in the American Hockey League. I decided to get up the nerve to call Mr. Hendy. I told tell him that we had a pretty good hockey team and asked if he would consider playing us in a couple of exhibition games during training camp. I told him how much I thought of him and that I knew all of his players. That sort of impressed him. Finally, he asked what days I was thinking about. He said that if we could play two days in a row, he would come up and play us. He asked about money and I told him he would get 70 percent of the gate. I didn't care about the money — it was the prestige of playing against an American League team that I wanted.

We played the first game in Whitby. I was on the bench coaching. At the end of the second period, we were leading Cleveland

and Mr. Hendy came down to talk to me. "I wonder if you would consider not coaching the last period and come up to the press box and sit and talk to me."

"Why, are you afraid we'll win if I continue coaching?"

He laughed and then said, "You're going to do all right in hockey because you have nerve. And in order to stay in the top echelon of hockey, you have to have that."

I agreed to bypass the third period and went to see Stan Waylett, my trainer, who always used to ride me that he could coach just as well as me. "You remember all the times you gave me that crap that you were as good a coach as I am. Well, tonight, you are going to get your chance. I'm going to go up and talk to Mr. Hendy and you're going to coach the last period."

My talk with Mr. Hendy was very enlightening. The first thing he asked me was if I was from this area. "You must find it very difficult to run a hockey club in your home town."

I agreed. "I do get rather tired, though, of the criticism and jealousy of the hometown people." I got all sorts of criticism from guys I grew up with, telling me to do this and that and blah, blah, blah because they were better hockey players than me. But as I told Mr. Hendy, you don't have to be a great player to be a coach. In fact, it might be a deficit. I explained to him that I was a great believer in movies and that I decided a long time ago that if I couldn't go any farther as a player, which I couldn't, just as movies needed directors and producers, so did hockey clubs need coaches and general managers.

"I've never heard it put that way before, but it is very true," he said. "Wren, let me tell you something. Don't ever worry when people are talking about you, good or bad. You worry when they're not talking about you at all. That's when your day is over." I always remembered that and I think people who know me can testify that I did not worry about being liked any longer, good or bad, but focused on staying on top. Politicians can be great, even though they are cut up constantly in the news.

As it turned out, Cleveland scored in the third period and we ended up tied. Mr. Hendy was very impressed with Harry Sinden, Ted O'Connor, and Alfie Treen. Later on, he tried to sign all three of them. The next night we went to Orillia to play the second game. I'll always remember that Marcel Paille, who later went to the Rangers, was in goal for Cleveland. I can't remember whether Long John Henderson had joined us yet, but both goaltenders were outstanding and the score was 0-0 late in the game. Eddie Redmond, one of our defencemen, had a great habit of whistling if he got caught on a play. It sounded just like a referee's whistle, and sometimes all the players stopped. In this game, it was about halfway through the third period when Ed, who was playing defence with Ted O'Connor, got caught and blew his famous whistle. The Barons waltzed in and scored. When Ed came to the bench, I yelled, "What the hell is wrong with you? You get caught and blow your stupid whistle and the only guy who quits is Ted".

We lost that game 1-0. I was heartbroken, even though we were playing an American League team. It was a great experience meeting Mr. Hendy, who later on sold Johnny Bower off his team to the Leafs, John Ferguson to the Canadiens, and many others. He was a master horse trader in selling players in order to keep his team going.

When the playoffs started that year, we pretty well breezed through our league. We went to the all-Ontario Senior B finals against the Woodstock Athletics. We beat them in six games to win our second Senior B championship and came home to a great reception in Whitby. But already, I was getting restless to move up to Senior A hockey, big time.

"I think we are as good as a lot of Senior A teams," Harry Sinden said one day. I then talked a bit to Bobby Attersley and a few other people about the idea. With their support, I contacted Bill Hanley, the secretary-manager of the Ontario Hockey Association. The league, at that time, was comprised of Hamilton, Kitchener, Owen Sound, Sarnia, Niagara Falls, Stratford, and Brantford. There was only one other professional league at the time, besides the NHL, and that was the American League. Tons of good Canadian players elected not to turn pro and stayed at home to work and play senior hockey. Senior A clubs were paying so well at that time that a player with a combined work and hockey salary was making much more than an American League pro, about $3,500 to $4,000 per season.

I attended the league's next meeting in Kitchener and made my pitch for the Whitby Dunlops to join the league. It never got resolved that day, but I could tell I wasn't getting the warmest reception. That was in June. About three weeks later another meeting was called in Stratford at the Queen's Hotel. Dutch Meier owned the hotel. I really put up a strong pitch that day to join the league. The executive group left the room, and when the group returned, the chairman of the executive group stood up and said, "Mr. Blair, we have great respect for the Whitby Dunlops and your accomplishments, but we think that Whitby is out of our area of configuration, geographically, so we reluctantly turn down your application for entry into our league, but we are accepting the Windsor application, by Mr. Bill Butcher."

I was really upset now. When I reached the door, I turned and said, "Gentlemen, let me tell you something. I am going back to the Eastern Ontario Senior B League and I'm going to turn that entire league Senior A and you guys will never see an Allan Cup again."

That became quite a challenge for them. I came back home to Oshawa and immediately began a tremendous dogfight with my partners in the Eastern Ontario Senior B League to turn our league Senior A. Cornwall, of course, had been Senior A and their manager, Ray Miron, who was also manager of the arena, wanted to move up. Pembroke Lumber Kings, headed by Art Bogart, had joined our league and they too wanted to move up because they had been Senior A in Northern Ontario. Whitby, of course, wanted to move up, but Belleville, Kingston, and Brockville wanted no part of it. I finally got Brockville to agree to move up, with the help of Ray Miron, so that left just Belleville and Kingston.

Reg Walton, President of the Kingston team, and I had sort of a love-hate relationship. We used to sit around after the meetings and games, have a few drinks, argue, and share a few laughs. After a league meeting in Peterborough, I told Reg that if he didn't vote to go Senior A, then Whitby was leaving the league anyway. We were still their best draw.

"Are you trying to intimidate me?" Reg asked.

"Call it whatever the hell you like," I said, "but Whitby is prepared to go to the OHA and take out a single Senior A entry and I will end up playing the winners of that big-shot Senior A League and they can't turn me down according to the OHA bylaws. I will play exhibition games all year, but I won't be playing in Kingston." The next day we talked and they agreed to join us. Their biggest worry was that they were already filling the building and it was going to cost more to operate as a Senior A entry. I told them to put their ticket prices up a little more and they would take in more money.

With Kingston finally in, that left just Belleville. I went down to Belleville to meet with Drury Denyes. "Drury, why won't you come in?"

"Wren, I can't get hockey players the way you do. You know more people than I do, you'll get all the players."

"Wait a minute. We don't need any more players. I'll tell you what, Drury, if you'll agree to go Senior A, I'll help you build your team, too, behind the scenes.

"Are you serious," he said. "You'd do that?" I said yes. "I want to think about it, but will you call me in a couple of days and tell me who I could get and I'll tell you what I think.

I went back to Oshawa that day and called "Bep Guidolin," who I knew was the playing-coach in Timmins of the Northern Ontario Senior A League. I had known Bep for years as a player growing up in Oshawa. Bep had played for the Oshawa Generals when he was only 15.

"Bep, how much money are you making as player-coach in Timmins?"

"$100 a week."

"How'd you like to make $250 a week as a playing-coach?" He immediately thought I meant coming to Whitby and said he'd love to come down as the playing-coach for me. "No," I said, "it's not in Whitby. We can't afford $250 a week." When I told him the job was in Belleville, he agreed. "However," I said, "there is a catch to this. You have to bring five good Senior A players with you to Belleville."

"That's no problem. I can get Moe Savard. I can get Floyd Crawford. I can get Gordie Bell. I can get Minnie Minard and Moe Benoit. I'll talk to them all tonight." I asked how much they were making, and when he told me, I said I was pretty sure I could get them more in Belleville. He promised he would talk to them that night and I was to call him the next day. I did and he verified that they were all ready to go. I called Drury and told him the players that he could have and the money it was going to cost. I could tell, almost immediately, that Drury was very excited. A few days later, we held our league meeting and our entire league voted to elevate to Senior A status.

Shortly after that, Drury got some pretty good players himself, like Al Dewsbury and Johnny McLelland. He was building a pretty good hockey club. The irony of this is that at the end of schedule, we finished first and Belleville finished second, just three points

behind us. In the first round of playoffs, we met Kingston and
Belleville met Cornwall. Then we met Belleville in the league final.
The series went seven games. At one point in the series, I thought,
oh my God, I've created a monster here to beat my own team. However, we prevailed in the seventh game and that meant that we
would now play the "big shots" from the west.

Kitchener had won the west but didn't have any ice, so the first
game was played in Guelph. Our guys were really uptight and nervous and we lost 5-2. I can remember while coming home on the
bus, Harry Sinden, Bobby Attersley, Ted O'Connor, and some of
our other guys were saying that we had never played a worse game.
Sinden was livid. "I wish we could play them again, right now!
Right now!"

When Kitchener came back to our small arena, we won 4-2.
They complained about the arena being a bandbox and that nobody
could win there. The third game was scheduled for Maple Leaf Gardens because Kitchener still didn't have any ice. After the first
game, I will never forget the headline in the *Toronto Telegram*:
"Dunnies find out difference between Senior A and Senior B." After
we tied the series in Whitby, all the papers were saying, wait until
the Dunlops play in Maple Leaf Gardens on the big ice surface. For
that third game, there were about 10,000 people in the stands. We
won. We went back to Whitby for the fourth game and won again,
putting us three games to one. The fifth game was now back in
Kitchener because they had ice again. We lost. The next game we
also lost, right in Whitby.

By this time people were starting to take notice of the Dunnies,
and we played the seventh game before a complete sellout of more
than 8,000 people in Kitchener. Our goaltender that game was Long
John Henderson, and I don't think he ever played a better game. We
went ahead 3-2 late in the game. In the last two or three minutes of
the game, they pulled their goalie and stormed our net. They hit

goal posts and crossbars and when he wasn't looking they were hitting Long John.

We won the game to take the Southern Ontario Senior A crown. There were many fans from Whitby and Oshawa in attendance, and they blew their car horns all the way home from Kitchener. We arrived to a tremendous reception in Whitby.

Then it was off to the North to meet with the North Bay Trappers of the Northern Ontario Senior A League, a very strong league. We had scouted the North Bay team and felt that they were a better team than Kitchener. I remember telling the guys that we had already scored a moral victory this year. At this point, the OHA forced us to move our home games to Maple Leaf Gardens because the Whitby Arena was too small. We played the first two games there and split, winning one and losing one. Now, we had to go to North Bay for the next three games of the series. Technically, all North Bay had to do was win their home games and we were gone. But we won two of three games in North Bay, and then we were going back to the Gardens for game six, leading three games to two. We lost that game to tie the series 3-3.

There were more than 13,000 fans on hand at Maple Leaf Gardens for the final game. We were down 4-3 at the end of the second period and I can remember going around our dressing room asking every player, individually, "Do you think we're out?"

The answers were all the same: "No way!"

Early in the third period Gordie Myles scored to tie it up. Then North Bay scored shortly after to go back in front 5-4. With the score at 5-4, Ted O'Connor put Tommy O'Connor in the clear — Ted could really pinpoint passes — and Tommy went in and deked Marcel Brodeur, the father of Martin Brodeur, the goaltender for the New Jersey Devils today, and scored. Right after that, Teddy put Tommy in the clear again and he scored to make it 6-5. North Bay was all over us and we were trying desperately just to hang on. They had pulled their goaltender and we were in big trouble until Fred Etcher grabbed the puck just inside our blue line. He backhanded the puck so high in the air it almost hit the roof of the Gardens and came down just in front of their goal and trickled into the open net. We won 7-5.

The Whitby Dunlops, in our first year of Senior A hockey, were now in the Allan Cup finals for the Senior A championship of Canada. Our dressing room was like bedlam after the game. To be in the Allan Cup final in our first year of operation was something we hadn't dreamed of. There were many fans still sitting in the stands 20 minutes after the game was over. They were exhausted. I went up into the stands to talk to some people that I knew, and on my way up, I felt someone tug at my coat. I looked down to see Mr. W.A. Hewitt, who had been secretary-manager of the CAHA for years and years and was the father of Foster Hewitt. He was probably in his mid-80s at that time, getting pretty feeble, including his voice. He motioned for me to lean over close to him.

"You know Wren," he said, "I've been involved in hockey for nearly 60 years and have never seen a game as exciting as this one tonight. It was outstanding and the CAHA badly needs an exciting year such as the Whitby Dunlops are providing to get the people in Canada excited about our various trophies again."

When we got back to Whitby, it seemed like the whole town was out in force to welcome us home. They put us on the fire trucks and paraded us around the community. It had to be getting around to 1 o'clock in the morning. Still, they held a big reception at the town square in Whitby.

For the Allan Cup, we were to face Spokane, Washington, who had won the west. At the time, there were two or three American cities playing in the British Columbia Senior A League. The entire Allan Cup series was to be played in Toronto Maple Leaf Gardens. The entire Spokane team was on hand for our final win over North

Bay to scout the series. The CAHA had believed so strongly that North Bay would win the series that the Spokane team had already been set up in a hotel in North Bay. If North Bay had won, the original schedule would have seen games in both North Bay and Toronto.

In the end, the Allan Cup final was somewhat anti-climatic as we beat Spokane in four straight games by lop-sided scores. Still, this was the Allan Cup we had won, the premier trophy in amateur hockey. The Dunnies would go on to achieve a greater goal, the World Championship in 1958.

PROFILE

Harry Sinden

HARRY SINDEN FIRST CAME TO Oshawa when he was a 16-year-old to play for the Oshawa Generals. Harry was from Weston, Ontario, and a year or so after he played for the Generals, I recruited him to play for a Junior A softball team in Oshawa that I was operating at that time. Harry was a good softball player, an outfielder and a catcher. And he was tough. At an exhibition game in Port Hope, Harry was hit smack in the jaw by a pitch during warm-up. The pitch flattened him but he picked himself up and played the rest of the game. Next day we discovered that his jaw was broken. He had to have it all wired up and drank nothing but liquids for the next five or six weeks.

We had a very good softball team in those days. Among Harry's team-mates were Bobby Booth, "Red" Mcdermaid, Joe Piontek, "Herky" Tutak, Des Selles, John Hruska, Teddy Jones, Herky's brother Mike Tutak, Bill Berwick, Nick Mroczeck, Gordie Myles, Gillie DePratto, Zip Thompson, Joe Bosco, Ziggy Benkowski, Sonny Hill, "Dingy" England, Dick Sciuk, and others. We won the Eastern Ontario Junior A Softball Championship several years running, but could never get past Toronto to win the Ontario Championship. Davesville Park Junior Team we met was a powerful squad, led by Peter Conacher, the son of Charlie Conacher, the famous forward of the Toronto Maple Leafs 'Kid Line' in the 1930s.

Besides our regular scheduled games, we also played exhibition games, most notably against my brother in-law's Senior team in Burlington, Ontario. They had their own clubhouse where we could have a few beers and play cards after the games. Near the park there was also a nightclub called the Pier Palace. One year, we played back-to-back games in Burlington on Saturday and Sunday afternoon. After the Sunday game we were drinking a couple of cold beers before leaving for home in our three or four cars, when all of a sudden Harry Sinden and Bill Berwick decided to go into the Pier Palace to see what was going on. In their blind enthusiasm, they walked through the rear door of the club, and ended up walking right out onto the stage just as the announcer was saying, "And for our next act we want to introduce the great so and so." The crowd started to give them a big hand, so Bill and Harry decided to bow. They soon ran from the stage and came back to the cars laughing like crazy. Just as they were telling us the story, I happened to notice a policeman come around the corner of the building at the far end. The Pier Palace employed their own security officers for crowd control at this club, but we thought they were the real thing. Our guys yelled, "Nix, here's the cops, let's get out of here." We all fired our beer bottles under the car and started running towards the canal.

Suddenly, I thought I heard a shot being fired and said to Gillie Deprato, "Are they shooting? Let's hit the ground." We were going to be the first ones shot, because we were bringing up the rear. We ran as far as we could, but there was a big wire fence in front of the canal, so we finally had nowhere to go. The cop pulled up to us waving his gun and lined us up against the wall near the bridge. He was puffing and panting something fierce.

Bill Berwick stepped forward and said to him, "Were you shooting at us?" When he said yes, Bill went on, "Are you nuts? How could I tell my wife, I got shot at a ball game?"

"Why didn't you guys stop?" the cop asked.

"Would you stop if somebody was shooting at you?" Bill replied.

"Ah you weren't shooting real bullets anyway," Zip Thompson interjected.

"Oh yeh?" and the cop stuck his gun through the opening of the fence and fired his gun. The bullet hit the water. That wasn't a blank. "What was going on?" he asked.

When we told him we were playing ball, he said, "Are you the guys that played here yesterday and again this afternoon? I saw both of those games. You guys have a great softball club." So now he starts getting real friendly. "Are you guys getting ready to go home to Oshawa?" In those years the traffic going over the Burlington Skyway on a Sunday was just bumper-to-bumper. "I'll go out onto the highway and stop the traffic, to let you guys out. You guys haven't been drinking too much have you?"

"Oh no!" So he goes out onto the highway, stops the traffic to let us get out. Underneath our cars were the empty beer bottles that we had pitched. As we drove away, he saw all these beer bottles and began to yell, "Hey, hey, hey," but we were on our way. We laughed all the way home.

In the 1953-54 Season, Harry Sinden turned overage from junior and started to play for our OHA Senior B team. He became a star defenceman. In the 1954-55 season, we financially really hit rock bottom. Part way through the year, I called a meeting with the players to tell them that the club could no longer pay them any money for playing. "The only thing we can do, if we plan to carry on, is to pay all the bills first, and if at the end of the year there is any money left, it will be divided among you guys." That used to be called playing for a "split." The split in this case would not be even. "You all get paid by the game now, in various amounts," I told them, "and I will decide, if we go on a split, what your percentage of any net gate left at the end will be. The split will be from 4 to 7 percent. I'll meet with each of you afterwards to let you know what your percentage will be, should you decide to carry on." Only two players quit, and I arranged meetings with the rest.

I met first with Bus Gagnon, my playing coach, and I gave Bus 7 percent. Next was Bobby Attersley, our star forward, who also received 7 percent. That was 14 percent out of 100 percent already gone, so felt I had better start pulling in my horns a little bit. I decided the next most important player to get signed to this new agreement was Harry Sinden. I called Harry late in the afternoon and asked him if he could meet me over at the Spruce Villa Hotel in Whitby that night to discuss his split. Harry said, "Sure I'll see you over there shortly after 7:30." We both arrived at the 'Spruce'within minutes of each other, sat down, and ordered a draft beer each. After some normal chit chat about the team, I said, Now, Harry let's talk about your split. I will give you 6 percent of the net money after expenses are paid." I was splitting hairs, I know, but I wanted to save something for another player.

Harry shot back. "No way! I'm a 7 percent player."

"Not in my book you're not!"

"Then I'm leaving."

As he left the hotel, I thought to myself, he'll probably quit the team now. I had already had two good players quit earlier. To his credit as a man, when we practised the next night, Harry was on the ice. He was still pretty mad at me, and for a while hardly spoke to me, but he did not quit. He stayed with the team through to the end of the season. At the end of the year, when we split-up the money left after expenses, there was no significant difference between a 4 percent and a seven percent split – maybe $15.00. For Harry the money was the issue — it was the principal of the thing. He believed he was a 7 percent player!

When we played the Kitchener-Waterloo Dutchmen for the Senior A Eastern Senior League title some years later, Harry was a powerhouse on defence in our victory, and when we went on to play North Bay on our way to the Allan Cup, Harry played the best hockey of his career. As Captain of the team, he led the Dunnies to the World Championship the next year. I was especially proud to see Harry, as our Team Captain, stand on the top tier of the World Championship podium and accept the Cup as winner of the World Championship. On the other two tiers stood the Captain of the Soviet Union team that had won the silver medal, and the Captain of the Czech team that had won the bronze medal.

Following the game, our sponsor, the Dunlop Rubber Company, rented the entire second floor banquet hall of the Viking Hotel to throw a huge party for all the teams competing in the series. When I joined the celebrations after a series of radio interviews, I noticed the Captain of the Soviet Team Solugabov talking in a very animated tone with our Captain Harry Sinden. A number of our players were also gathered around the table. Captain Solugabov was challenging Captain Sinden to a wrist-wrestling contest for that championship of the world. I guess "Solly," as we nicknamed Solugabov, felt that if they couldn't win the World Championship in hockey, they might save face by beating our Captain in wrist twisting. Solly was much bigger than Harry, but I knew Harry wouldn't back down. When the contest started, Solly brought Harry's arm down close to the table, then Harry summoned every bit of strength he had and reversed the advantage. They went back and forth for some time. Sweat was beginning to show on Harry's brow, but he hung in there. Finally in one huge surge, Harry started Solly's arm moving towards the table and gathered just enough momentum to pin him. We were so proud of Harry. Not only were we World Hockey Champions, but now our Captain had made us World Wrist Twisting Champions. We toasted Harry and had some more drinks to celebrate this championship.

In February 1960, a number of our players were added to the Canadian Olympic Team that played in Squaw Valley, California. Harry Sinden was one of them, together with George Samolenko, Fred Etcher, and Bobby Attersley. That summer I worked feverously to try and get Harry to turn pro and come to Kingston with me to play for the Frontenacs in the EPHL. Harry was not anxious to become a pro. He had a good job at General Motors as a second or third class engineer. Harry and his wife Eleanor had three young children at that time. And he was already 27 years of age. Eventually, I was able to obtain a contract for Harry from Lynn Patrick in Boston that was sufficient for his needs. I was very grateful to Lynn Patrick, as I'm sure Harry was, when he gave me enough funds for Harry to see his way clear to turn pro with Kingston.

I immediately made Harry Captain of the Kingston Frontenacs. He provided strong leadership for two years before I asked him to become a playing-coach. That was our last year in Kingston, but we were able to go out in style by winning the Championship of the EPHL. The next year, we moved the team to Minneapolis, becoming the Minneapolis Bruins. I suggested to Harry that I wouldn't be around as much in my management role and that he should consider retiring as a player to become the full-time coach. He did so, and after one year in Minneapolis, the Bruins moved the team on to Oklahoma City, where a new arena had been built.

Just a few years later, Boston beckoned Harry to move up as coach of the Bruins in the NHL. We had signed a strong cast of young players the year or so before Harry had arrived – indeed, many of these future NHL stars arrived in Boston the same year that Harry took over as coach. Not the least of course of those players was Bobby Orr. Among the others were Derek Sanderson, Dallas Smith, Rick Smith, Wayne Cashman, Don Marcotte, and Gilles Marcotte. The Bruins had recently made a great trade with Chicago, acquiring Phil Esposito, Ken Hodge, and Freddy Stanfield. Harry led this team to a Stanley Cup victory.

Shortly after winning the Stanley Cup, Harry became involved in a contract dispute with the owner Weston Adams. Always strong willed with a mind of his own, Harry quit the Bruins to go into private business. The hockey world was somewhat shocked, me included, when I heard that Harry had left hockey. But Harry was far too good of a hockey man to stay out of the game too long. In 1972, Al Eagleson made perhaps his greatest contribution to Canadian hockey when he engaged Harry as the coach of Team Canada for the Summit Series against the Soviet Union. After embarrassing losses in the Canadian end of the series, Harry surely had a difficult job trying to maintain morale on the Canadian team, but none of us can forget that eighth game in Moscow, as Team Canada, led by Phil Esposito on the ice and Harry Sinden on the bench, managed to fight back in the dying minutes with that heart-stirring goal scored by Paul Henderson.

Soon after the Summit Series, the ownership of the Boston Bruins passed from Weston Adams to a new enterprise known as the Storer Corporation, who hired Sinden to become the general manager of the Boston Bruins. Later, the Bruins were sold to the Jacobs Family, who still own the team. Given the limited seating capacity of the old Boston Garden, the Jacobs Family and Harry Sinden had to operate on a very tight budget to keep the team alive financially. Often criticized for his tight hold on the purse strings, Harry's teams have remained competitive in most years. He has always known the difference between a 6 and a 7 percent player.

*Whitby Dunlops celebrate first Allan Cup Victory
at Maple Leaf Gardens Toronto, 1956–57*

Whitby Dunlops 1958-59 Allan Cup Champions

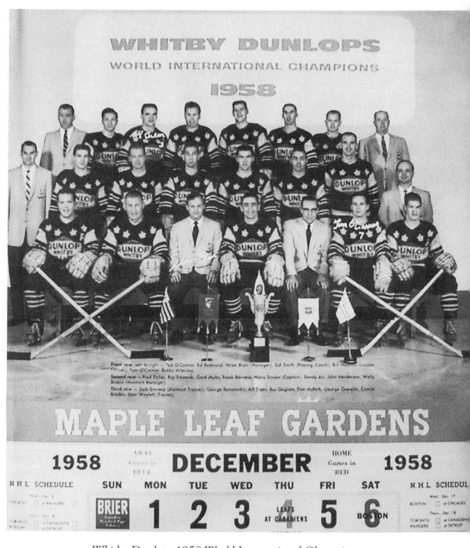

Whitby Dunlops 1958 World International Champions

   Front Row (from left) – Ted O'Connor, Ed Redmond, Wren Blair (Manager), Sid Smith (Playing Coach), Bill Hannah (Liaison Officer), Tom O'Connor, Bobby Attersley.

   Second Row – Fred Etcher, Roy Edwards, Gord Myles, Frank Bonnelo, Harry Sinden (Captain), Sandy Air, John Henderson, Wally Brabin (Assistant Manager).

   Third Row – Jack Donlevy (Assistant Trainer), George Samolenko, Alf Treen, Bus Gagnon, Don McBeth, George Gosselin, Connie Broden, Stan Waylett (Trainer).

4 Champions of the World

IMMEDIATELY AFTER OUR ALLAN Cup victory, I started thinking about going to the annual CAHA convention in Edmonton, Alberta in late May to make a bid for the Dunlops to represent Canada in the World Hockey Championship in March 1958. I talked it over with our players, and with the Dunlop Rubber Company from a sponsorship point of view, because it was certainly going to be expensive. Dunlop was extremely interested because they had plants all over the world. You could see that the wheels were turning in their heads as they imagined what could be accomplished for them on the world stage. I wrote a 16-page brief, and armed with that brief, I traveled to Edmonton. I was extremely excited about this proposition, but also very apprehensive because we had only been in Senior A hockey for one year. Much to my surprise, the CAHA delegates approved us unanimously to represent Canada. I don't think the CAHA had ever approved anything unanimously before.

When I brought the news home to our team, I told them that one of the conditions the CAHA had approved us on was that we had to be suitably strengthened to the satisfaction of the CAHA committee that had been formed at the convention. That meant that every player who had played on the Allan Cup team might not play in Oslo. However, I assured every player from that winning team, they would definitely go to Europe, whether they played or not because if they hadn't won the Allan Cup, we wouldn't have been in a position to apply for the trip in the first place. With all of this in mind, we now began to prepare over the summer months and into the next season to represent the Town of Whitby, the Dunlop Rubber Company, Durham County and all of Canada in our effort win the World championship back for Canada. There had been a world championship in 1957, but the United States and Canada had withdrawn because of the Hungarian uprisings. In 1956, Canada had competed in Cortina, Italy, represented by the Kitchener-Waterloo Dutchmen, but had lost to the Soviet Union. The Soviets had won for the second time in three years, and the Canadian hockey fans were not happy.

The summer of 1957 was a worrisome summer for me. Many of the newspaper people and other hockey people were beginning to grumble that Whitby wouldn't be good enough to restore Canada's hockey championship status in world hockey. It began to grate on my nerves and on the nerves of a great many of the players. I can remember Harry Sinden, Bob Attersley, Charlie Burns, Alf Treen, Frank Bonello, Sandy Air, and Ted O'Connor talking. They were just livid that we had so little respect. We didn't come up in our first year of Senior A hockey and win the Allan Cup because we were off a turnip truck. The media called us a Cinderella team.

At that time, the Dunlop Rubber Company hired Bob Hesketh away from the *Toronto Telegram* to become the publicity director of our team. He was a well-respected feature writer in Toronto at the time. Bob was a very enterprising publicity guy and he knew that he had a very "hot" property in me — I would react to any kind of criticism — so he started prompting guys who would criticize our team publicly in order to get a reaction back from me. I always remember one article late in summer where Harold Ballard was quoted. It was headlines in all three Toronto papers. Harold said that the Dunlops were a silly choice by CAHA, but what's new with the CAHA — they could never run anything right. Right after it came out in the papers, Bob called me and said, "What do you think of that bastard, Ballard?" Oh, Bob, you put me on!

I had no idea that Hesketh had set up the whole thing, but I reacted. I said, "Well that fat ol' bastard Ballard, what does he know about hockey? He's only in hockey because he's riding on Stafford Smythe's coattails." Of course, Bob writes this, and releases it all over the country, and the Dunlop Rubber Company got their name spread right across the nation and even into Europe.

We had decided early that we would withdraw from competition in the Eastern Ontario League around January 25 because we were going to sail to Europe on the 29th from New York on the new *Queen Elizabeth* ship. We had told all of the other clubs in our league that although we would be involved in the standings, the Dunlops would not be a candidate for the playoffs. The season started on those conditions. We played an accelerated schedule, four and sometimes five games a week to get as many games in before we left. We were probably the best drawing card in the league and the teams were worried about losing money if we weren't coming into their buildings, so we resolved this by agreeing to play extra games.

The next thing that we heard was that the Soviet Union, for the first time in history, was coming to Canada for an eight-game tour. The CAHA had set it up so that the Whitby Dunlops and the Soviet Union would kick off the tour with a game at Maple Leaf Gardens. I recall that the Soviets came over about November 15 and practiced every day in Maple Leaf Gardens. The Toronto media were at the practices every day. I believe the Soviets pulled off the greatest con job of the media in history. They did everything the exact opposite of the way we practiced. They only practiced the goaltenders in the corner of the rinks, not in the nets. They marked off areas in the corner of the rinks, put one goalie in each corner, and shot at them. They had a tremendous skating team.

As we played league games and drifted towards this showdown on November 22 with the Soviets, I began to take our team to the Soviet practices. Our guys were mystified as to what was going on.

By the time the game arrived, the Gardens was completely sold out. When we started the game, it just seemed to me that our whole team was just 18 more spectators. Our players were so busy watching what the Soviets were doing that they completely lost track of their own game. The Soviets scored in the first minute of play. In the second minute of the game, they scored again. I can remember walking up and down behind the bench saying to myself: Oh my God, a goal a minute, we could lose 60-0.

Finally, I got so mad that I went to the front of the bench and talked loudly enough so that everybody could hear. "Look, there's about 16,000 people in here and they all paid about $10 to get in. I have a feeling that all I've got is about 18 more spectators on this bench, which is fine by me. But if that's the case, and I believe it is, then at least have the decency to get off this damn bench, go the box office and pay your admission the same as all these people have and we'll all watch this game together. Otherwise, Alfie start slamming some of these guys out there; Teddy knock somebody over." The players weren't too happy with me over those stinging remarks, but it seemed to snap them out of their lethargic state and we started to hit. The Soviets were great if you let them roll in those days — it's not the same today where they can hit every bit as much as we can — but in those days they didn't have much experience with hard-hitting. They liked to wheel and deal with their heads down, but if you hit them it was a different story. They just seemed to collapse. We scored the next five goals to come out of the first period ahead 5-2. We scored two more goals in the game to win 7-2.

It was probably a good thing that the Canadian public got a glimpse of just how good a team we would face overseas, but then we started hearing rumors that this wasn't really the Soviet national team. The rumors were true. So, then the media started all over again, saying if that wasn't the national team, then what was going to happen in March. The Soviets also played the Montreal Junior

Canadiens during this tour and won big, then trounced the Toronto Marlboros and a team from the United States. They only lost two games on their tour.

In late November, after the Soviet game, I began to sense that Long John Henderson, who had played so brilliantly for us the year before, was not playing that well. John and I had a bitter contract dispute in the summer. He was asking for more money than he knew the Whitby Dunlops could afford to pay, especially with our small rink. I refused to budge and he was really ugly. I think he missed a game or two. He finally signed, but it was sort of a protest signing. I've found that no matter who is involved, in all contract battles between club and player, it always seems to affect the player. The relationship between the club and players deteriorates; the relationship with their own teammates slips. All of the players then felt that they were a team and should be compensated almost on the same level, whereas today players love it when a teammate goes for a big raise because it might get them more, if he wins.

I started dropping the word around in hockey circles that I was looking for a goaltender. One day, I got a call from Bob Wilson, who at that time was the chief scout of the Chicago Blackhawks. "Wren, I understand, you're looking for a goaltender," he said.

"I certainly am."

"How would you like Roy Edwards?" he asked. I knew Roy Edwards from the year before when he had played for St. Catharines in junior. He was a hot prospect. "He's playing in Fort Wayne, in the International League."

"If I did want him, Bob, how could you get him away from Fort Wayne?"

"Well, we put him there," said Wilson, "we can certainly take him out."

"If that's the case, Bob, then get him up here as fast as you can."

Edwards arrived a couple of days later and a couple of days after that, I called both him and Long John into my office. "Look, we're playing an accelerated schedule, so I'm going to alternate you two every game. In the end, Sid Smith (who was my playing-coach then) and I will decide who is going to play in the world championship. And whoever that is, the other guy will not play unless we have an injury." In the end, young Roy just took that job away from Long John. He was just tremendous and at the end, there was no hesitation, by either Sid or myself, on who would be our goaltender in the tournament. We played 27 games overseas and Edwards was in goal for all of them

We made several additions to the team from the year before and I'm still amazed at how well the newcomers fit in with our team. We got Sid Smith from the Leafs early in the year. Sometime in early October, I had noticed that Smitty wasn't playing very much, so I called Stafford Smythe. I didn't even know Stafford at the time.

"Stafford, this is Wren Blair calling."

"What do you want?" he answered, a very nice opening salvo. I thought: Oh my God, what am I doing?

"Mr. Smythe. As you know, Whitby Dunlops are going to represent Canada in the world hockey championships and I notice that you aren't playing Sid Smith very much and I was wondering if I was to make him my playing-coach, would you consider loaning him to us for the world championships?"

"What the hell's the matter with you? Do you know the rules in hockey?"

"Well, I do in amateur, but I don't know what you're talking about."

"Well, in pro hockey, every player has to be waived out of the league. Have you ever tried getting a player past Eddie Shore?"

"Well, no sir, I don't even know Eddie Shore.

"Well, I don't know how you expect me to do that."

"I'm sorry, I said, I'm only asking."

"Call me at my home, a week from today, in the afternoon, and I'll have an answer for you." He gave me his home phone number and hung up. I felt, Oh, Jesus, I don't want to make that call . . . he'll only start yelling at me again. I made that call, a week later.

"This is Wren Blair calling."

"You got him," he yelled into the phone.

In those days, if you got a player from minor pro, you had to pay to have a player reinstated. So at that point, I said, "Just a minute, Mr. Smythe, for how much?"

"What do you mean, you jerk; do you think you're the only Canadian who cares about Canada? For nothing, stupid! When do you want him there?"

We continued to play in the Eastern Ontario league and finished our schedule in January. We were way out in front in the standings, in fact, I believe when the season ended we were still in first place. We took a bus to New York City and our wives came with us. We had a night out in New York City and got on the ship the next day. The bus waited because it had to take our wives back home to Whitby. About an hour and half after our wives left, we pulled away from the dock and sailed past the Statue of Liberty. I don't think any of us had ever been overseas before. The amazing thing was that five or six of our players were seasick before we even got out of the harbor and headed for their bunks. Many of them never left there the entire trip. Jack Donnelly was really sick and so were Eddie Redmond and Goose Gosselin. I had talked to a doctor about seasickness before we left and he had told me that seasickness was a case of mind over matter. Anytime you feel like you're going to get sick, get up on that deck and walk and walk until you get rid of that feeling.

I was rooming with Bob Attersley and Frank Bonnello. I told Bob this, so every so often, I would look at Bob and say, "You look a little peaked, let's go." So up we'd go and walk and walk and walk. Neither one of us was ill. They had great food on this ship, and we'd go down and have dinner. After dinner, Bob would say, "Let's go down and see the guys who are sick." Bob would walk in and say, "Boy, what a great dinner we had — do you know what we had?" And then he'd go into great detail about the menu. Guys would be throwing stuff at him and cursing him, saying, "Get out of here, you goof."

We had a great trip overseas. We got to know the captain, the purser, and a lot of the staff. They all treated us like royalty because they knew who we were and what we were going after. We stopped in Cherbourg, France and they let us off the ship for three hours. We did a little shopping, and I can still remember that almost everybody there was on bicycles. We got back on the ship and sailed on to Southampton, England. There was a train waiting for us and it took us to London where we had to play the next night in the Wembley Arena. We played in Brighton the next night. I always remember that game against the Brighton Tigers. They had packed about 5,500 people in the stands. Hockey was big in the British Isles then. Every once in a while the crowd would start singing, "Up the Tigers, Up the Tigers." They played pretty well against us, but we won by five or six goals. After that game, we played the next night in Herringa arena and then were scheduled to fly to Zwybruken, Germany to play against the Canadian Air Force team stationed there.

The reason we took the ship overseas instead of flying is that I wouldn't fly at that time. They players weren't upset because they enjoyed the passage. Now were scheduled to fly to Germany, but I still wouldn't get on an airplane. To complicate matters for me, the day before, a plane carrying the Manchester Football Team had crashed, killing everybody on board. Then the players were saying: "We're not flying." But I made them get on that plane because we had made a commitment and we'd have been in a helluva mess with

Bunny Ahearne, the President of the International Ice Hockey Federation, if we didn't honor it. They went without me, though. Don McBeth and I took a boat across the English Channel. It was an overnight trip and the channel was rough as hell. We landed in the Hook of Holland the next morning and took a Scandanavian Express straight to Stockholm where our team was scheduled to play two games.

That was a very eventful trip for Mac and I. Before we left Canada, the town of Whitby had given us all Bolex movie cameras and we were shooting everything that moved. As we were heading for Stockholm, the train stopped in Hamburg, Germany. The train had a 40-minute stop, so I said to Mac let's get off take some pictures of real live Germans. We were in a compartment with a whole bunch of Norwegian sailors and they were getting pretty bombed. We grabbed our cameras, left our topcoats on the train, and left. We were in the town square shooting movies of pretty girls. Finally, Mac and I went back downstairs to where the train was. But there was no train there. I thought maybe it had backed up for a minute to get something done.

Standing near the end of the platform was a great big kind of a guard in uniform, looking like Schultz in *Hogan's Heroes*. We walked over to him and asked him where the train had gone.

"Stockholm Express?"

"Yes, Stockholm Express, we were on that train."

"Stockholm Express. Bye. Bye."

We had four trunks of equipment on that train, all painted in Dunlop colors. Finally, the officer directed us upstairs to talk with someone who understood English. We were told that there was another train due out shortly and that by making a few changes, we might to be able to catch our train in Copenhagen. We took a couple of local trains and then got on a little boat and went across this channel in rough water. But we spent most of the time up in the cabin with the captain drinking rum. We got off at some little town and back on another train and pretty soon we're traveling into Copenhagen. We're thoroughly discouraged now, blaming each other for getting us into this predicament.

All of a sudden, Mac says to me, "There's our train, there's our equipment, right there."

"Look we've got to get off this train," which was still moving at this point. So we grabbed our cameras and off we go. We started running across the tracks and the other train just started to move. We managed to get somebody's attention and they stopped the train and we got on. We walked back into our compartment and by this time the Norwegian sailors are really drunk.

"Where'd you go? Where'd you go?"

"Oh, we went down to the front of the train and talked to some of our friends." We never did tell them where we'd been. We had been gone for eight hours. Well, Mac and I laughed all the way to Stockholm. We agreed then and there that we wouldn't tell the other guys that we missed the train and lost all the equipment for eight hours. We never told them for ages.

We were met at the Stockholm station by an interpreter hired by Dunlop. His name was Bengt, a good-looking guy about 25 years of age. We just called him Benny. He was a great guy. We beat the Swedish national team two games there and they had about 12,000 at each game. We played a game in Sojetelin, a suburb of Stockholm, and then we went down to Malmo, which is right on the coast, and played another outdoor game. We had to walk through the snowbanks from these little huts, which were the dressing rooms, to get to the rink.

The players got into a terrible fight that day. There was a little guy on the Malmo team who reminded me of Mickey Rooney. He was skating around and running at everybody. Ted O'Connor came to me during the game and said, "That little bastard is getting on my nerves. He's running everybody and high sticking them. I'd like to run him."

"Look, Ted, if you can keep it undetected, go ahead, he's getting to me, too. I don't think the Swedes had ever seen the one where you go into the corner and leave the shaft of your stick open and let them take that right in their guts. The little Swede went into the corner one time and all of sudden he's down on the ice and he's rolling and moaning. I said to the players, "Teddy got him." And then I turned to the Swedish people and yelled, "Heart attack, heart attack."

It turned out to be a pretty rough game after that. The referees started giving us all sorts of penalties and the crowd was going nuts. When the game ended, the pathway toward our dressing room area was lined with all these hissing Swedes. I stopped the players and said, "Hold it, guys. Get your sticks at high mast and the first person that moves give it to them, right over the head, and let them know that to take a step means we're going to react." We walked all the way to the dressing room and there was no problem because they knew we meant business.

That night the Malmo Hockey Association threw a banquet for us. The guy who ran the team came over to my table. During the game, he had been yelling at the referee about our play and finally went out on the ice and started yelling again. At that point, I had gone on the ice, too, and told him to get back on his bench. At my table he says, "Mr. Blair, we have a little trouble, but no hard feelings."

"No, no, don't worry about it, it happens all the time in Canada."

"Oh good," he says, "the only problem is that four times you say to me that bad English word." Now, he's made me really mad because he can't let it go.

So, I say, "Four times?

And he says, "Yes."

"Well, make it five: "F. . . off!" Well, all the guys at our table, broke right up . . . they talked about it for days.

We played 10 games all over Sweden, a great hockey country. It's really amazing to me how many countries are playing our national game now. After we finished our games in Sweden, we traveled by train to Oslo, Norway, where we were met by another interpreter, Chic. Before the tournament started, I invited him up to my room for a drink. He got pretty plastered. (It's always the other guy who gets plastered, I never do!) I had seen many movies involving the Norwegian underground during the war, and it always seemed to me that they had been the bravest of the resistance fighters. I asked Chic about this one particular movie that had intrigued me, and quizzed him on whether he thought the underground stories were true. He went to the window and looked down at the square below. "See this square here . . . we call it the town circle. The Norwegian underground published a newspaper every day telling the truth to the people about who was winning the war. We would get the real truth from Britain. Finally, the German officers handed an ultimatum to the Norwegian people that if the underground didn't stop printing that paper, they would smash the presses every day. But we continued to publish. In response, the Germans would go into a Norwegian classroom every day and pick out one teenager at random, take him from the class, bring him to the circle and shoot him at 5 o'clock every day."

"Chic, that can't be true," I said.

"Can't be true," he said, and now he was crying. "I stood here. I watched every day. A boy one day, a girl the next. Shot. But you know, Wren, that newspaper never stopped coming out." I've always wondered if our Canadians and Americans really understand what went on in those countries during the war and appreciate the bravery of the people involved in fighting the invaders.

I had heard many times that the Norwegian hockey players were a lot tougher than the Swedish players. I asked Chic what he thought. He looked at me and said, "Ach, Sweden."

"You don't like the Swedes."

"Ach, let me tell you about the Swedes. You know what they do Wren. When the Germans came, they could not get in from the sea because the British boats were patrolling the North Sea, so they made a deal with the Swedish people to let the Germans come in through Sweden and cross by land to Norway. The deal was that Swedes would let them do that if they promised never to declare war on Sweden. They came from behind, out of the trees, big surprise, and Oslo fell in four days. You know Wren, we had a saying in Norway, '10,000 Swedes ran through the weeds, while one Norwegian chased them.' Can you remember that saying? Tell everybody in Canada, because that's the way we feel."

"The first day they came into Oslo, they went to the North section where all our big homes are, walked into the homes and threw the people out. They said, 'Out, a German officer is going to live here now.' They'd bring their ladies in from Germany and move into those homes."

When the Allies finally landed in Norway to liberate Norway, Chic said the Allies took back Oslo without one shot being fired. The Allies lined up on one side of the street and the German troops were on the other side. Suddenly, the Germans bolted and ran back into the trees through Sweden and were gone. I could tell from the way Chic was crying that our talk had brought back some very painful memories for him.

The next day the Whitby Dunlops took to the ice in the World Championship.

We had finished our two final pre-tournament games in Norway and were set to start the 1958 World Hockey Championship series. We had moved into the Viking Hotel, with two other teams from the tournament – the Americans and the Russians. The tournament was going to be played in the Yodelamphi Stadium, built by Sonja Henie, who had won the figure skating championships in the 1936 Olympics and shortly after that moved to Hollywood, where she became a movie star. She made a lot of money in the movies and in the Ice Follies, which she used in her later years to build this stadium for the Norwegian people. The stadium seated around 10,000 people; it was open at the top and partially covered along the sides.

To our original Whitby team, we had added Roy Edwards in goal from the Chicago Blackhawks and Sid Smith from the Toronto Maple Leafs, as our playing-coach. We also added a defenceman – Jean Paul Lamirande – from Quebec City. Punch Imlach and Joe Crozier owned the Quebec Aces of the Quebec Pro League at that time. We were loaned Lammy, as we called him, under the condition that we would play a game in Quebec City after the tournament ended and Quebec would keep the entire gate. We also added George Gosselin, a left winger from the North Bay Trapper team. We acquired him to replace Fred Etcher, who had broken his leg about a month or so before we were to leave to go overseas. Our other big addition was Connie Broden from the Montreal Canadiens. After we picked up Sid Smith, I traveled to Montreal to talk to Mr. Frank Selke, General Manager of the Canadiens, and to Sam Pollock, who was the director of the Canadiens' farm system, to see what kind of a contribution we could get from the Montreal Canadiens. When I got into Mr. Selke's office, he asked me if I had any idea who I would like?

"Yes," I responded, "you own a player by the name of Connie Broden and I don't even know where he is playing right now, but I know he is a good hockey player."

He looked at me and said, "You don't make things very easy, do you?" Connie Broden was now owned by Springfield. He had refused to report to Springfield and had been suspended by Eddie

Shore. I asked, if perhaps he could call in some past favors to Eddie Shore and see if he couldn't get him to drop the suspension. If he could, I promised that the Montreal Canadiens would receive substantial publicity for this contribution to our cause. He promised me he would try, but also cautioned me that Eddie Shore was a very difficult person to deal with. Eventually, Sam called me and told me that they had made a deal with Shore. They had to give him another player, but Broden wasn't going to play there anyway. He then gave me all the information on Connie and said it's now up to me to get him to play. I talked with Connie and was able to persuade him to play with us. He didn't join us until late in the year, but was added to our team to go overseas.

A couple of our regular players did not accompany us overseas when we left in late January, but arrived before the tournament started. Sandy Air, who was not going to play in the tournament, and Doug Williams, a school teacher who could not get the amount of time off we needed, flew over just before the tournament started. We paid for their flights because we wanted the entire team that had won the Allan Cup the year before to be part of this world tournament. Mr. Bill Hannah had also been added to our tournament team as the laison officer between the hockey club and Dunlop Rubber Company. Bob Hesketh was with us, along with Wally Brabin, our assistant manager, and our trainer, Stan Waylett. They made up our contingent of 27 people.

On the ship, I had talked to the team about our conduct. It was not my intention to suppress a good time, but I reminded them of the bad behavior of teams that had gone before. If we were going to have a few drinks, I suggested that we get to our hotel rooms behind closed doors and not be caught sitting around bars with the press watching every move we make. I wanted to come out of this with an impeccable reputation for our sake and for the sake of the Dunlop Rubber Company. "If you do this for me, voluntarily," I promised, "I won't check curfews or anything else. But I can assure you that when the tournament ends, win, lose or draw, you can do whatever the hell you want." The guys were great. When the tournament ended, Milt Dunnell of the *Toronto Star* commented as he was interviewing me, "Wren, I want to tell you something. Of all the teams that have come over here — and I have covered many of them back to 1930 — this is the very best-behaved team that ever represented Canada. I want to compliment you on that because those things just don't always happen." I thought to myself, if he had been behind the closed doors a few nights he might not have thought that. In truth, they did a great job as ambassadors.

One of the things that really concerned me as we prepared for the opening of the tournament was the mental pressure that was being placed on the team. We had received telegrams from all over Canada — from the Prime Minister, from the Premiers of all the provinces, and the executives of many of the biggest corporations in the country. I made a mistake when I jammed all the telegrams we received into three bushel baskets, dumped them in the middle of the dressing room, and started reading some of them to the team before our game against the Soviets. All of the telegrams carried the same tone: Don't forget you are Canadians; bring home the bacon; don't let us down. I don't believe there was one telegram that said: Win, lose or draw, we're with you.

We opened the tournament against Poland and won 14-1. Next, we shut out Norway 12-0, and then in game three we beat Finland 24-0. This was the first time that Finland had ever played in an international hockey tournament. Today they are one of the world powerhouses. We really only had to concentrate on the Soviet Union, Czechoslovakia, Sweden, and the United States. As a result, I kept some of our better players under wraps in these games so as not to expose them to the scouting of the Soviet Union, who were at every one of our games as we were at theirs. In many games,

I hardly played Bobby Attersley, who I felt was our best forward, so the Soviets wouldn't concentrate on him when we played them.

Our next game was against the United States and we beat the Americans 8-3. I turned all our cannons loose in that game. Our next game was against Sweden. I can remember telling our guys that we had to hammer these Swedes — we couldn't let them skate. We took a ton of penalties en route to a 10-2 win. We had a couple of days off before our next game against Czechoslovakia, which was to be our toughest game before the Soviets. Roy Edwards was just outstanding in this game. I can always remember Baz Bastien, who had worked with Detroit during Edwards' days in the Detroit net, telling me years later that he was one of the best goaltenders he had ever seen. I really think that the Czechs outplayed us and may have even out shot us, but Roy just stoned them as we won 6-0.

We had another day off before meeting the Soviet Union in the final game. FINAL GAME! The Soviets had been tied 5-5 by the Czechs, so, technically, we only needed a tie in the final game to win. However, our players wouldn't hear of that. All of Canada wanted us to beat the Soviets. I spent a lot of time the night before the final with Bob Atterlsey, Harry Sinden, and Ted O'Connor going over a game plan for the next day. I finally ended up alone with Bob in my room and told him, you know Bob, how you go tomorrow, is how we go. You have to come up with the best game of your life and so does Harry, Charlie Burns, Sid Smith, Roy Edwards, and others. But you, especially, Bob.

The tension in our dressing room was unbelievable and it certainly showed in our play to start. The Soviets scored early in the first period to go up 1-0, and they seemed content to keep it that way. They were masters at protecting the lead. They would string five players across the blue line, making it very difficult for us to get any flow in our game. Late in the second period we were still scoreless. Their goaltender was outstanding and their defence was playing extremely well. I can remember looking at Attersley on the bench. His face was just white from the tension. I remembered him telling me the night before that all of the mind games I used on other players wouldn't work on him. I agreed. He was a self-motivated player, just like Harry Sinden was. For others I have to get the needle out in order to motivate them, to get them to achieve new heights. There are guys like that on every team.

I had to think of something to get Bobby riled, get him mad at me if that's what it was going to take. I wracked my brain to come up with something. Suddenly, it struck me. Bob is the President of the Young Conservative Party of Ontario riding and no one is further from a Communist than a Conservative. Our players' bench was like a baseball dugout — I was in front of the players, not behind them as we are in Canada. We had a line change and Bob came off the ice. He sort of glanced at me and went and sat down. I went down the bench, leaned down over him, looked in his eyes, and then whispered, "You know Bob, the way you're playing today, I'm beginning to doubt your political beliefs."

He jerked back, looked at me, and said, "What did you say?"

"Aw shut up, don't talk to me. You see those red shirts out there. You show them. You show them, not me!" He charged off the bench.

With a couple of minutes to go in the period, Jean-Paul Lamirande let a shot go from the blue line. He had an extremely, low accurate shot that enabled our forwards to tip them at the net. Attersley deflected the shot to tie the score. As Bobby came off the ice, I thought, well I'm not going to let up now. I don't think that was the reason he scored, but I had to keep on him. He was now so mad at me, he forgot all about being uptight. When he went by me, I said, "Can you imagine that, you fluked a goal?" He turned, glared back at me, and muttered something. I kept that tone up with him for the rest of the game.

In the third period, Connie Broden scored to put us ahead 2-1, but two or three minutes later, the Soviets scored again to tie it up. They were a helluva team — it seemed when they needed to score, they could score. They had been playing "kitty-bar-the-door," but when we went ahead they opened up and tied it up quickly. The tension was building. If they had scored the next goal, I don't know if we could have come back. It stayed 2-2 until about four minutes to go when Alexandrov of the Soviets broke through in the clear and went right in on Edwards. I remember turning to somebody on the bench and saying, "I can't watch this, let me know what happens." Usually, when any European team scores against Canada, there is a great uproar in the rink. Even though it was the Soviet Union, they were seen as a European team by the fans. But as I turned back to watch the play, there was no outburst from the crowd. Alexandrov had gone right in on Roy, deked him until he fell, and then flipped a backhander that went off the crossbar.

As I'm talking, I look out on the ice and there's Attersley streaking down the ice. As so often happens in hockey, when somebody misses an opportunity, the other team takes over because you're still in shock. Atterlsey picked up that shot off the crossbar and turned up ice. He went right in on Pucsnov, deked him, and scored to put us up 3-2 with a little more than three minutes to go. Our team went nuts. It was all I could do to keep them on the bench.

The teams went back to center ice for the faceoff. Bob won the faceoff, went down the right side, pulled a defenceman with him, and then fired a perfect pass to Bus Gagnon, who was streaking down the left wing. He buried it to put us ahead 4-2. The goal came 15 seconds after Attersley had scored. The guys were cheering, some were crying on the bench. All of the players who were not dressed came out of the stands and jammed our bench for the last three minutes until the game was over. The players were hugging each other and saluting our Canadian fans who had made the trip over.

They finally got our players lined up at the blue line for the playing of O *Canada* as they slowly raised our flag. Canadians are usually not demonstrative in their patriotism, although I feel they should be. You always see Americans, for instance, putting their hands over their hearts and singing the *Star-Spangled Banner* at sporting events. But as I looked down the line of our players, they were just belting out the words of O *Canada* and it got louder and louder.

Gold medals were awarded to the team members before a speech from Bunny Ahearne, and, finally, the World Championship trophy was presented to our captain, Harry Sinden. It's a picture that is forever etched in my mind — and I'm sure in the minds of every member of our Canadian contingent.

PROFILE

Dunnies

ALTHOUGH BOB ATTERSLEY, Harry Sinden, Bus Gagnon, Ted and Tommy O'Connor, Alf Treen, and Long John Henderson certainly stood out among the Whitby Dunlop World Champion team other 'Dunnies' made significant contributions to the victory, players who understood the importance of quality checking and defensive play. Three defensive-minded forwards on the team come quickly to mind, Sandy Air, Frank Bonello, and Charlie Burns. Not only did these players score important goals for the club from time to time, we were seldom scored against when they were on the ice.

Sandy Air first came to my attention when he played for the Oshawa Generals in the later 1940s and checked opposition players in the corners with great skill. There is an old saying in hockey that games are won in the corners, be it in your own end or in the opposition end. Sandy drove opposing players crazy trying to get out of their own end. He would dog them relentlessly. If they finally got away from him, he would scamper back to be on their case again. Once when we were playing the Belleville McFarlands in the Eastern Final of the OHA Senior A league, Sandy Air dogged and dogged one of their players in their end until he finally took the puck away from them. He quickly moved to the net and scored a beautiful goal on Gordie Bell, an outstanding goaltender. Sandy threw the puck high over Bell's shoulder and into the net, which stood up as the winning goal, and put the Dunnies into the next series with the Kitchener-Waterloo Dutchmen. Today Sandy is a very prominent employee of the HSBC Firm. I talk to Sandy every two weeks or so and our families get together from time to time.

Sandy's linemate, Frank Bonello, was another forward who understood the art of defence in the game of hockey. The hard checking of Frank and Sandy gave their other linemate, Gordie Myles, the chance to score tons of goals for the Dunnies. Frank was a guy with a very droll sense of humor. At one time, I had sold a small amount of shares in the team to a friend of mine named Wally Brabin. Wally had very little connection to the game of hockey, but because of our friendship and his support, I gave him the title of Assistant Manager. Wally was always dressed up to the nines, and he would come into the dressing room and talk to the guys from time to time. Frank knew that Wally didn't have a lot of experience with hockey. One game he called Wally aside, and in a mock serious way, quietly said to Wally, "I don't like the way that Stan, our trainer, tapes my sticks. Wally, I don't want you to hurt Stan's feelings, so if you see him taping my sticks, could you try in a nice way to get them away from him, and you tape them for me." Well, this made Wally feel important. "Frank, don't worry about it. I'll make sure that I take care of your sticks." Meanwhile Frank goes to Stan shortly after Wally started taping a couple of Frank's sticks, and said, "I've noticed Wally taping my sticks lately. He doesn't know anything about taping sticks. I don't want you to let him tape my sticks. Nobody knows as well as you do how I like my sticks taped."

Frank had told me on the side what he had done, and so I was quietly watching for the results of this set up. Wally would jerk Frank's sticks away from Stan, Stan would resist. This went on for a week or so, and finally one night in a bit of anger, Wally said, "Stan, I do not want to hurt your feelings, but Frank told me he doesn't like the way you tape his sticks, and not to let you do them." Stan looked at Wally for a second and said, "That bastard Frank. He told me the same not to let you tape his sticks." At this point our whole dressing room broke up because by this time most of the players were in on the joke.

Frank had played for Galt in Major Junior "A" Hockey, and moved up to play for the Chatham Maroons in Senior A Hockey. He was living the Toronto area when I got in touch with him about playing for us in Whitby, which meant that he could live at home and keep his day job there while also playing hockey. When Frank retired from playing, he became Coach of the Markham team in the Metro Junior A League when I was operating the Oshawa Generals in that same league. Sandy Air was the General Manager of the Brampton team, Bob Attersley the coach of the Whitby team, and Dougie Williams, who played for me in Whitby, was my coach with Oshawa. Frank has stayed close to his hockey routes over the years, and today he is Director of Central Scouting for the NHL in Toronto. My brother Gerald is a scout who works under Frank.

Charlie Burns was another player who understood the value of forechecking. I don't think I've ever seen a player at any level who could forecheck better than Charlie. Charlie was such a great skater. In the World Championship final game against the Soviet Union, they went ahead 1-0. A few minutes later, we were called for two double minor penalties only seconds apart. If the Soviets had had ever gone ahead 2-0, I think it could very well have spelled curtains for us. The Soviets were masters of protecting a lead. To kill the penalties, I put Charlie on the ice as our lone forward with Ted O'Connor and Harry Sinden on defence. Charlie hounded the Soviet players so hard in their own end that they had great difficulty in getting rolling. When they did, Charlie charged back to assist our defenceman. Eventually, we killed the clock on that double penalty. In the early years of NHL expansion, I was able to acquire Charlie for the Minnesota North Stars, where he served for me as playing coach and became a key player in our early success with this franchise before coaching in the minor pro leagues.

Another Dunnie who understood the art of defence was Doug Williams. Doug was a Whitby native who had played Major Junior A Hockey in Stratford, but when I signed him to play for us, he was playing for Peoples Credit Jewelers in the THL in Toronto. Not only could Doug check, he could scrap with the best of them. I remember one night in Kingston when we had got into a big scrap that flowed over into the crowd. Kingston fans started coming at us out of the stands in droves. The police were unable to keep them away from our bench. They had some of our players down under the bench. Doug got up onto the boards, skates and all, gave a yell and jumped skates first right into that melee. The Kingston fans scattered in every direction. Doug became my first coach when I returned the Oshawa Generals to the Motor City. Doug and his wife Marion have remained great friends of ours over the years.

Tommy O'Connor and his brother Ted added a touch of levity to the team. Tommy was a great comedian who often used his brother Ted as a prop for his jokes. Ted was a bit always on the heavy side, and Tommy would needle him, "Here comes the beach ball with legs on it." Ted let himself be the butt of some of Tommy's jokes for the fun of the team. Tommy wasn't a great skater, but he was a wizard in handling the puck when he got in tight on goaltenders.

In the later years of the Dunnies, we added a few new players who made great contributions to the team. Bob Hassard battled his way up to play for the Toronto Maple Leafs in the NHL after playing for us. He used to always call me "Blairs." I would come in the dressing room and say, "How are you doing Bobby?" He'd say, "I'm doing great Blairs, how about you?" Bob was a good checking forward who had a dry sense of humor like Frank Bonello.

Another great player we added in this same era Pete Babando. We nicknamed him "Hass." Pete had played in the National Hockey League for the Detroit Red Wings and was credited with scoring a sudden death overtime goal that won the Stanley Cup for the Red Wings, when, on a line change, he flipped the puck into the opposition end and it bounced on rough ice and skipped past the goaltender. Signing Pete to a contract each year drove me nuts. No matter what I offered him, he wouldn't answer at all. He would just sit there. So, finally I had to say, "Well what do you think Pete?" Finally, he would look at me, and with a big sigh, say, "Jeez, I don't know Wren." He didn't say no, he didn't say yes, but I'm sure he got some better money from me than I had in mind just because I wanted to get on with things. Pete came to play for my team in Clinton, New York after the Dunlops folded.

Another player who followed me to Clinton was Jack Kane. Jack was only about 21 years of age when I acquired him from Chatham to play for the Dunnies. He was from Peterbrough, so he commuted back and forth to practices and games the same as Eddie Redmond and Jack Donlevy were doing. Jack still lives in Clinton, New York.

Without these hard-working, defensive-minded players, the Whitby Dunlops would not have won the Allan Cup or the World Championship. I still appreciate their contribution to the success of our team.

5 The Clinton Comets and the Squaw Valley Olympics

THE MORNING AFTER OUR GOLD medal victory, the phone screeched in my room. I reached over from my bed and picked it up. A Norwegian operator was on the line. "Meeester Blaaair, this is the overseas operator calling and you have a long distance call coming in from Canada. If you hang up, I will call you back in two or three minutes and connect you." That's the way they handled overseas calls in those days. A couple of minutes later, the phone rang again and this voice came on, almost a snarl, and said, "Wren, congratulations." That was the extent of the conversation about our world championship win. "This is Stafford Smythe calling."

'Oh, Staff. Where are you?'

"In my office, in Toronto. Where do you think I'd be? I don't want to take too long on this. We've had our eye on you for some time in the Toronto Maple Leaf organization and I want you to make me a promise." I said, I will, if I can. "I want you to promise me that you will not talk to any other NHL team until you return and talk to me first."

"Stafford, since no other NHL team has contacted me that is a pretty easy promise to make."

"Good, call me when you get home," and with that, he hung up the phone. There were only six teams in the NHL at that time, so I was kind of excited by the call, but I'd have to wait a few weeks before seeing Mr. Smythe.

We went home by boat, sailing out of Liverpool, England, on the *Empress of Britain*, a Canadian ship. We had to play several more exhibition games in Switzerland, Paris, Scotland and London, so it was quite a while before we got back to Canada. A day or two after returning home, I phoned Stafford Smythe, and he invited me to meet with him. I ended up having four meetings with Stafford and you could almost write a book on each one of them.

At the first meeting, he said, "We want to offer you a position in the Toronto Maple Leaf organization."

"Doing what?" I asked.

"We don't know, yet. We just want to get you into our organization."

"I had never heard anything like that before."

"What do you mean, you don't want it," he barked.

"I didn't say that. I don't like it, that's all."

"Why?" he asked.

"Well, if you decided to start a team in Nome, Alaska, and send me there, I ain't going. I think it's only fair you tell me what you have in mind."

"Nope, we're not saying. That's the way it is. Take it or leave it."

"What I'd like to do is to talk this over with my family and some other hockey people and then have another meeting, if that's okay with you?"

"OK," he said, "be here next Tuesday."

When we next met, I decided to take a little different approach and ask what kind of money he was talking about if I took this job. In 1958 guys on the line at General Motors were making about $5,000 a year. Before I left to go to Europe, I was working as an appraiser at Central Mortgage and Housing making $6,000 a year.

"We'll pay you $8,000 a year," he offered.

"I think it's only fair to tell you Stafford, that if I was to take this job it would be my goal to become the General Manager of the Toronto Maple Leafs in the not too distant future."

"What the hell do you think we're talking to you for," he yelled back.

"You're not offering me that now."

"No, we're not, " he said.

"Well, just so I know what I am shooting for, what would you pay a General Manager?" The Leafs didn't have a General Manager at that time, so I wasn't stepping on anybody's toes trying to get his job. The Leafs had a group called the 'Silver Seven' who ran the team and Billy Reay was the coach. "Stafford, I have no idea what a General Manager makes in the National Hockey League, so I just want to know what kind of a salary I could be looking at."

"Last year, we paid Howie Meeker this." When he named the amount I was surprised.

"Is that all you pay for a GM?"

"Don't be cheeky, that's the going rate for a General Manager."

"But you fellows hired Howie Meeker in August and fired him before training camp opened. I figure you are a fairly ruthless bunch of guys around here."

"You've got that right. We are ruthless."

I thought to myself, $8,000 now and not knowing where you are going to work and not too much more down the line if I get the big job. Finally, I said, "Do you think I'd be cheeky now if I asked to think about this and meet again next week."

"See you next week, same time."

The next week we talked some more.

"You know, Stafford, I am a great believer in the law of supply and demand and you must have a helluva lineup for this job because I'm not getting anywhere here."

"No, we haven't. We've only got one other man in mind and if you don't take it, we'll offer it to him."

"Do you mind if I ask who the other man is?"

"Not at all," he said. "It's Punch Imlach." Most people in

Canada didn't know who Punch Imlach was then. I knew him from the time he worked for the Boston Bruins and ran their team in Springfield in the American Hockey League.

"Okay, I'm going to need a few days to think this over. I'm going to talk to my boss, where I'm working now and my family, and if we can meet a week from today I'll definitely give you my answer."

The next day, I was at home when the phone rang. It was Ed Stanley, the general manager-operator of the Clinton Comets of the United States Eastern Hockey League. Clinton is a suburb of Utica, New York. I knew Ed very well because at one time when I was with Whitby, we had played a partial interlocking schedule with Clinton with points to count in both leagues.

"Wren, I haven't talked to you for a while. I just wanted to congratulate you on winning the World Championship. It must have been a very exciting time for you and your team." We chit chatted back and forth about a number of things until finally, he said, "Wren, we have fallen on very tough times with the Clinton Hockey Club. There are 11 teams in our league and we finished dead last. We had a meeting with our directors and decided to either hire somebody to turn this thing around or fold up. My question to you is, would you take a position as General Manager, hire a coach and do some recruiting to turn this team around? You can do it in absenteeism because I will still be here and can oversee the day-to-day operations of the hockey club."

"That's a very interesting proposal. How are you structured to pay me?

"We will give you a salary of $7,500 U.S. per year, with a very generous bonus plan," he said. "We are prepared to give you a $1,000 bonus for every position we move up in the standings from last year."

"If we move up four positions, I would get a $4,000 bonus on top of my $7,500 salary."

"Absolutely," he said.

"Ed, let me ask you something strange. Would you have any opposition if I continued to run the Whitby club?"

"None, whatsoever, as long as you recruit for us. In fact, I think you would be foolish to give up the Whitby team," he said. I thought a little more about his proposal and asked if he would let me talk with the Dunlop people and I would get back to him the next day. At this point, I was thinking I wanted to get something done before I had to meet again with Stafford Smythe.

I had managed to get some prominent business people in the community involved in the Whitby team, so after my phone call with Ed Stanley, I talked with the team president Norm Irwin and vice-president Don Wilson and asked them if they had any objections to my running both Whitby and Clinton. They said, no, as long as I felt I could continue to raise enough money in Whitby through program ads, gate receipts, and various sponsorships to pay myself. I phoned Ed back the next day and told him that the directors in Whitby, even though they didn't say this, wanted to be on hand and sign both agreements in front of each other. We met in Buffalo a couple of days later and signed a joint contract for three years. That was a Saturday morning. I was now ready to meet Stafford Smythe on Tuesday.

At the meeting on Tuesday, I said to Stafford, "Punch Imlach may work for you at the money you offered me, but I'm not going to take the job."

"Thank you very much. You will never ever work for the Toronto Maple Leafs." He walked out.

In the meantime, I had talked to my boss Bob Ballard, General Manager of the Central Housing office. Bob had flown over to Oslo for the World Tournament and was with me most of time. He helped me with all sorts of tasks while he was there. I told him everything that was going on.

"I am the manager here and here is what I am making," he confided. "I can't go any higher. I want you to look me in the eye and tell me that you don't want to be involved in hockey on a full-time basis."

"Bob, you know, it will only take me two seconds to answer that." He then said that if things didn't work out, he would take me back.

I was a full-time hockey man. That year, 1958-59, the Whitby Dunlops came back and won the Allan Cup all over again. I believe we were the only team on record ever to win the Allan Cup, the World Championship and the Allan Cup, again, in a span of three seasons. In the meantime, in Clinton, we went from last place in the Eastern Hockey League to first place. My playing-coach in Clinton was "Whipper" Billy Watson, who was from Ottawa. I acquired him right out of the American Hockey League from Jim Hendy in Cleveland. My first training camp with the Comets was held in Whitby. Over the summer, I had released a number of players from the previous year when the Comets had finished in last place. In fact, the only players from that team that I retained were Art Rose, a right winger; Angie Defelice, who played both centre and wing; Norm Defelice, the goaltender; Willie Pawchuk, another winger; and Eddie Calhoun, who had been the interim playing-coach the previous year. All other players had been released.

When camp finished, I had added the following players to the lineup: "Spider" Brown, Tim Hook (a right winger), Mike Kardash (a defenceman), and Rudy Balone (a defenceman). Other new players were Doug McPhee, Jerry Stringle (a centerman), Lennie Speck (a good defenceman), and Ted Sydlowski. We added two players as the season went on. Our goaltender, Norm Defelice, got hurt and I had heard about a good young goaltender from Sudbury, Ontario, Eddie Giacomin. Eddie was 18 at the time and later went on to star in the National Hockey League with the New York Rangers. Part way through the year, I also brought in a right winger named Dickie Wray, who had been playing in the Quebec League for the Montreal Royals. Dickie was a small guy, but a tremendous goal scorer. He was from Stratford, Ontario.

We finally broke camp in Whitby and headed for Clinton. It wasn't long before the fans in Clinton realized that the club carrying the Clinton colors this year was vastly different from the one the year before. The fans started coming out in droves. Clinton itself was only a town of about 2,500, but they had a larger population in Utica and up-state New York to draw from.

Early in the season, we had climbed into first place in the Northern Division of the Eastern Hockey League, and we pretty well stayed there for the remainder of the season. The Northern Division was comprised of teams from Johnstown, Pennsylvania; New Haven, Connecticut; Long Island, New York; and New Jersey. The Southern Division had teams from Charlotte and Greensboro, North Carolina; Nashville and Knoxville Tennessee; and Washington, DC.

The Dunlops were also playing very strongly, after their World Championship and Allan Cup victories the year before. The Belleville McFarlands had been chosen to represent Canada at the World championships in 1959, so, they withdrew from league competition early in the new year. The Senior League had diminished somewhat, with teams from Belleville, Whitby, Kingston, Cornwall, and Kitchener. As Clinton had moved into first place in the Eastern Hockey League, the Dunlops were in first place in the Senior League.

After Eddie Giacomin arrived in Clinton, he was so outstanding that Norm Defelice came to me one day, after he had been out a month or so. Normie was upset and agitated when he walked into my office. I asked him what was bothering him? "I know you are in love with Giacomin . . . and I know that when I'm ready to play again that I'm going to be history, so why don't you trade me to hell out of here now," he demanded.

That bothered me to no end, so I said, "Sit down you little hot-headed Italian. I will make the decisions around here and I have not even remotely thought about that at all. I will deal with you when you are ready to play. I am not going to deal damaged goods to any team, so no trade will ever take place until you are ready to play." I had no intention of trading Normie. About three weeks later, Normie was ready to return. I kept Eddie for a little while until I was sure Normie was healthy, then dealt Eddie to another club.

Spider Brown, who had played Major A hockey in Guelph, Tim Hook, who had played Major A in Toronto, and Mike Kardash, who had played Junior hockey in Winnipeg were all rookies with Clinton but were playing tremendous hockey for us. With our veteran players, like Rose and Speck, who played for Windsor in the OHA Senior A League, and our playing-coach Watson, a former American Leaguer, it gave us a very nice blend of veterans and rookies. After finishing first in the regular season standings, we moved into the playoffs and won every series we played in, culminating our season by winning the Tom Lockhart Trophy as champions of the United States Eastern Hockey League in the first year that I was in Clinton. The trophy was named after Tom Lockhart, who had been President and commissioner of the league for many, many years. We had come from last place the previous year in the 11-team league, all the way to first and the league championship.

We met Long Island in the first round of the playoffs that year and had lost the first two games. After the second loss, Billy Watson phoned me and asked if I would come down and talk to the guys. We had finished first, but they just weren't putting out in the playoffs. I went down, raised a lot of hell, and talked to a lot of the guys about the year we had had. That night we won and then won the fourth game to tie the series. Now we had to play the fifth game, back in Long Island. Billy urged me to go to the fifth game and then asked me to go on the bench and coach the team that night so that he could concentrate solely on playing. We ended up winning the game, in overtime, to eliminate Long Island. After a scary walk from our bench to the dressing room, where we had to threaten the boisterous Long Island fans with our sticks in order to get through, we had a magnificent celebration that night.

Meanwhile, back in Whitby, the Dunlops again finished first in the Senior A Division and eliminated every team in the playoffs, en route to another Allan Cup. Whitby became the first and only team ever to win the Allan Cup, the World Championship and the Allan Cup again in a span of two seasons. For me, 1958-59 was a tremendous year with league championships in the Eastern League in the United States and the Allan Cup, the top amateur hockey trophy at that time, in Canada. It was a once in a lifetime experience for me and something that has never been done before or since.

With all of the bonus clauses in my contract with the Comets, I ended up drawing a salary roughly three times higher than the base rate offered, which had to be twice the amount of money any General Manager in the NHL made in those days. On top of that Whitby had won the Allan Cup, so with my salary and bonuses there, it was quite a lucrative year. I could have gone to Toronto on an ego trip, but I didn't like the money and I didn't like not knowing what I was going to do. We had won the ultimate championships on both sides of the border. Yes, 1958-59 was a great year.

That summer while I was meeting with Ed Stanley, he asked me, "That bonus clause we put in your contract, do you think that covers the whole three years?" I didn't answer him for a minute. "If it does, we'll be bankrupt. The amount of bonus money we paid out last year, especially to you, was phenomenal. We just can't afford that every year." I told him what I'd like to do was negotiate a new contract with lower bonus clauses. I didn't want to bankrupt my team!

THE KITCHENER-WATERLOO Dutchmen had been picked to represent Canada at the 1960 Olympic Games in Squaw Valley, California. George Dudley and Gordon Juckes of the Canadian Amateur Hockey Association asked for my assistance in securing players from Whitby to strengthen the Dutchmen. They wanted Bobby Attersley, Fred Etcher, George Samalenko, and Harry Sinden. Then, Dudley kind of stunned me when he said, "We would also like you to join the team as a consultant." I was a bit apprehensive because there was no love lost between Ernie Goman of the Dutchmen and me. He had been extremely bitter towards me ever since we had beaten them out in the Allan Cup playdowns that first year. I told Mr. Dudley my concerns. However, he assured me that this was too important to put personalities ahead of hockey for the good of Canada. I talked to my players and they wanted me to come because they said they would have nobody there to back them up. I agreed to go.

The first part of the journey saw the team go by train to Winnipeg, Manitoba for an exhibition game. I made this trip, but returned home while the team continued to play exhibition games all through the West until they finished up in Penticton and then flew out of Vancouver for Squaw Valley. Because I still didn't fly at this time, I took a train out of Toronto all the way to Truckee, California. Truckee was very close to Squaw Valley, about 20 minutes south. I was four days on the train to get there. When I arrived, my players had got a car from the Olympic car pool and picked me up to drive me to the Olympic Village. When I arrived in Squaw Valley, Mr. Juckes, the President of the CAHA, met me and told me that the Canadian section of the Olympic

Village was just jammed and asked if I would mind bunking in with the Australian team.

The Australian team was comprised of a bunch of guys who had got together, formed a team, and paid their own way to the Olympics. They said they'd love to have a Canuck with them, especially a hockey guy. That turned out to be one of the best experiences of my life. The Aussies have a special sense of humor and they are tough. The night before their first game, they said to me, "Listen Canuck, we play tomorrow on an outdoor rink at 7 a.m. against Sweden and we want you there."

In those days, I didn't get up that early, so I said, "Hey boys, I'll do anything for you, but I'm not getting up that early." So the next morning off they went and about three hours later, they were back in the hut. When I asked how it went, they said, "Oh, not bad."

"What was the score?

"Sweden 18, us 1."

"If you call that not too bad, you've got a lot to learn about hockey."

The next day they were playing the Czechoslovakia "B" team and off they went again to the game, bright and early in the morning. When they returned, I asked them again, how you'd do today?

"Oh, a lot better today. "Czechoslovkia 17, Australia 2. Not bad, eh, a lot better."

The next day they are playing Japan. During the war, there was no love lost between the Japanese and Australians and they had never forgotten it. So the next day, off they go again and about an hour later they're back. "Who won?" I asked.

"We never finished the game. We got in a fight, those little bastards jumped over the boards (they played the "B" games on an outdoor rink) and ran up into the hills. We went right after them, caught them, and beat the hell out of them." I think they got expelled for this, but it didn't matter to them. They said it was the best time they had ever had.

After that, I sat around drinking Foster's beer with them and telling them all sorts of hockey stories. They asked if they could come with me to our games in the A Pool, and although I couldn't get tickets for the whole team, but I did manage to get four for each game and took various players with me.

I like to sit up high in the stands when I'm watching a game and I can remember during one game, I looked down and saw Janet Leigh and Tony Curtis. I walked over to them and introduced myself, told them that I was connected with the Canadian team. Tony then asked me if I would mind sitting with them and telling them about some of the rules of the game. I said that I'd be glad to sit here, but I would just as soon you left and I would explain the game to Janet. "I've heard that line before," he said, "but it's not going to happen today." I had a lovely time with them.

Shirley Harmer, a Canadian singer from Oshawa who knew several of the players, got in touch with us and asked us to come over to Harrods in Las Vegas, where she was singing, and be her guests for the night. All of us from the Dunnies headed out for Vegas. Shirley met us before the show started, then during her act, she told the audience that she was having a special treat for herself. "I have five men here from my hometown of Oshawa, who are with the Canadian Olympic Hockey Team, as my guests," she announced. Then she introduced every one of us to the crowd. A couple of days later, we learned there was a front page story in the *Oshawa Times* with a story about local hockey heroes having dinner with another Oshawa hero, Shirley Harmer.

In between games with the Dutchmen, Harry Sinden, Bobby Atterlsey, Ken Laufman Moe Benoit, and I rented a car. We wanted to go to Carson City because there was some gambling there. Boy, what a night we had! The next day, after we got back, Ernie Goman and Bobby Bauer called me and started questioning me about where we were the night before. They inferred they didn't care what my players did after hours, but they didn't want me taking one of their players with us. They read the riot act to me. I was really upset. I had a return ticket to Toronto, so I arranged for Harry to drive me back to Truckee. I was going home. My players were really upset, but I said, no, I'm going . . . I've got tons of work to do with Whitby and Clinton. The next day, the U.S. beat Canada 2-1 with Jack McCartan in goal. McCartan was just outstanding in that game. I didn't see the headlines until I got home.

George Gross, who was writing for the *Toronto Telegram*, wrote a column that started out, "Wren Blair, who was an addition to the Kitchener-Waterloo Dutchmen at Squaw Valley, mysteriously disappeared yesterday. We have been trying to get a hold of Mr. Blair for his comments, but have been unable to do so. However, one must feel, from a hockey standpoint, that Mr. Blair could fall in a toilet and come up with roses in his hand, because the moment he left, the Canadians promptly lost to the Americans."

Upon my return to Canada, I turned attention to my teams in Whitby and Clinton. The Dunlops never re-captured their momentum from the previous year and were eliminated by the Chatham Maroons. But the Comets rose to the occasion. In my second year in Clinton, we still had Art Rose, Spider Brown, Tim Hook, Mike Kardash, playing-coach Billy Watson, Ted Skylowski, Angie Defelice, Dickie Wray, and Norm Defelice. I added John Ayotte, a big, big forward, who had played junior in Winnipeg, and a couple of other players. We played well that year, but we didn't seem to have quite the punch needed to win the championship.

In Whitby we were going into the last season of the Dunlops history. The Eastern Professional Hockey League had been formed in the 1959-60 season. Kingston left Senior A hockey to join the EPHL as did Kitchener. Senior A hockey in Ontario dwindled down to only five teams (Cornwall, Belleville, Whitby, Chatham and Windsor) in total from both the East and West Divisions. In the north, Sudbury had left Senior A to join the EPHL along with Sault Ste. Marie. This was the beginning of the end for Senior A hockey in Ontario.

In the summer of 1960, I signed a contract with Lynn Patrick of the Boston Bruins and was assigned to Kingston as General Manager-Coach of the Kingston Frontenacs of the EPHL. Cal Gardner had been the coach the year before. The Dunlops also folded and ceased operations that year.

One of the things that I had asked for in my contract with Boston was that I still be allowed to operate as General Manager of the Clinton Comets, and the Bruins granted that request. In 1960-61 we added some more new players, Skippy Teal, who had played the year before with the Kingston Frontenacs, along with Jack Kane, who played with me in Whitby, and J.P. Lamirande, who had been a tower of strength for the Dunlops when we won the World championship. J.P. had played the following year in the World Championship of 1959, also with Belleville. I also added Weiner Brown from the Belleville Senior A team, which had also folded. Earlier that year after Billy Watson had retired, and I signed Irwin Gross, who had played Senior A in Whitby, as the playing coach for the Comets.

In 1961-62, we again won the Tom Lockhart Trophy. I had signed Benny Woit to succeed Irwin Gross. Benny had played in the NHL, in Detroit and Chicago, then in Rochester in the American Hockey League. By Eastern league standards, Benny was a premier player. We only played three defencemen in the Eastern League in those years because the league had the rosters set at 13 players — three defencemen, a goaltender, and three forward lines — so the defencemen played tons of hockey. I believe the first year that Benny played was the strongest team I ever had in Clinton.

In 1962-63 we continued to ice strong teams. I added Orval
Tessier, who had played for me in Kingston, and was an outstanding
right winger. We added another great player, Hector Lalonde, and
Jack Kane, who had played in Whitby. Another strong addition to
the club was Pete Babando, who had also played in Whitby. Pete
had been a great player in the NHL for Detroit; as a matter of fact,
he's in the history books for an overtime goal, one of the longest in
NHL history, when he scored to win the Stanley Cup for Detroit.
Pete had lobbed the puck into the opposition end in order to make
a line change, and by the time he got to the bench the puck had
bounced once over the goaltender's stick, and he was sitting on the
bench watching when the puck entered the goal and gave Detroit a
1-0 win for the Stanley Cup.

Also joining the team over the years were Jacques Faubert and
Jeannot Gilbert, who had played the year before with Kingston in
the EPHL, Jimmy Jago, and Billy Bannerman. Bob Attersley came
out of retirement in the 1962-63 season to help us out when we ran
into a ton of injuries. I appealed to Bob to see if he could come to
Clinton and help us out for the balance of the season and the playoffs. I flew him around the country to places like Greensboro, New
Haven, and Long Island. He played well for us and was very popular
with all the members of the team. We also added Reg Mulholland in
the 1967-68 season.

We won the Eastern League title again that year. By this time,
Pat Kelly was my playing-coach. Pat coached the Comets for nine
years following that until I bought my own team in Saginaw, Michigan, in the spring of 1972. Some of the other players on that championship team were Davey Armstrong, Borden Smith, Lenny Speck,
and Ian Anderson. Anderson came to me on the recommendation
of George Maguire, who was working with me for Boston. He was a
big, strong defenceman and we called him "The Bear." Other players
on that team were Howie Dietrich, goaltender Eddie Babiuk, Don

Davidson, who had played in Greensboro, Bill Heindl, who had graduated from the Oshawa Generals, Pat Draper, and Rod Zaine, who had also graduated from the Generals.

Ed Stanley, who was one of the owners of the team and also the business manager, commented on the success of the Clinton team in an article in the *Utica Observer Dispatch*, on March 10, 1968: "'Wren Blair's the fellow who did it,'" said Stanley, as he reviewed the Comets' amazing season. Blair, who is also coach of the NHL's Minnesota North Stars, also doubles as the Comets' General Manager. Three years ago Blair traded with the Jersey Devils, for Ed Babiuk, Borden Smith and Pat Kelly. In return, the Comets gave up Benny Woit, Norm Defelice, Ted Skylowski, Lorne O'Donnell and Hector Lalonde. Babiuk, Smith and Kelly have been sensational for us in the three years since they joined us and are key players on this year's championship club. On the other hand, Woit, Defelice and Lalonde have all retired out of this league. Only O'Donnell and Skylowski are still with the Jersey club. In winning the Northern Division title, the Comets scored a record 55 wins that broke Nashville's record of 54 in the 1964-65 season. Since Kelly took over the coaching reigns three years ago, the worst he did was in his first season when the club finished second with 41 wins. The following two years the Comets have finished in first place. This year's 55 wins also betters the Comets' 1964-65 season when they won 50 games for Benny Woit."

At the end of the 1964-65 season, I had felt that Benny Woit might soon retire from playing. If a player in that league retired as a player, he is also out as a coach since we could only afford playing coaches. So I made a deal to trade Benny, Norm Defelice, Lorne O'Donnell, Orval Tessier, and Hector Lalonde, but once the trade was completed, both Benny and Orval advised me that they were retiring. I appealed to Benny to play just one more season so it wouldn't screw up my trade, but he said he wasn't sure. Then I explained to him that I had told the Jersey team that he was making considerably more money as playing coach for the Comets than he actually was. "If you will go," I pointed out, "you will get close to a 25% increase." That quickly changed things. But Orval Tessier wouldn't budge, no matter how hard I tried. I talked with Len Gaudette, the manager of the Jersey team, and told him that Tessier would not report. I didn't say anything about Benny. I told Gaudette that I would replace Tessier with a younger player in Ted Szydlowski. Gaudette accepted and the trade was made.

Ed Stanley is gone today, but he was an outstanding gentleman. He had a fiery temper, as I have, but we were always able to get along, as is apparent by the fact that I stayed there for 14 years. In those 14 years, we never finished lower than third, finishing first nine times, second four times, and one year we finished third. We won three EHL championships. Benny Woit was from the Lakehead, and his nephew was the singer Bobby Curtola. A few years ago, I went to Las Vegas, and Bobby was singing there. I had a chat with him between sets, and when he went back on the stage, he mentioned that his uncle's former general manager from Clinton was in the audience, which I thought was a very professional thing to do on his part. Pat Kelly coached for me for nine years after that trade for Benny Woit, then he worked for us in Haliburton at our camp for several years in the late '60s and early '70s. His wife June was a good potter and she made me a lovely lamp with the Minnesota North Stars crest on it. I still have it on my desk. Pat went on to work as a commissioner in hockey for some time.

I had always wanted to own my own team in minor pro somewhere and eventually the opportunity presented itself in Saginaw, Michigan. I bought a new franchise there. Late in my final year in Clinton, I had obtained a player from Muskegon Mohawks, on loan, to play in Clinton. His name was Dennis Desrosiers. "Rosie" played very well for us in Clinton. At the end of that year, when I left for

Saginaw, it appeared that the Clinton Comets might not be operating in the same manner they had in the past. As I started to build my team in Saginaw, I got in touch with Jerry Deslisle, the owner of the Muskegon team and told him I would like to bring Desrosiers to Saginaw. He immediately said he wouldn't release him, except for a substantial price. We finally struck a deal for $1,000 and Desrosiers became the first player that I signed for the Saginaw Gears Hockey Club. A new chapter had opened in my hockey life as a team owner. But I am getting ahead of myself . . . there were those years in Kingston with the Frontenacs and then the Minnesota North Stars entered the NHL . . ..

PROFILE

Paul Rimstead

THE FIRST TIME I TRAVELED TO Kingston when I took over the management of the Frontenacs franchise in the EPHL, I went down by train, from Oshawa to Kingston. In those days, they had the old-fashioned club cars on the train, instead of the first-class sections we have today. After I boarded the train, I wandered into the club car. There was only one other person in the car. After the steward brought my drink, the other chap in the car got up and walked over to my table and sat down.

"I'm Paul Rimstead," he said, and I, in turn, introduced myself. I asked him where he was going, and he said Kingston.

"What are you going to Kingston for?"

"I've just been appointed Sports Editor of *The Kingston Whig-Standard* and I'm moving to Kingston."

I looked at him strangely and then said, "Guess what I'm going to Kingston for? I'm the new General Manager-Coach of the Kingston

Frontenacs. Do you think we'll be running into each other again?"

"Boy, oh boy, this is great."

Paul Rimstead was a very colorful guy, one of the very brightest minds that got wasted in the media business. He was very inventive. We forged a very good friendship, but because he was so talented, he moved on, and eventually I did too. I can always remember when we used to talk that if there was nothing really newsworthy going on, he'd say, "Well, we'll invent something."

However, sometimes, he'd invent stuff that I didn't know about. One day he phoned me and asked, "How come Murph Chamberlain hates you so badly?" Murph Chamberlain was the coach of the Sudbury Wolves in the EPHL at the time and before that he coached the Chatham Maroons in the Senior A days when I was in Whitby. I had always thought that Murph and I were pretty good friends, so I was surprised to hear from Paul that he hated me.

Paul said, "Well, he said you never played in the NHL, you're this, you're that, you really don't know what the hell you're doing." Well, I just erupted when I heard that and said: Why, that beer-drinking jerk, what the hell does he know? Well, Paul writes all this and also forwards it on to *The Sudbury Star*, where he had worked before coming to Kingston. It just happened that we were playing Sudbury at home the next night.

The Kingston people were just eating this stuff up and the place was jammed for the game. After the games, I always had a gathering in my office and many people would drop in. Danny McLeod and his wife would come in, Jim Magee and his wife, and Gary Young, along with many others. Eventually all the people had left and I was there all alone cleaning up some paperwork when I became aware of someone standing in my doorway. I looked up and there was Murph Chamberlain, a big hulk of a man, looking at me menacingly. "What the hell is wrong with you, you little son of a bitch," he said.

"What's wrong with me, what the hell is wrong with you."

"What did I ever do to you," he bellered.

"Well, you cut me up pretty good in the paper. Rimstead called me and told me everything you said."

"Rimstead, I never talked to him."

I sat there for a moment and then said, "Murph, do you think, maybe we've been had?"

"I think so." We looked at each other, had a big laugh and then adjourned to the Town and Country for a few drinks. When I challenged Rimstead about this later, he responded, "What are you bitching about? You had a sellout, didn't you?" When Paul was in Kingston, we led the league in attendance and he had a lot to do with it. Many fans used to tell me that they couldn't wait to get home after work to see what Rimstead and I were up to.

Paul was also a great friend of Bob Attersley and he used to call us from time to time when we were meeting in Bob's office to ask, "What are you two rascals up to today?" He was married while he was in Kingston. It was a very small wedding and I can remember the night of his wedding my phone rang and it was Paul. I didn't realize it, but they had their honeymoon right in Kingston. It was about 3:30 in the morning when the call came into my home.

"Do you have any idea what time it is?"

"Yeah, between 3 and 4?"

"Where are you?"

"At the Town and Country, we're lonely here, we want you to come down and have a few drinks."

"Paul, for chrissakes, it's your honeymoon night."

"Aw, we're all finished with that stuff. Come on down." So, in the middle of the night away I go, and didn't get home until after daylight.

After Paul left *The Whig-Standard*, he went on to work for *The Globe and Mail*, *The Toronto Star*, and *The Toronto Sun* before he died in his early 50s. He was one of my greatest friends.

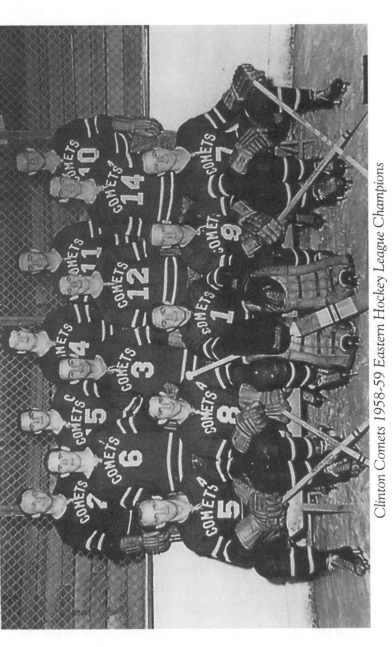

Clinton Comets 1958-59 Eastern Hockey League Champions

Front Row — Fern Bernaquez, Angie Defelice, Norm Defelice, Dick Wray, Coach Bill Watson. Middle — Tim Hook, Leon Bouchard, Spider Brown, Jerry Stringle. Back — Mike Kardash, Captain Ed Calhoun, Rudy Balone, Doug MacPhee, Willie Pawchuck.

Clinton Comets 1961-62 Eastern Hockey League Champions

Front Row — Jack Kane, Art Rose, Norm Defelice, Angie Defelice, Captain Pete Babando. Middle — Lennie Speck, Tim Hook, Coach Benny Woit, Ted Szydlowsk. Back — Jacques Faubert, Jeannot Gilbert, Skip Teal, Reg Mulholland.

The Kingston Frontenacs and the EPHL Championship

6

SHORTLY AFTER THE 1960 HOCKEY season, I received a call from Lynn Patrick, General Manager of the Boston Bruins. He asked me if I was free the following Saturday to go to Toronto and have a talk with him at the Royal York Hotel? Lynn had been over in Oslo when we won the World Championship, so he was familiar with many of the players and me. We sat around in his suite and chatted a bit about the guys and our win and finally he said, "I would like you to consider joining the Boston Bruins organization." Immediately, I thought, here we go again, thinking back to my dealings with Stafford Smythe. "Are you interested?" I told him, yes, but I pointed up that I was awfully busy running two hockey clubs in Whitby and Clinton. "I know you are," he recognized.

"What would you want me to do with the Bruins?" I asked.

"Well, we have a professional team in Kingston in the Eastern Professional Hockey League that was coached last year by Cal Gardner. As you probably know, it was the first year of this new league and we want to hire somebody who would become General Manager-Coach of the team. We'd like you to consider going to Kingston to operate that team. Harold Cotton is our head scout, but we have nobody from our organization to watch our junior teams and keep us informed on what is happening with our prospects."

All I could think of at this time, was, God, go to Kingston. That's the city that probably hates me the most of any in Canada because I used to taunt them and wave towels at them during my heydays in Whitby. I asked him how much money the Bruins would be willing to pay if I took the jobs. He offered $11,000 a year, which was $3,000 more than the Leafs had offered me. I told him that I was interested, but only under the condition that I still be allowed to operate the Clinton team in the Eastern Hockey League. I told him that I knew I wouldn't be able to carry on with Whitby in any event. We worked out the finances and my duties, then I asked him about signing a contract.

"I have two plane tickets for Montreal tomorrow on my way back to Boston," Lynn proposed. "I want you to meet me at the airport and we'll fly to Montreal and sign the contract at the NHL offices in Montreal." Of course, I didn't fly and this created a major problem for me.

Finally, I said to Lynn, "Do you know I don't fly?" He said, he was quite aware of that, it had been the talk of the World Tournament, where we went over by boat and that I traveled all around Europe on trains, while the players flew.

"However, you certainly can't work for the Boston Bruins if you don't fly. All I'm going to do is leave this with you. If you want this job bad enough, you'll meet me at the airport tomorrow. If you don't, then I'll understand, and there will be no hard feelings."

I left the meeting and went back home. All night I anguished over this, but the next morning I was on my way back to Toronto. When I met Lynn, he kind of grinned, but never said much. We got on the plane, a four-engine Vanguard, and I white-knuckled it all the way to Montreal. When we finally landed and I got off the plane, I got down on my knees and kissed the ground. I'm not stupid, I knew planes flew every day, but I had this fixation in my mind that any plane I flew on would not reach its destination. The funniest part of all is that from that day forward I was on planes almost every day, sometimes twice a day, in my seven years with the Bruins, followed by 10 years in Minnesota and then Pittsburgh and Los

Angeles. I probably did more flying during those years than most people do in their entire life.

After signing my contract that day, I began to work on my move to Kingston. My wife and I decided that she and our children, Jill and Danny, would not go to Kingston that year. The kids were pretty young. Jill was born in 1957, so she was three years old and Danny was born in 1953 so he was coming on to eight. I could tell Elma was more comfortable to just let me go and be on my own for my first year in professional hockey.

During my time at the Olympics in Squaw Valley, I had seen Tommy Williams play for the U.S. Olympic team. He was just 19 years old and could skate like the wind.

After getting my affairs in order, Lynn Patrick called me and asked what I would like to do in the off-season. I said I would like to go to Duluth, Minn., and try and sign Tommy Williams to a pro contract. He was already on the Bruins' negotiation list. Lynn thought that was a great idea. The only thing I want is your word that if I turn Tommy pro, he plays in Kingston, not Springfield, where we still had another minor pro team that Punch Imlach had run. Lynn agreed.

I went to Duluth and met with Tommy's father, Rick Williams, who was involved with minor hockey in that area. This was a very difficult meeting because Rick wanted his son to go to college in the U.S. I stayed there for three days and finally began to crack Tommy. He asked for a couple of things that weren't too costly, so I contacted Lynn and he agreed. Finally, he signed, and when I left Duluth, I had Tommy Williams' name on a contract to play in the EPHL for Kingston.

Technically, Tommy became the second player I had signed to a pro contract. The first was Harry Sinden, who I had persuaded to sign a four-year pro contract to come to Kingston and become my captain. I had to do a real selling job with the Bruins to sign Harry. I wanted to give him about twice as much as players were making in that league, and when I told Lynn he said, facetiously, "That's just what the Bruins need, a 27-year-old defenceman, who is not an NHL type skater."

"I'm not talking about him as a player," I said.

"What are you talking about, then," said Patrick.

"Well, you know you and Milt Schmidt [coach and general manager of the Bruins) are not going to be in Boston forever. And, I think, down the road, I can help Harry to become a pretty good coach and eventually a general manager.

Lynn then surprised the hell out of me. "I agree wholeheartedly with that. He is a bright young man and I concur that down the road he will become a coach and GM, so go ahead and give him the contract."

The EPHL team that had been in Kingston the year before was a very old team but now was suddenly starting to take on a new look. The whole idea behind the formation of the EPHL was to take players right out of Junior A and groom them for the NHL. That year, on our Niagara Falls junior team, Randy Miller and Nelson Leclair had graduated. I then discussed several young players with Lynn, such as Dick Meissner, who I wanted in Kingston. I also asked Lynn to try and get Lorne Ferguson back from the Detroit organization and put him in Kingston. Fergie was from Kingston and I thought he would do a lot for our crowds. He was still a damn good hockey player. The biggest player, name-wise, over the summer that I convinced Lynn to let me have was Real Chevrifies. "Chevy" had played for Sudbury the year before, even though he belonged to Boston. I told Lynn that I wanted every player Boston owned and I would decide who would or wouldn't play in Kingston.

We were scheduled to open training camp in mid-September at the Kingston Memorial Centre. One has to realize that I had never worked in pro hockey before, so a lot of older players on the

Frontenacs, such as Skippy Teal, Bob Blackburn, Don Blackburn, Pete Panagabko, Red Ouellete and a couple of goaltenders didn't really know who the hell I was. We skated on the ice that first day and I could hear mumblings from the players, who is this guy, where'd he come from? He was in amateur hockey and that's why Sinden's here and is going to be captain, etc., etc. They were setting Harry and me up for a fall. Finally, I stopped the team and had them gather around one of the nets. I was trying to SET them up. "Okay, you guys, I wasn't here last year, as you know, so I want to ask you a couple of questions. Where did you finish last year?"

"Sixth," one of the players answered.

"How many teams are in the league?"

Another one answered, "Six."

"What! You guys, and I know a lot of your backgrounds in pro hockey, finished in last place!"

By this time, they are starting to look a little sheepish. I told them to wait just a minute, stay right where you are . . . and I turned and skated slowly down the ice as if I was pondering some major decision. I came back and asked, "Who was your coach here last year?"

"Cal Gardner," said one of the players.

"What did you think of him," I asked Buddy Boone.

"One of the finest," he said.

"What did you think, Skippy?"

"He always treated me great," said Skippy.

"What about you, Blackie?"

"Good guy, great," said Blackburn.

"Isn't that strange," I said. "Do you know that Cal got fired and Mr. Patrick hired me to take his place? I would like to know if any of you guys sent Cal any bread tickets or meal tickets. He's out of work and all of you guys are still here, for cripes sake." I could see by the look on their faces that they were thinking, what kind of stupid questions are these? So, I told them again to wait just a minute, don't move . . . and I turned and slowly skated to the other end of the ice again, pondering another major decision.

I asked them a couple more questions and then said, "Listen, gentlemen, my name is Wren Blair and I have never been a coach in pro hockey before and I might get fired this year, maybe even before this year is over, but let me tell you one thing. When I leave, if anybody ever asks you what kind of a guy was Blair, I doubt you are going to say one of the finest, a great guy or all that kind of stuff. And, secondly, let me tell you another thing, I may go, but before I go a lot of you guys are going to be gone before me. And with those words, gentlemen, let me tell you that this training camp is now on."

I then blasted the whistle and yelled, "Now move." They started to skate around the ice. I told them that when I blow, you go double time; and when I blow a second time, you ease up; and when I blow again, go double time. I continued to drive them, a lot harder than normal.

Harry Sinden skated by and said, "Will you ease up, I'm dying out here?"

"You're the captain, don't talk that way."

When I finally finished, the guys just dropped to their knees. They were exhausted. After a brief rest, I blew the whistle and said, okay, let's go again. I kept that up for the whole practice, nothing but skating and stops and starts. I can tell you one thing that when that training camp ended, they were in the best shape of their entire careers.

I had told the guys that all bars in Kingston, especially the Indian Room at the Prince George Hotel, were out of bounds. "Any guy that's caught drinking in a Kingston hotel will be sent home. If you want to drink, go home or go to Napanee, Gananoque, or across the bridge to the U.S. You are not drinking in this town. All I've heard since I got here is that if you want to see the Frontenacs, go to any bar and you'll find them there. I don't want to hear any more of that crap."

We opened the season and I was paranoid that we weren't going to make the playoffs. We played a 76-game schedule in those days and only four teams would make the playoffs. One of the key players on our team that year was Real Chevrifies, who had been a big star with the Bruins in Boston. Early in his career, Chevy never drank, but, apparently, he married a woman who liked to drink and eventually Chevy started drinking with her, especially over the summer months in Timmins. He was the type of person who really couldn't handle alcohol. Early that year, Chevy had 18 goals in the first two months and was playing well. I relayed that message to Lynn Patrick in Boston and he told me that he had Chevy living with him at one time when he was in Boston and he almost got divorced over his drinking. He then warned me, "The day that Chevy tells you, 'Honest to God, Chief, I'll never do it again,' is the time to move him on."

Jim Magee was the club president of the Kingston Frontenac Hockey Club and we became pretty good friends. One day Jim Magee and I had been away at a meeting and decided to stop at the Indian Room on our way back into Kingston. We walked into the hotel, which had a long standup bar, which reminded you of something out of a western movie. And who do you think is standing at the bar, holding court, with the patrons, none other than Chevy. As I walked by him, he yelled at me, "Hey, Chief, how are you?" I ignored him, and Jim and I proceeded to a table at the back of the room. A few minutes later, Chevy arrives at our table with three beers and plunks them down at our table.

"Damn, now I can't even have a beer," I complained.

"What do you mean?"

"Do you think the people don't know that I've said Kingston

bars are out of bounds to the players and you make a fool of me like this. Drink the beer yourself." I then said to Jim, "C'mon, Jim, we're out of here."

When I got home, I phoned Bun Cook, our trainer, and said, "Bun, I want you to take Chevy's equipment down off the pegs and put it away, and then tell Chevy when he comes in for practice tomorrow to come into my office and see me." The next morning I'm in my office, which was attached to the dressing room. After a few minutes, in comes Chevy, with his head down, a sorrowful look on his face, and he slumps down in the chair.

I sat there for a minute and then said to him, "What'd you think of your performance in the Prince George yesterday."

"Terrible," he said. "Honest to God, Chief, I'll never do that again."

Oh my God, don't tell me that, I thought. I'm right where Lynn was. "Okay, Chevy, I'm going to try and give you another chance." He practiced hard for the next two or three days until I got a phone call from a woman.

"Mr. Blair, I am Real Chevrifies's landlady. I don't mind him having beer cases piled to the ceiling all over his room, but when he lays on the bed and starts firing wine bottles into the waste basket and breaking them all over the room and my sister gave herself a terrible gash trying to clean up, then I've had it. I want him out of here."

"I can promise you he'll be gone. Give me four or five days." Right after that, I called Lynn in Boston and the Winnipeg Warriors in the Western League and arranged to move Chevy. I then called him into my office. I didn't bother going into the drinking, I just told him he'd been traded to Winnipeg.

"Here's your plane ticket for 2 o'clock this afternoon out of Toronto. Be there." "What do you mean?"

"Chevy, I don't want to discuss it. Go and see Bun and he'll get your skates and be on that plane if you want to get paid.

Early in the New Year, we were going to play in Hull-Ottawa on a Sunday afternoon. We had played at home on Saturday night. Red Ouellette had an appendicitis operation about six weeks before and still wasn't back, and at that time I was convinced he was a hypochondriac. After our game on Saturday night, I went into the dressing room and "Tess" (Orville Tessier) was trying to bend down. I went over to him and said, "What's wrong?"

"It's my back. It's so sore, I can hardly move." With that, I said, just a minute, I'll be right back. I then walked over to another section of the dressing room to where Red Ouellette was standing and said, "Red, you're playing tomorrow. Get your stuff packed."

Tess could hear me at this point and he hobbles over and says, "Wait a minute, I can probably play tomorrow."

"You just told me, you couldn't, so you're not. Red's playing."

We left bright and early the next morning, by bus, and stopped in Smiths Falls about 10 o'clock so the guys could eat. I wasn't feeling very good that day, so I stayed on the bus and was stretched out on the back seat. Pretty soon, I hear the bus door open and five or six guys get on. They all sit up at the front of the bus, and Buddy Boone, who was playing pretty well for us at this time, decides to hold court with the rest of them, who don't know that I'm on the bus. "Did you hear him this morning," said Boone, in reference to me. "Telling Red he has to play. He doesn't know if Red is well enough to play. You know that sonofabitch has been on my back all year." I never got up, so he didn't realize that I was there. Finally, the rest of the guys got back on the bus and away we go again.

During the pre-game warm-up while the guys are skating around, I called Pete Panagabko over to the boards. "I just wanted you to know that I was on the bus this morning when Buddy Boone was holding his little union meeting. Do you believe all that stuff he was saying?"

"No, it wasn't my thoughts. Leave me out of it. I had nothing to do with it," he said.

"I'm glad to hear that." So I said to him, "Send Blackie over."

Blackburn came over and I asked him the same questions I asked Pete. He said, "No, I don't want any part of it. It was his thoughts, not mine."

So away, he goes. Pretty soon, I can see them skating with Boonie, saying: "The Bird was on the bus . . . The Bird was on the bus. He heard everything you said." I could see Boone's head drop. He still played a great game that day.

After we got back into Kingston, Boone still had a real long face. I then went over to Bun, our trainer, and told him to take Boone's stuff down and put it away and when he comes in for practice tomorrow, tell him to come and see me. Bun looks at and me and says, "Is he going west?"

"Ask me no questions and I'll tell you no lies. Just tell Boone to see me when he comes in tomorrow." The next day Buddy slinks into my office and sits down. I make out that I'm doing something really important and let him sit there and stew for a few minutes. Then, I look up and cross my arms, and say, "Well, I guess you know from the other fellows that I was on the bus when you conducted your high profile union meeting yesterday."

"Yeah, I heard that," he answered in a real soft voice.

"Well, I just want you to know, here's a plane ticket for a plane that leaves Toronto at 3:50 p.m. for Winnipeg."

He looks at me for a minute and says, "Sonofabitch, I'm having the best year I've had in years."

"Boonie, why do you think you're having your best year? It wouldn't be because I've been on your back since Day One would it? Don't give that any credit."

"It probably is that."

Nevertheless, I answered, "Out. By the way Buddy, I talked to

Chevy (which I hadn't) and he tells me that the Warriors are dead last with no chance of making the playoffs, so don't spend your play-off money too early because you're not getting any from here."

That night, Paul Rimstead, the Sports Editor of *The Kingston Whig-Standard*, phoned me. "I understand your fired Buddy Boone today. Would you mind telling me why?"

"Sorry, Paul, it was club business and I'm not about to discuss that publicly."

"Well, I'm a reporter and I want to know." I told him that I didn't divulge that stuff to the media. "Well," said Rimstead, "Buddy gave me a helluva story and if you don't talk, then I'm going to use his version and it's not very flattering to you."

"Look, Paul, don't you try to intimidate me. You write whatever the hell you want," and I slammed down the phone.

The next day, when *The Whig-Standard* came out, there was Rimstead's column and it started out something like this: "Wren Blair, getting bigger and more important every day, yesterday traded his leading scorer, Buddy Boone, probably canceling any chance the Frontenacs had of making the playoffs." Then he proceeded to quote Boone extensively. I never said a word to Paul. I just let it go.

About this time in the season, Tommy Williams started to slump and I couldn't figure out why. Finally, I called Tommy into my office and asked, "Tommy, what's going on?"

"Why?"

"Well you haven't done a thing for the past two weeks. Do you have a problem? "Nope," he said.

"Are you having a problem with your mom and dad?

Again, he said, "Nope."

"Do you have a girlfriend?"

"Yep."

"Where is she?"

"In Duluth, Minn."

Do you have any problem with her? "Nope."

"Look it, Tommy, I know you have a problem, but I can't help you if you don't tell me what it is, so please quit lying to me. I know something is going on.

"Well," he said, "this is just between you and me." I said, yes. "Well, my girlfriend in Duluth is pregnant." How old is she? "Seventeen." Do you love her? "Yes." Well, then I said, get the hell home and marry her. "You won't give me the time off."

"Who said, I wouldn't? I said, I'll give you 10 days off to go home and marry Emmie on one condition."

"What's that?"

"After you're married, I want you to bring Emmie back here with you. I'm sick and tired of the way you've been running around here anyway." Tommy went home, got married and came back to Kingston with his new wife and started playing great hockey once again.

Looking back, I think Tommy was probably the most exciting player in Kingston that year. He could pick the puck up and just fly up the ice. But like a lot of Americans back then, he kept his head down and got hit a lot. I can remember one game we were playing in Hull-Ottawa and big Jean Gauthier lined Tommy up and just flattened him. He was out cold. They carried him off the ice to the first-aid room, and when I went over there, he didn't know who he was or what happened. I thought he might be a goner as far as playing hockey was concerned. We waited for a couple of hours after the game and they finally released him from the hospital and let us take him back home. I talked to the doctor before we left the hospital and he told me to keep him off the ice for a few days. I guess what happened to him was a high-level concussion, something that is becoming quite common in the game today, but was never talked about back then. He was hit as hard as any player I've ever seen, but yet he came back and made the Bruins the next year.

Early in my first year in Kingston, we had played eight games when I called Harry Sinden into my office. I asked Harry what he thought of our team. He thought we had a pretty good team, but we were not very strong down the center. I agreed with his assessment and said to Harry, "I know a guy, who played with us in Whitby who is better than any centerman we've got."

"Atterlsey, right? Well, get the hell up to Whitby and turn him pro."

"Harry, it's not going to be that easy. He just opened a new business, Attersley Tire, in downtown Whitby." I asked Harry if he would run the next couple of days at practice, while I went up to Whitby to see Bob.

I went up to Oshawa that day and stayed overnight at my home and the next morning I got up, picked up a bottle of Walker's Imperial, which Bob and I drank in those days, and headed for his office in Whitby. I went in the side door and met ol' Jack, as we used to call him. He was working for Bob as jack-of-all-trades — security, errand boy, whatever. Anyway, I asked Jack if Bob was in, and he said yes, he is in his office at the back of the building. I then asked Jack, if he would make sure we weren't disturbed.

"Are you going to try and sign him," he asked? I nodded affirmatively and he said. "Nobody'll get near you."

I proceeded out to Bob's office, opened the jug, poured a couple of drinks and we started chatting about all sorts of things. I had written out a whole schedule on how Bob could play in Kingston, commute and hardly miss any games, maybe none. Finally, I said, Bob, I talked with Harry the other day and asked him for an assessment of our team. He said he thought we weren't too bad, but were weak at center ice. I agreed and told him I knew of somebody who could fill that spot. Your name came up immediately and Harry said, "Why don't you go up to Whitby and sign him."

"Hey, I can't go down there to live and play," he said.

"Nobody asked you to move down to Kingston and live. And who the hell asked you to go down and practice. You can skate here in Whitby at night. Bob, I'll pay you by the game and here's what I'll give you. And if you multiply that out, it's more money than some NHL players are making."

He sat there for a minute and then said, "You know, if I do this, I wouldn't have to take any money out of the business to live on for the first year." The hardest thing for any person to do in starting a new business is to live day-to-day while trying to get yourself established. "Do you have copies on the schedule you worked out?"

"We play our home games on Saturday, so you can take the train down. We usually play Hull or Montreal on Sunday afternoons and I'll fly you back from those games. When we play in Kitchener, we'll pick you up on the way through. When we go to Sudbury and the Sault, we'll pick you up on the way through and those games are usually the weekends."

He looked it all over and said, "You know, I guess I could play."

The amazing thing, when I look back on it now, is that Bob missed the first eight games and yet at the end of the season led our entire team in scoring and finished about fifth in the league scoring race. And that was at a time when Phil Esposito, Cliff Pennington, and Jean Ratelle were all centers in our league.

Over the summer of 1961, I knew that we had to improve our team. I talked at length with Lynn Patrick and he told me of a few players that he was going to try for in the intra-league draft that he would then place in Kingston. We had some fairly good players coming out of our Major Junior A farm teams in Niagara Falls, Estevan, Saskatchewan, and Shawinigan Falls, Quebec.

Our No. 1 line from the year before was Bob Attersley at center with Tom McCarthy and Orv Tessier on the wings. Tessier was one of the greatest scorers I've ever seen, but he was short in the wheels department and that's why he never stuck in the National League.

When Tess got in range of the goal, I never saw a player who could pinpoint shots the way he could. In practice, he used to bet the players a quarter that he could hit the posts. "We'll do 10 pucks," he used to say, "and you pick the post you want me to hit. Every time I hit a post, you pay me a quarter." Tess used to make quite a bit of money doing that because he hit a helluva lot more posts than he missed. Tom McCarthy was a big rangy player and he was kind of moody, but he was dynamite around the net.

Players that we graduated from junior ranks to play in Kingston that second year were right winger Ron Willey, centermen Billy Knibbs, Jeannot Gilbert, and Bobby Leiter, and defenceman Ken Stephanson. Ed Chadwick, who had played in the NHL, came in to play goal for us. In the first year, we had Long John Henderson, Ed Babiuk and even the great Harry Lumley played a bit. Most of them were gone in the second year when "Chad" took over and played just great for us.

Speaking of Chadwick reminds me of the time that the players were complaining to me about the floor in our dressing room. I had told the players that we had no money to fix the floor properly, and the rink management had no intention of helping. One day I came across an ad in the newspaper, advertising rubber tiles for sale at 10 cents a tile. It struck me that rubber would be great for our dressing room, especially when our players had their skates on. I went into the store and talked to the salesman and gave him the dimensions of our dressing room. He told me how many tiles I would need and how much it would cost. The cost was nominal and I got permission from the Bruins to buy them. The reason the tiles were on sale was they were odd colors, every color in the rainbow. I called them Joseph's coat of many colors in tiles.

I then had a meeting with the players and told them that I had bought the tiles, but they would have to install them. I asked if there was anyone on the team who had any experience in laying tiles.

Chadwick immediately piped up. "I know how to lay tiles. I do it all summer."

"Okay, you're the foremen for the rest of these monkeys here." I then told them I had to go to a meeting in Ottawa on the Sunday and I would buy them a couple of cases of beer to 'help' lay the tiles. I also told them that I wanted the job completed when I returned later that night.

Eddie said, "No problem, it'll be finished." When I returned from the meeting, I stopped by the rink, walked in the dressing room, and turned on the lights. I was amazed. It really looked marvelous. I think what really happened that day is the players quickly polished off the two cases of beer I bought them and bought three or four and had a real party.

At about this same time, Harry Sinden had led a bit of a charge to change my name from "The Bird" to "The Penguin" because of the way I walked on some occasions. Often times, I'd see him doing the Penguin waddle in front of his teammates. After I walked around the dressing room and headed back to my office, I stopped in my tracks. On the back of my office door, the side facing the dressing room, there was a huge picture of a penguin painted on the door. I stood there and laughed like crazy because it was so funny. But I said to myself, I'm never going to let on to the players that I'd seen it. For days I never said a word and the players are stewing like crazy because I hadn't said anything.

Finally, one of the players asked me, "What did you think of the penguin we painted on the door?"

"What penguin? I never saw it." They then took me into the room to show it to me." That's great. I think if people can paint that and have a lot of fun, I think it's great. I can take it, but now you can take a can of brown paint and cover it up." Eddie, who still scouts for the NHL, often talks about the tile job and the penguin painting.

We were a much improved hockey club that second year and

moved from fourth place in the standings to third at the end of the season, even though we had a lot of rookies in the lineup. League rules set down that we had to have 12 players under the age of 23 because the NHL wanted to develop players in this league. We acquired Dick Cherry that year. He was attending teacher's college in Peterborough came home on weekends to play and joined us for mid-week games whenever he could. When we got to the playoffs, I used to fly Dick to our away games. We were playing Sudbury and he would fly out of Peterborough in a private plane and join us on the road. That cost quite a bit of money, but it was worth it because he was a great player and a real asset to us.

We went to the league and met Hull-Ottawa. In the final game, played in Kingston, Harry Sinden and one of the Plager brothers went into the corner after the puck and collided. They both went down in a heap. When they got up, Harry was really incensed and took a swing at Plager. Nobody could figure out why Harry did that because he wasn't the type of player that got riled up. Tom McCarthy said to me, "What's wrong with Harry. That's not like him." Tom skated over to the penalty box and asked Harry what the problem was. Harry said that while he was down on the ice, Plager tried to kick him. As soon as Tom heard this, he skated to the other side of the penalty box, where Plager was sitting, and hit him with his stick, opening up a deep gash on his head. McCarthy then turned, skated off the ice, and went right to our dressing room. He knew he was in trouble. He took off his equipment and left the building before we ever finished the game. That's the last time I ever saw Tom McCarthy.

As a result of McCarthy's action, we received a 10-minute minor penalty, which I had never heard of before. Harry had taken a five-minute penalty, so we were shorthanded for the next 10 minutes. We killed off those two penalties and the game remained tied until a third overtime period when Hull-Ottawa was in our end and Chuck Hamilton scored to eliminate us.

That summer of 1962, I had made a deal with Stafford Smythe of the Toronto Maple Leafs to put a junior team from Oshawa into the Metro Junior A League. Stafford had become disenchanted with the Ontario Hockey Association earlier that year and had pulled the Toronto Marlboros out of the OHA and told them he was forming his own league. The league was comprised of the Marlboros, Neil McNeil Maroons, who succeeded St. Mike's, Brampton, Markham Waxers, Oshawa, and Whitby. Steve Stavro, who now owns the Maple Leafs, owned that Markham team. Over the summer, on Labour Day, I signed Bobby Orr, at age 14, to play for Oshawa, which also gave the Boston Bruins his playing rights.

My third season managing and coaching the Kingston Frontenacs turned out to be our final year in the EPHL, as the NHL decided to move the entire league to the United States and rename it the Central Professional Hockey League. With my work as the general manager of the Oshawa Generals and the Clinton Comets, in addition to the extra duties I had been handed by the Boston Bruins, I was beginning to have such a heavy workload that I talked Harry Sinden into becoming an assistant playing-coach with the Frontenacs. Harry not only gave it his best shot, but he did an outstanding job. He ran almost all of the practices that year as I had started the Oshawa Generals up again. I was really only behind the bench during the games. Harry handled almost everything else, including curfew checks.

During the summer, the Bruins made a trade to get goaltender Bruce Gamble. Gamble was a great goaltender, but didn't make the Bruins that year so he was sent to Kingston. Our backup goaltender that season was Wayne Rutledge, who had graduated from our junior team in Niagara Falls. On defence, we had Harry Sinden, Alf Treen, Wayne Schultz, and Ken Stephanson. Later in the season, the Bruins made a trade with the Chicago Blackhawks to get Pat "Whitey" Stapleton. Lynn didn't feel that he was big enough to play in the NHL, although I felt differently along with many others in the NHL, and he was eventually sent down to Kingston. With Stapleton, we probably had the best defence in the league that year. We also had Eddie Westfall playing for us off and on. Also up front, we had Randy Miller, who was starting his third season with us, Don Blackburn, Red Ouellette, Pete Panagabko, Dick Cherry, Ron Willey, Jeannot Gilbert, Bobby Leiter, Billy Knibbs and Stan Maxwell. This was probably the best team we ever had in the EPHL.

Early that season, I got a call from Lynn Patrick in Boston and he told me that he had been talking with Sam Pollock of Montreal about the possibility of trading for Cliff Pennington, who was playing in the EPHL with Hull-Ottawa. If the trade was to be made, the Canadiens wanted Stan Maxwell from our club. I told Lynn that would be a tremendous loss to our club. Even though I was down on Maxwell from time to time because of his defensive shortcomings, he was a big offensive weapon for us. However, if you feel you have to make the trade for the benefit of the Bruins, then make it. Personally, I told him, I don't think Pennington can play in the National League. "He is a good playmaker, but I don't think his skating will hold up. What I want from you is your word that if Pennington doesn't stick with the Bruins, then I want him sent to Kingston, not to another Bruin farm team."

Later on that week, Lynn phoned me and told me that he had made the trade – Pennington for Maxwell. Pennington was eventually sent to us and he was a big cog in our wheel. As for Maxwell, it wasn't long before Sam traded him away.

The Frontenacs set an EPHL record in their final season, finishing in first place with 49 wins, only 19 losses and 11 ties for 95 points. We finished nine points ahead of the second-place Hull-Ottawa Canadiens, the defending league champions, who had 87 points, and 29 ahead of the third-place Sudbury Wolves. The St. Louis Braves, who had started the season as the Syracuse Braves, finished fourth and out the playoffs with 61 points, six behind the Wolves. Only three of the four teams in the league that year made the playoffs. Because the Frontenacs' first-place finish, we gained a bye to the league final and met the Wolves, who had upset the Canadiens in a best-of-five semi-final. Sudbury was no match for the high-flying Frontenacs in the best-of-seven final. We opened the final series on home ice and romped to a 6-2 victory as Kingston native Dick Cherry notched three goals. Singles were added by Don Blackburn, Pete Panagabko, and Wayne Connelly, while Norm "Red" Armstrong and Mike McMahon scored for the Wolves. The Wolves got outstanding goaltending from Gerry Cheevers in game two in Sudbury and upset the Frontenacs 5-3. Dunc McCallum, Jim Johnson, Dave Richardson, "Red" Armstrong, and Mike McMahon scored for Sudbury, while Pat Stapleton, Cliff Pennington, and Pete Panagabko replied for the Frontenacs.

But that was the only blemish on the Frontenacs' playoff record as they breezed to 5-3, 4-0, and 6-2 victories to clinch the championship. Stapleton notched the winner in the 5-3 victory when he scored with just 25 seconds remaining and Pennington scored three seconds later, into an empty net, to clinch it. Don Blackburn had a pair of goals in that game and Cherry added a single, while Gord Labossiere, with two, and Dave Richardson scored for Sudbury. A perfect goaltending performance by Bruce Gamble moved the Frontenacs to within one win of the title when he backstopped his mates to a 4-0 win in Sudbury in game four. Kingston scorers in that game were, Cherry, Stapleton, playing-coach Harry Sinden, and Jeannot Gilbert.

Before more than 3,500 boisterous fans in Kingston, the Frontenacs clinched the championship with a 6-3 triumph. Panagabko again sparked the Frontenacs with a pair of goals, while singles were added by Cherry, Blackburn, Stapleton, and Sinden. Len Ronson, Marc Dufour and Labossiere scored for the Wolves.

In the final league playoff scoring stats for that year, the Frontenacs occupied the top five positions, even though they only played
five games. Pennington was the playoffs' top point-getter with 12
on three goals and nine assists, followed by Cherry with a playoff-
leading six goals and three assists for nine points. Blackburn, with
four goals and four assists; Panagabko, with four goals and two
assists; and Stapleton, with four goals and two assists, rounded out
the top five.

The playoff victory marked the first time in the history of
Kingston that it had won a professional hockey league championship. We were awarded the Tom Foley Memorial Trophy. Tom
Foley had been a prominent broadcaster on Hockey Night in
Canada and had been killed in Toronto taking a taxi down to
Maple Leafs Gardens to do a hockey game after having flown in
from Ottawa. Both of the presidents from the EPHL had been
from Ottawa — Ed Houston and Jack Urie. Both had strong ties
with Foley, which was the reason behind the naming of the trophy in his honor.

In the summer of 1963, all members of the EPHL were all
notified by the NHL that the entire league was moving to the
United States. The Kingston team was moved to Minneapolis, Minnesota, to be called the Minneapolis Bruins. The Bruins would own
51% of the team with the other 49% being owned by three Minneapolis businessmen — Walter Bush, Gordon Ritz, and Bob
McNulty. This was my first contact with these gentlemen, who later
would become some of the owners of the Minnesota North Stars.

At this time, I sat down with Harry Sinden and explained to
him that my workload was getting even greater with the Boston
Bruins. I was now General Manager of the Minneapolis Bruins, the
Clinton Comets, and the new Oshawa Generals. In addition to
that, Lynn had asked me to scout for players who we could turn into
pros. I told Harry that it was time he hung up his skates and became

the full-time coach of the Minneapolis Bruins. Harry was a bit wist-
ful about giving up playing, but finally agreed.

We opened training camp that year in Minneapolis and most of
the players from Kingston had moved down to the Twin Cities area.
Like other years, we also had graduates from our junior farm teams.
One of the players who really caught my eye at training camp that
year was a young defenceman who had played for the Estevan Bruins, Joe Watson. He was from Smithers, B.C. Once training camp
progressed, Harry would tell me the players he wanted on the team
and I would sign them. He indicated to me that he felt Joe could
play, so I called him to my office.

In those days, if you were signed to a minor league contract, you
got a $1,000 bonus to turn pro. When I told Joe about his bonus, he
was not very happy at all. He said he was not going to sign for that
amount and left my office. I talked to him one more time and still
made no headway.

So I had lunch with Harry and asked him, "Do you really want
Joe Watson on this team?"

"Oh, yeah, he's even better than I thought."

'Then you better have a talk with that young man this afternoon because I'm not getting anywhere with him. You can tell him
that I want to see him in my office at 5 o'clock and I'll have the contract ready along with a train ticket home. He either signs or goes
home the next day."

It's kind of funny because all through that practice, Harry never
worked with the team, but skated round and round that rink talking
to Joe. Harry finally told me that he was going to sign. I asked Harry
what he had said to him to change his mind.

"I told him that I have played for you for many years and when
you say that is your final offer, it is. I also told him that I wanted him
on this team and that he had too good a future in pro hockey to
pack it in at this juncture in his career."

At 5 o'clock that day, Joe came into my office and I said to him, "Joe, there is a train reservation here and a contract here, you either take the contract and sign it or pick up the train ticket and leave."

He finally picked up the contract, signed it, got up and left. He turned around and said, "Thanks very much," and stormed out of my office. Later Joe was drafted by the Philadelphia Flyers in the original expansion draft and became a key player for them during their Stanley Cup years.

When I traveled to Minneapolis to check in on Harry during the season, I always went out to dinner with the local owners and became quite good friends with them. A little more than halfway through the year, Walter said to me, "Wren, you know we're going to get an expansion franchise in the NHL when the NHL expands and we want you to come back here and be our General Manager." I can remember saying to Walter, "Heck, by the time you guys get into the NHL, I will have a beard down to my ankles." Two years down the road the league did indeed expand and Minneapolis was one of the new teams.

Minneapolis is a major-league sports town. They had the Minnesota Twins in baseball, the Minnesota Vikings in football, and the Minneapolis Lakers, who today are the Los Angeles Lakers, in basketball. As a result, as a minor pro team, we did not draw that well. We lost tons of money and the team moved on to Oklahoma City the next year into a brand new building. I was still the GM of the team, but Harry was running more and more of the operation. I have some good memories of the players who played in Oklahoma City — Wayne Cashman, Dick Cherry, Joe Watson, Ron Buchanan, and Peter Panagabko. They had all played for my Kingston Frontenacs or Oshawa Generals Junior A team, whose star player was a young kid from Parry Sound, Bobby Orr.

PROFILE

J.P. Parise

JEAN-PAUL "J.P." PARISE WAS raised in Smooth Rock Falls, Ontario. He used to say that he was an Ontario French-Canadian, not a Quebec French-Canadian. I don't know what that means, but it must mean something in Smooth Rock Falls.

J.P. first came to my attention when he was playing for the Bruins Junior B team in St. Marys, Ontario. He moved up to the Niagara Falls Flyers, the Bruins Major Junior A team, before turning pro with the Kingston Frontenacs. When I offered J.P. our standard salary, he accepted without a question. You could tell that money wasn't an object with J.P. He just wanted to play.

J.P. Parise was one of the best-checking wingers in minor pro hockey and went on to do the same in the NHL. He was also one of the best players in the corners who ever played for me, a skill that Harry Sinden recognized when he added J.P. to the Team Canada roster in 1972. Not only was he a great checker, but he went about that task without taking too many penalties.

When I started to build the Minnesota North Stars team, I saw J.P. as a potentially important member of our team and I was able to acquire him in a trade. He became one of our most reliable players and one of my favorites.

During the years when the WHL was threatening to entice players away from the North Stars with higher salaries, I set out to sign our players to long-term contracts. My first job was to negotiate a new agreement with Danny Grant, who had won the Calder Trophy as rookie of the year in his first year with us. I signed Danny to a new contract in the $20,000 range, but when the morning papers came out, splashed across the top of the sports page was a headline saying that we were paying Danny $30,000. Very few players other than the big time stars made $30,000 in those days. Later that day I had scheduled a contract meeting with J.P. and thought to myself, he's going to come in here with visions of grandeur because the players think everything they read in the papers is the gospel truth.

Before J.P. arrived, I asked my secretary, Marilyn Vaughan, to bring me Danny Grant's contract along with J.P.'s file. When he arrived, we chit-chatted away for a bit before I asked, "J.P., do you read the newspapers?" When he gestured yes, I continued. "Do you believe everything you read?" He answered, "One never knows," and then I set the trap. "Well, J.P., I don't want to waste too much time on this. I know what you read this morning and I'm telling you that Danny Grant did not get the money the papers are saying he got. As a matter of fact, he got less than you got last year. As you know J.P., you did not have a good year last year, which is unusual for you, but I am still prepared to offer you the same amount of money you got last year, which is more than Danny Grant signed for yesterday. I have never done this before J.P., but if I have to I will show you Danny Grant's contract. However, if you ask me to show it to you, you will have to agree to take the same money as Danny received. I turned the contract over so he couldn't see it and left it on my desk.

J.P. was in a bit of quandary, but finally he said, "Aw, to hell with it, I didn't have a great year last year . . . give me the contract . . . I'll sign."

I never did have to show him the contract. A few years later, J.P. was scouting for the North Stars and I was with the Los Angeles Kings, around 1979. I went up into the press box at old Chicago Stadium and suddenly a guy came in and sat down beside me. I looked over my shoulder and it was J.P. We chatted a bit — there were still a few minutes before the game started — then J.P. asked me, "Wren, remember the time I signed the contract when you told me that I was making more than Danny Grant, and you told me that if I looked at his contract, I would have to take the same money as he was getting." I nodded yes. "Well, can you tell me now what would have happened if I had looked at his contract?"

"J.P., honestly, I have never lied to any player and I have too much respect for you to lie now. J.P., you would have lost a $1,000."

Soon after I left the North Stars, Jack Gordon traded J.P. and Jude Drouin to the New York Islanders. The day that trade was announced, I called Bill Torrey, the General Manager of the Islanders. "Billy, you must have got down on your knees and thanked God the day I left the North Stars." When he asked why, I said, "Do you think if I was still there, I would have traded J.P. and Jude for the players the North Stars received from you in return? You stole Minnesota blind on that deal." It wasn't long before both these players tipped the Stanley Cup and tasted champagne as they helped the Islanders on the road to their fourth straight Stanley Cup victory.

J.P. is back in Minnesota today, the head coach at a private school with an extensive hockey program. A few years ago, J.P. called me to see if I was going to the Silver Stick Bantam Tournament in Port Huron, Michigan. He then told me that he was bringing his bantam team to that tournament and perhaps we could get together for a few evenings. He also said that he had an excellent player on his team that had to see play. "He wears No. 11," J.P. said. When I asked for his name, J.P. seemed to ignore me and went on with the conversation. At the time I was involved with the Kingston Frontenacs Major Junior A franchise, so I decided to go to Port Huron and have a look at this kid J.P. was so high on.

When J.P.'s team took the ice, I noticed No. 11 immediately, then took a double look when I saw the name "Parise" on his sweater above the number. J.P. had always worn No. 11, which should have tipped me, but it didn't. J.P. was certainly not wrong in his assessment of his son. He could skate and he could lug the puck. I kidded J.P. after that game that I would have never known it was his son, even though he had the same last name. "Why?" he asked "Because he can skate . . ." I arranged for another one of J.P.'s sons, a goaltender, to try out with the Kingston Voyageurs with Pat Anson, but in the end, he didn't come to training camp.

My memories of J.P. are always fond. I enjoy looking back at the tapes of the '72 series against the Soviet Union and seeing him play the greatest hockey of his career. I'm glad that he had chance to win a Stanley Cup ring with the Islanders. J.P. is high on my list of the best guys I have met in my hockey career.

Kingston Frontenacs 1962-63 Eastern Professional Hockey League Champions

Back Row (from left) – Dick Cherry, Jeannot Gilbert, Wayne Shultz, Billy Knibbs, Cliff Pennington, Ken Stephanson, Howie Dietrich.

Middle Row — Bun Cook (Trainer), Red Ouellette, Pete Panagabko, Jean Paul Parise, Ron Willy, Randy Miller, Alf Treen, Tom Dickinson (Ass. Trainer).

Front Row — Bob Goy (sub-goalie), Wayne Connelly, Pat Stapleton, Jim Magee (President), Wren Blair (General Manager/Coach), Harry Sinden (Asst. Coach), Don Blackburn, Bruce Gamble.

A Great Line: Tom McCarthy (left wing) shows the "58" puck, Bob Attersley (centre) shows the "53", and Orval Tessier (right winger) holds the "57" puck and the "168" puck, signifying that this line had scored a total of 168 points at mid-season.

Signing Bobby Orr and the Revival of the Oshawa Generals

7

"WREN, HOW CAN WE GET the Bruins out of the cellar? If something positive does not happen soon, I'm going to get fired." Lynn Patrick, my boss with the Boston Bruins, and I were talking in his hotel suite at the old LaSalle Hotel in downtown Kingston shortly after I had joined the Bruins in 1960.

"Lynn," I replied, "several of the NHL teams sponsor more than one Major Junior A Hockey Club in Ontario. For instance, the Montreal Canadiens sponsor the Junior Canadiens and the Peterborough Petes. The Toronto Maple Leafs have sponsored the Toronto Marlboros and Toronto St. Michaels for years, yet we have only one Major Junior A Club in Ontario, the Niagara Falls Flyers."

"What's your point?" asked Lynn.

"I remember when the Oshawa Arena burned down in September of 1953. The Bruins then sponsored the Oshawa Generals and you were in town watching the team at training camp. In a newspaper story, you said that Oshawa was a great Junior Hockey town, and if ever a new arena was built, the Bruins would return to Oshawa, to again sponsor the Generals."

"You sure have a good memory, because I remember saying something like that," Lynn replied.

"That's exactly what you said Lynn, because I still have a copy of that newspaper.

Do you want to read it?"

"No, no," said Lynn, "you're obviously correct about this." He

151

then asked, "Why are we talking about Oshawa, when they don't have an arena at this time?"

"No, but Oshawa is getting ready to build a new arena. I had lunch with Terry Kelly (a prominent Oshawa lawyer) the other day, and during lunch he told me that he was going to spearhead a fund raising drive to raise enough money to get a new arena for Oshawa." Actually Terry added, "You get busy and bring the Generals back to this city."

Lynn looked at me a bit surprised for a few moments and then he said , "Wren, Hap will never agree to splitting the junior hockey talent between Niagara Falls and Oshawa as they did in the past." Lynn was speaking of Hap Emms, the owner, the GM and coach of the Niagara Falls Flyers

"To hell with Hap. We'll enter the Generals in the new Metro Major Junior A Hockey League Stafford Smythe has put together."

Lynn looked at me somewhat astounded. "Wren, you can't get in that league, it's an all Toronto League."

"How do you know Lynn that I can't get into that league?"

Lynn looked at me for a moment. "I'll tell you what Wren, if you can get a Boston team from Oshawa in the Metro Junior A League, you've got $50,000.00 of Boston money to bring the Generals back." Fifty thousand dollars in 1960 was a lot of money.

Later that year when the Frontenacs had completed the season, I drove into Toronto and called Stafford Smythe on the phone.

"This is Wren Blair calling," I said.

He snarled back, "I know who the hell it is. What do you want?"

"I want to put a team in the Metro Junior Hockey League from Oshawa."

He laughed, "Yea doesn't everybody." Most of us in hockey knew the Metro League was in trouble financially.

"Mr. Smythe, I am serious."

"Will you pay your own bills?" he questioned. "We are going nuts trying to fund five teams in this league now."

"Certainly we will pay our own bills."

"Will you get your own players?"

"Certainly, we will get our own players, it's a Boston team Mr. Smythe, not a Toronto team."

There was a pause on the phone for a few seconds, and then he totally surprised me by saying, "Ok you're in the league."

"Hold it!" I said. "I can't be in the league, I don't have an arena to play out of."

Then he really shocked me. "Oh yes you do. You'll play double headers on Tuesdays and Sundays out of Maple Leaf Gardens."

I couldn't believe it. No sooner did I get off the phone with Stafford, I called Lynn in Boston. I can certainly remember how excited I was when Lynn came on the phone. "Lynn, it's Wren. I just finished talking with Stafford Smythe, and we are in the Metro Junior League from Oshawa." I then told him about Stafford's offer to let us play in Maple Leaf Gardens. Lynn was astounded. Then I asked, "When do I get the $50,000.00?"

"Very shortly, but a hockey club has to be established in Oshawa before I can get Weston to ok it." He was speaking of Weston Adams, the Bruins Owner.

Then I had another thought. "Lynn why don't you ask Weston to put in $51,000.00 and I will capitalize the club at a $100,000.00 by selling shares to seven Oshawa businessmen for $7,000.00 each for the other 49%." That meant that the local business people would own 49% and the Bruins would own 51%, which was control.

I always remember Lynn's reply. "You're not only a good hockey man, you're a pretty damn good businessman as well. I think that's a great idea, and I will talk to Weston today and call you tomorrow."

The next day Lynn called to say Weston liked the whole plan. He then gave Lynn permission to work with me in setting up the return of the Oshawa Generals. Since we had to begin play the next season, and this was already late May, I didn't have too much time to put the financial structure in place, find players, hire a coach and trainer for the team, and be ready to start at training camp in early October 1962.

I'll never forget putting together the local Oshawa shareholder group to purchase 7% each in the "Oshawa Generals Hockey Club Limited." The first person I approached in Oshawa was Mr. Russ Humphreys. I really didn't know Mr. Humphreys at that time very well, but he was a lawyer with offices right downtown. I made an appointment with him to visit him in his office the next day. After I explained everything to him, he said, "So what you are saying Mr. Blair, is that for $7,000.00 that I would invest, I would own 7% of the new Oshawa Generals. I like this idea, so you can count on me to purchase 7%." He then asked me whom he should make the check out to, and I said to the Oshawa Generals Hockey Club Limited.

As I took the check, I said, "You are the first local person to buy stock in the new Generals, and I would like you to become the President of the Club."

He looked at me for a moment and he said, "Wren, may I call you Wren?"

"Yes, if I could call you Russ?"

"I don't know anything about how to be the President of a hockey club."

"Oh, you don't have to know anything about that Russ, I'll just tell you what you should do."

He looked at me with a glimmer in his eye. "Okay, you tell me what to do and I'll be the President." Russ Humphreys was a great gentleman. He had a good sense of humor, and we had many good times together over the next few years.

The next day I went to see Mr. Murray Johnston, owner and operator of a successful men's clothing store, named Murray Johnston Men's Clothing Ltd. I told Murray the same story as I told Russ.

I mentioned to him that Russ Humphreys had bought the first share in Oshawa, and that he had agreed to become the Club President. Murray's Clothing Store was right across the street from Russ's office, and they were obviously good friends. Murray then said, "If Russ is in , I'm in." So now I had two of the seven required local investors in the fold. The next day I went to see Dr. Charlie McIlveen and told the same story to Charlie. I knew Charlie fairly well, and he knew me at least from my activity in hockey, because Charlie was then and still is a great hockey fan. He quickly agreed to come in. By now, I was really getting excited about the fine group of business people in Oshawa that I was assembling. The remaining local Oshawa shareholders were Joe Bolahood, who operated a very successful Sporting Goods Store in Oshawa, Dr. "Bud" Shaw, a very well known and successful doctor in Oshawa, and Dr. Peter Zakarow, a successful local dentist who had followed my exploits with the Dunlops when we won the World Championship in 1958 over in Whitby. Two or three days later I traveled over to Whitby to the Court Building to talk with a good friend of mine, Bruce Affleck. At that time, Bruce was the Crown Attorney in this region. He was very enthused about the idea and quickly bought the remaining 7% holding in the Generals. I then asked Bruce if he would agree to perform the duties of Treasurer of the Hockey Club, which he agreed to do. Bruce and I became very good friends over the next few years as we wrote payroll checks and paid the accounts of the club.

The Generals truly became part of the community. Terry Kelly raised funds for the new arena, leading an initiative among employees of General Motors who contributed to the cause through a payroll deduction plan. Usually when Terry starts a drive on something of this nature, it culminates in success. Later in my life, I was thrilled to be inducted into the Oshawa Sports Hall of Fame together with 29 others in its first year of existence; again Terry

Kelly was involved with Bill Kurelo, Walter Branch, and Effie Hezzelwood in creating this hall of fame. My brother Gerald, who took over my duties as a sport columnist with the Whitby newspaper, traveled with us a great deal. My son Danny had became a stick boy with the team in the later years, and he still fondly remembers those days. The late Jim Bishop broadcast those games and reported on the Generals with great enthusiasm. The late George Campbell and later the late Eric Weselby, together with Jim Shaw and others, did a good job of bringing the news of the Generals to the sporting public of the Oshawa area.

I was busy that year. I was still operating the Kingston Frontenacs and was now also the General Manager of the Clinton Comets. I was the League Governor of the team in Kingston and the Alternate Governor of the Clinton Comets. Now I began attending the Governors' Meetings of the Metro Junior A League as the Governor of the Generals. Steve Stavro was the owner of the Markham team, and Frank Bonello, who had played for me with the Whitby Dunlops, became Steve's General Manager and Coach. Sandy Air, who had also played for me with the Dunlops, was the General Manager of the Brampton team. That summer I hired Doug Williams, another player from Whitby, to be the first coach of the returning Oshawa Generals. Shortly thereafter four former Dunnies were coaching in the league when Bob Attersley became the coach of the Whitby Dunlops Junior Team.

We opened training camp in the Oshawa Children's Arena, the only ice surface in the city. Construction of the new Oshawa Civic Arena had just begun. Because we had no place to store our equipment in, I made arrangements with the Oshawa Kinsmen Club to rent space for our equipment following practices and games. When the season started, our players used to gather at the Oshawa Kinsmen Centre, and we would load up the bus there to go into Toronto or over to Whitby or to Brampton and Markham. We had to go into

Toronto a great deal that year, since all of our home games were played in Maple Leaf Gardens. A number of people from Oshawa traveled into Toronto, especially for the Sunday afternoon double-headers, to see our games in that first season.

JUST BEFORE CAMP OPENED, I had signed 14-year-old Bobby Orr in Parry Sound. He would become the heart of the Oshawa Generals, leading us to a Memorial Cup victory before graduating to the Boston Bruins and leading them to the Stanley Cup. I clearly remember how I managed to persuade him to sign with us.

When I was managing the Kingston Frontenacs, at the end of season in the first year of 1960-61, we made the playoffs in the final game of the schedule, on the road in Montreal, against the Montreal Royals. That put us up against the Sault Ste. Marie Thunderbirds in the first round of the playoffs. One weekend, nearly the entire Boston organization came to Kingston because we had two home games. Weston Adams had come down, the Owner of the Bruins, Lynn Patrick, the General Manager, Milt Schmidt, who had been our coach and was now the Assistant General Manager, Phil Watson, the new coach who had been hired by Lynn to succeed Milt, Harold Cotton, our chief Scout, "Hap" Emms, who was the owner of the Niagara Falls Flyers at that time, and Scotty Monroe, who ran our team in Estevan, Saskatchewan. We were having an executive meeting.

Following the game Friday night, Lynn and I went down to his hotel, the old LaSalle Hotel on Princess Street to chat and have a drink after the game. During the conversation, I said to Lynn, "There's a Bantam playoff game tomorrow afternoon over in Gananoque. There are two pretty good Bantam players on the Gananoque team I've been watching for awhile. Would you like to go over? They are playing in the Eastern Ontario Finals in their division against Parry Sound." So we went over the next afternoon. Nearly the entire Boston group was in attendance.

The game started. In those days, there were no program line-ups or things like we have today, so you had to kind of struggle to figure out who was who and so on. Lynn stood behind the screen at one end of the rink. I was a little further down the side looking straight on so I could get a good vision of the ice. After about three or four minutes of play, I walked down to speak to Lynn. "There is a kid on that Parry Sound Team that I think is just out of this world. Forget the Gananoque team for a minute, and just watch Parry Sound, and see if you spot the same kid that I am talking about."

"Who, that little guy number #2 on defence for Parry Sound? Man, isn't he something?"

I didn't know his name until the game was over. The kid had played the entire game. He never left the ice, except once when he got a two-minute penalty. I found out later that he was only 12 years of age. I think if I remember right, Parry Sound lost the game, and Gananoque went on to win the Ontario Bantam playoffs. When the game was over, I went searching for the coach of the Parry Sound team, Bucko MacDonald. I knew Bucko. He was from Sundridge, Ontario and a Member of Parliament at that time. He had been an NHL player in both Detroit and Toronto and was now a part-time scout for the Red Wings. I was directed to the visitor dressing room area, in a little narrow hallway, and there were several people talking to Bucko. He was holding court outside the Parry Sound dressing room. When I caught his eye, he came over to speak to me. "Hi Wren, how are you doing?"

"Good Bucko. Who was that little guy #2 on your team?"

Bucko was a great orator, and he put on his political voice when he said to me, "Wren, his name is Robert Gordon Orr." That was the first time I had ever heard this young man's name. "As you know

Wren, I am a part time scout for the Detroit Red Wings, and he is going to Detroit, so I wouldn't waste my time."

"Oh, heck Bucko, he's not that good. He's a pretty good little player, but I am not that interested in him." I've often been asked by many people if I discovered Bobby Orr. I certainly did not discover Bobby Orr, probably none of us from Boston did. Bucko already knew that Orr was a great talent before we saw him that day.

Bobby was certainly all the talk of our Boston group after that game. The minute we finished our playoffs that year, I immediately traveled to Parry Sound to meet with Bob and his family. He lived in a big stucco home, right by the river in Parry Sound. I think it was 24 Great North Road. I went to the house, but Bob wasn't home from school yet. I spoke to his mother and said that I would just sit out on the back porch and wait. It was in early May, so the weather was nice. Eventually, Bob came home from school, I introduced myself, and we chatted for a while. Nothing came of the meeting except for the good will I wanted to create between us.

The next season in Kingston, I changed our travel route that we used to take to go north (from Kingston to Smiths Falls, then on to Highway #17 to North Bay, onward to Sudbury and then north to Sault Ste. Marie). The new route I chose that season was going by Highway #401 from Kingston, west to Highway #400 north, up Highway #400 to connect with Highway #69 that went through Parry Sound. Highway #69 was just starting major construction, and was in pretty bad shape. When we got to Parry Sound, we used to go to the Brunswick Hotel for our pre-game meal. I would then leave the team and go over to see Bobby or his Mother just to keep my association current. I was keeping my foot in the door, so to speak, because in those days, a boy could not sign a Major Junior A card until he was 14. I remained hopeful that I could get him to sign with a Boston sponsored Junior Club the next year. The minute you signed a Junior A Playing Card with any NHL-sponsored Junior A team, that NHL team could then place your name on their reserved list. For instance, if you signed with the Marlboros or St. Mikes, you would become a future Toronto Maple Leaf player. If you signed a Hamilton Junior A Card, it meant that you would be a future Detroit Red Wing. In those days, if NHL teams saw a good kid in some small town, they would give the local minor hockey association a few dollars to only release players to their sponsored Major Junior A teams. I talked this approach over with Lynn Patrick, who agreed we should sponsor the Parry Sound Minor Hockey Association, so that we could get them to release players only to our sponsored Major Junior A teams.

I also suggested that Milt Schmidt should fly to Toronto, where I would pick him up to travel to Parry Sound to meet with the Parry Sound Minor Hockey Association. Milt had been a great NHL player. When I was real young, he was probably my favorite hockey player. He wore number #15, was a real hard-nosed centerman. I was astounded to find out that the meeting with the Parry Sound Minor Hockey Association was to be held in the Town Hall. The Town Hall was one of those old fashion ones with a balcony. It seemed like everybody in town was there to watch the proceedings. If I remember correctly, the meeting table was down on the main floor, and I think it was equipped with a sound system. After we made our presentation, we allowed the people in attendance and the minor hockey executives to ask us questions. In those days NHL teams would offer the minor hockey associations around $500.00 to $750.00 to release players only to their Major Junior A teams. Milt and I had been authorized by Lynn Patrick and Weston Adams to offer Parry Sound $1,000.00. Eventually the Parry Sound Minor Hockey Association agreed to the transaction.

I continued to see Bobby as often as I could. One night, which I will never forget, we were on the road, and when the game was over, Harry Sinden came to my hotel room. He knocked on my door, and when I answered he said, "Can I talk to you for a few minutes?" I thought this was most unusual because most of the time the players went out somewhere for a beer. Harry had been elected to come and chat with me. I opened a beer and gave it to him, opened one for myself, and we sat and chatted about the game that night and so on. Finally Harry said to me, "I've been asked by a lot of our guys on the team to come and talk to you about something. (Of course that's what captains are for, to be a liaison between management and the players.) To get to Sault Ste. Marie, we used to go through Smiths Falls, across Highway #17 and up to North Bay and Sudbury, but all this season, we have been going on the #401 to the #400 and that horrible #69 that's under construction. And we always stop in Parry Sound for our pre-game meal. Then you seem to disappear. The guys have asked that I ask you why we have changed the route." At first I told him it was none of his business. I didn't have to explain myself. "I know you don't, but I'd like to stay in hockey," Harry continued. "I'm trying to learn the hockey business, as well as play, and because the guys know I want to do my job as captain properly and therefore ask you." I told him how I visited Bobby Orr and his family when we stopped in Parry Sound and explained that we thought he was going to be an outstanding player, even a superstar. The same year that Harry became the coach of the Boston Bruins, a young man named Robert Gordon Orr graduated to the Bruins as well.

In March 1962, Bobby turned 14 years of age. He would now be eligible to play Major Junior A hockey in the fall for the 1962-63 season. In those days, we used to operate what we called a Junior tryout camp, nearly always held the last week in August, heading into the Labour Day Weekend. The camp was mostly scrimmages, which is the best way to tell if a young lad is getting anywhere close to the quality of being able to play Junior A. Our camp was held every year in Niagara Falls. I talked at length to Bobby and his family and finally convinced him to attend our camp in the last week in August. There were all kinds of young kids on the ice at that time who hadn't yet played Junior. I can remember Derek Sanderson, a little skinny lad. I believe it was the first time Bernie Parent attended as well. Even at 14, Bobby was a standout during that whole week.

When the camp ended on Saturday, I was planning to take our children and head up to our cottage to spend the weekend. We were going with my brother Gerald and his wife Marilyn and their kids. I had been away for over a week, and was looking forward to this weekend. Right after lunch that day, Weston Adams had decided that he would now talk to Bobby and his father Doug, who had come down to pick Bobby up to take him home. I don't know what really transpired there because I wasn't asked to even participate by Weston Adams, even though for over two years I had spent a lot of time with Bobby and his parents. Weston decided that he would take the reigns of this important decision. I don't know whether Bobby wasn't thrilled with him moving in at that time, or he wasn't ready, or his dad didn't want to do anything. But the net result was that Bobby did not sign anything. He kept saying to his dad, "I want to go home, I want to go."

I was in my room packing and getting ready to leave when the phone rang. It was Weston Adams. "Wren, what's your plans this weekend?"

"Well, I'm going to Haliburton with my family, and my brother and his family, for Labour Day Weekend. I'm leaving right now to pick up my family and head to Haliburton. How did you make out?"

"Well, I didn't get too far. Wren, what I would like you to do is go to Parry Sound this weekend." I couldn't believe him asking me to do that — I'd been away all week — and I guess I lightly resisted. "No, wait a minute, let's talk about this. If you don't get up there and sign this boy, we are going to lose this young man."

I drove home from Niagara Falls to Oshawa, picked up my

family, and headed to the cottage in Haliburton. My brother and his family arrived to take care of the kids. Elma and I left to run across from Haliburton to Parry Sound and checked into the Brunswick Hotel. Shortly after that, my wife and I went down to visit the Orrs. The visit was scheduled for early evening — I think we got there sometime around 7:00 p.m. It was still daylight. Mrs. Orr and Bobby were there, but there was no sign of Doug Orr. We talked for some time about the high cost of living. When it started to get dark, Mrs. Orr said to Bobby, "By the way young man, it's well past 9:00 p.m. It's your bedtime, and I want you to get up those stairs to bed." Bobby was sitting on the stairs leading from the living room up to the bedroom level. He didn't sound too thrilled when he protested, "Ah Mom."

"No young man, you say good night to Mr. & Mrs. Blair, and head up those stairs." I can always remember thinking, this young lad has been well trained at home. He's had discipline. I knew I would certainly like to get him even more because having a kid coming from a good family who already knew the value of discipline was very important to a hockey club at the Junior level. Bobby reluctantly said, "Good night, Mr. & Mrs. Blair," and went up the stairs. We continued to talk to his Mom for a while, and finally decided to leave. I told her that I planned to come back the next day, if I could. She said that was fine.

Weston had asked me to call him no matter how late to let him know how I was making out. I reported that I didn't think I was getting too far, but Weston insisted that I keep trying. On Sunday, we spent a little time having breakfast in the morning, and shortly after lunch we ventured over to the Orrs again. I could tell that as a family they wanted to talk more and I didn't want to wear out our welcome, so we just stayed for awhile. Mrs. Orr didn't want Bobby leaving home at 14 to go and play Junior A hockey. As a parent myself, I could understand that.

I told Doug that I would be back Monday morning to talk to him and Bobby some more. He said that was fine. I called Weston again, and told him that I hadn't tried too hard that day because I sensed that as a family they were wrestling with this decision, and maybe I should not wear out my welcome this time. Weston reiterated again to stay in the trenches. I sat in the hotel room and started to list in writing everything that I had offered to Bobby and his family up to this point. I wanted to have it recorded in a manner that he and his family could read the next day. In view of what happened, its good that I did that. The next morning, Labour Day, we went over early to get done whatever we could so we could get back over to our cottage. Elma decided to stay in the car, and I went into their home by myself. Bobby and his father Doug were sitting in the kitchen. As we chatted, I showed Doug and Bobby what I had written up concerning our responsibilities for taking care of Bobby if he played with our Major Junior A team. Doug read through it and said to me, "Do you mind if I take this over to our Lawyer to read? He is playing golf on our local golf course because of the holiday." I told him that was fine by me.

A short while later Doug returned, and I heard Doug say to his wife, "Joe said this looks pretty good to him." I assumed that Joe was the name of their Attorney. As far as I could hear, she did not reply. Doug came back in the kitchen and we chatted a little bit more. I then told him that Bob would not have to move to Oshawa that year to play Major Junior A hockey. We were going to be playing in the new Metro Junior A League, with our home games played out of Maple Leaf Gardens in Toronto. Bob would only have to come down and play on the weekends, therefore missing no school whatsoever in Parry Sound. As it turned out, we had a few mid-week games and I can't remember him missing any of them. Someone would drive him down mid-week and take him back home after the game.

This seemed to make a big difference to Doug. He turned to Bob and said, "What do you want to do Buck?"

Bobby looked at him and quickly responded, "You know what I want to do."

"Get up to the table here and sign this OHA Playing Card. Let's get this over with." Bobby signed the card, and Doug signed also as his father. With that, I put the Playing Card inside my jacket pocket and said goodbye to Bobby and Doug. I told Bob he would be hearing from the Oshawa Generals in the next few days about training camp. I didn't see Mrs. Orr when I left.

I got in the car and said to Elma, "I've got him signed." I then put the car in gear and took off out of Parry Sound.

"I thought you were supposed to call Weston as soon as you got him signed?" Elma questioned.

"No way. I'm not going to call Weston until we get over to Huntsville. I just need a little while to digest this whole thing. I feel that I might have signed a player that may very well become one of the greatest players in the history of this game."

When I got to Huntsville, which was a little over half an hour from Parry Sound, I stopped the car and went to a pay telephone and called Weston, who was extremely excited. "Wren, please try and find Lynn as soon as possible, and have him send that young man and his family our money right away. When you find Lynn, tell him to send that money in U.S. Dollars." In 1962, as unbelievable as it may sound today, the Canadian dollar was worth about 11 cents more than the American dollar. Weston's attempt to save 11 cents on the dollar still bothers me to this day.

I called Lynn at his farm in Cape Cod. "Lynn, just a half an hour ago I signed Bobby Orr to an Oshawa Junior A Playing Card."

"God bless you, Wren. That's going to be the salvation of the Boston Bruins." At that time, the Bruins had been in either 5th or 6th place in the six-team NHL standings for eight years. When I told

Lynn that Weston had told me to tell him to get the money out right away, but to make sure that it was sent in U.S. Dollars, I told Lynn that really bothered the hell out of me. "It bothers me too Wren, and I will damn well send the money in Canadian dollars." By the time Bobby arrived in Boston, Lynn had been replaced as General Manager by Hap Emms. As a Bruin, Lynn unfortunately never got to see Bobby play for his team.

Bobby went on to become perhaps the greatest player in the history of the NHL. There have been many great players in the NHL, and I am not trying to take anything away from them, but I cannot help feeling today that Bobby just had something else. Two or three years ago, there was a very fine film done, I believe by Bobby's own Company called Great North Productions, named after the street he lived on in Parry Sound. I was interviewed about Bobby. When the film was edited, they sent me a copy of it, and shortly thereafter, it aired on the CBC network. When I watched it together with several other people, I remember remarking that after all the years he played for me in Oshawa, and for all the years I watched him play in the NHL for Boston, I had forgotten just how great he really was. Some of the kids who were playing for me on the Kingston team said they couldn't believe his powerful skating, his tremendous moves, skating through the entire opposition team on many occasions. Bobby Orr was probably the most powerful skater in the NHL in those years. He could go from a standing stop, to full speed coming out of his own end, faster than any player I can ever remember both then and now.

It really was a great tragedy that Bobby was forced to retire when he was 29 years of age because of many injuries to his knees, probably ten years earlier than he normally would have. Bobby was never one to shy away from checks, going into corners, or indeed trying to squeeze between the boards and a player, when he probably should not have. But he just didn't know any other way to play.

It cost him, even worse, it cost our great game of hockey even more to lose a player like Orr in his prime. Thank goodness other great players came along shortly thereafter, like Wayne Gretzky and Mario Lemieux.

In Boston, Bobby Orr continues to be a sports idol, joining great Boston athletes such as Ted Williams and Eddie Shore. Bobby continues to be associated with our game as a player agent with the Boston-based Talent Agency and Woolf Associates. I know that I am likely prejudiced, but to me he was "One of a Kind."

Other players of note in that first year Generals team were Terry and George Vail, Jimmy Peters, Paul Gibbons, Terry Peters, Billy White, Jim Crouch, Mike Dubeau, Billy Little, Rickie Eaton, and Paul Domm, to name a few. I had decided to take players right from midget hockey, which would then give them four years of junior eligibility. For the most part these midget players were some of the best in the province of Ontario at that time. My rationale was that if they were the best Midgets at 16, it should follow that they would be some of the best Major Junior A players in their final year of junior. The weakness in that theory was that we would probably get beaten in most games in that first year. I figured that since we were going to have no home rink to play out of the first year, and knowing that its tough to draw fans if you're losing, it really didn't matter from an attendance standpoint, since we weren't playing in Oshawa in any event. I still felt the idea was right because these kids would get experience before we moved into the new Oshawa Civic Arena to play. Which is exactly what happened. However, I often felt sorry for the kids on our club that first year, and also my coach, Doug Williams, because we certainly got hammered on many nights.

I remember the first game we played, which was against the Marlboros at Maple Leaf Gardens. I believe the score was 18-1 in their favor. However, the Marlboros had many players in their final year of junior. Wayne Carleton was about 6'4" in height at that time in his final year of junior. I can still remember watching little Bobby Orr, 127 lbs, going in the corner with Carleton. It was comical. Although Bobby was only 14, he was still the best player on the ice for our club.

Lynn Patrick came up from Boston for that opening game at the Gardens. We sat together right behind the bench. Midway through the game we got a penalty, and Bobby Orr, who was already on the ice, came over to the bench. We could hear Doug Williams say to Bobby "Are you OK?" Bobby hated to come off the ice at anytime and said he was fine. "Bob just take a few seconds rest and I'll put you right out again at the next whistle." After the game, I advised Doug that a tired Bobby Orr was better than any other well-rested player we had.

DURING THE SUMMER OF 1963 I began to hear rumors that the Metro League might fold, and that Stafford Smythe would be returning the Toronto Marlboros to the powerful OHA Major "A" League. When I heard that, I went into the Gardens to see Stafford to see if he would confirm or deny that rumour. He was very quick to confirm it, which became one of the traits that I came to like about Stafford Smythe. Many people thought he was extremely blunt, almost sarcastic. But there was nothing phoney about Stafford, and I admire that because at least if you ask them a question, they always tell you exactly what they think. I prefer that to trying to window dress to spare people's feelings. People who do that are trying too hard to be liked by flattering you or they are evading issues, but in the end I think a great deal of danger can come out of that way of behaving. When Stafford said that was right, I asked him if could he try to get my Oshawa Generals back into that league as well as Marlboros. Stafford said quickly, "I'm sure I can." I told him how Lynn had mentioned that Hap Emms would never vote for Oshawa to come back again, but Stafford assured me. "Don't worry about that, I've got enough on Hap Emms from other hockey shenanigans and we'll get Oshawa back in." He informed me that the league was having a meeting within the next two weeks and suggested that I write Bill Hanley (Secretary/Manager of the OHA) and apply for Oshawa to join the league.

At the league meeting, the Marlboros were accepted whole-heartedly, but when Oshawa came up Hap wouldn't hear tell of it. Stafford asked for a recess, and took Hap outside the meeting room to talk to him. They were gone for about 20 minutes, and when Stafford came back, one of the other Governors from the league asked for a role call vote on the admission of the Toronto Marlboros and the Oshawa Generals. It was approved by the Board of Governors, unanimously. I don't know to this day — and Stafford is gone — what Staff said to Hap out in that hallway, but he never raised a whimper as he obviously voted in favor.

Upon our approval, I quickly went over to Bowmanville and made arrangements with their Arena Board for the Generals to play their home games that season of 1963-64, in the old OHA Major Junior A Hockey League. We added a number of new players to our kids from the year before who had become very good Major "A" players. Some quality guys we added for that season were Ron (Bucky) Buchanan, Nick Beverley, Chris Roberts, Wayne Cashman, George Babcock, Rod Zane, Bill Lastic, Jim Blair, Rickie Gay, Brian Fletcher, Billy Smith, Bob Kilger, Terry Lane, Darryl Leach, and Ian Young and Dennis Gibson in goal.

We had a pretty good club that year, especially when we were playing at home in that small rink in Bowmanville, but several other teams in the league were strong, with players who went on to play big time in the NHL — Jacques Laperriere, Wayne Carleton, Ken Hodge, Doug Jarret, Dennis Hull, Ron Schock, Bernie Parent, Yvan Cournoyer, Tom Reid, Wayne Maki, Andre Lacroix,

Brad Park, Jim Dorey, Derek Sanderson, Gilles Marotte, Don Marcotte, Andre Savard, Jacques Lemaire, Bill Barber, Donnie Luce, Sheldon Kannegiesser, Walt Tkaczuk, Gary Unger, and many, many others.

Wayne Cashman played three years for the Generals and served as a policeman, taking care of all the guys on the team in that department, especially Bobby Orr. Bobby was very young then, but as he got older, he didn't need anyone to take care of him. Part way through that year in Bowmanville, Doug Williams got incensed on the bench when Bobby Orr was roughed up along the boards. No penalty was called. Doug got in a bit of a shouting match, and all of a sudden several players on the opposition club started trying to provoke a scrap with some of our guys. As it progressed, Doug became livid. He made the mistake of going out on the ice to try to break up some of the fights and became physically involved with the referee. The police were called and went out on the ice to remove Doug. Several officers dragged him from the ice and straight out of the building and down to the Bowmanville jail. Since we had no coach, I came down out of the Press Box and finished coaching the balance of the game. When the game was over and I had talked to the team, I then told my trainer, Stan Waylett, that I was going to go down to the jail and bail Dougie out. The police officers took me down to Doug's cell. He was sitting on a stool in the cell, and when we saw each other, we both broke out laughing.

"Look at this?" he said. "They took my suit coat, my tie, my belt, what the hell do they think I'm going to do, commit suicide?"

This all hit the papers. Doug was suspended for the rest of the year by the OHA. After all this negative publicity for our club and for Doug, the Oshawa School Board (Doug was a Vice-Principal in an Oshawa high school at that time) asked Doug to refrain from any further coaching in hockey while he was still teaching. However, Doug rallied to become the Principal of that school where he worked for the rest of his life. To replace Doug, I hired Jim Cherry from Pickering.

That year the kids on our club battled hard and made the play-offs. Bobby Orr scored 30 goals, breaking Jacques Laperriere's previous record of 29 goals in OHA Junior A competition in the 1961-62 Season. When Bobby scored his 30th goal to break Laperriere's record, his teammates swarmed on the ice in excitement to congratulate him. Only a minute later Ron "Bucky" Buchanan scored his 50th goal, only the second player to do so. Also that same night Rickie Gay and Nick Beverley, brought up from the Whitby Junior "B" Club, scored their first goals in Junior A competition. Other members of the team were Dennis Gibson and Ian Young in goal; on defence with Bobby Orr and Nick Beverley were Chris Roberts and Bob Kilger. Besides Bucky and Rickie Gay on forward were Billy Smith, Danny O'Shea, Wayne Cashman, George Vail, Billy Little, Terry Lane, Bill Lastic, Jim Blair, Rod Zaine, Darryl Leach, and Mike Dubeau.

The next season, the Generals opened the new Civic Auditorium in the City of Oshawa on December 19, 1964. Chairman of the Arena Board Walter Branch and the Manager of the new Civic Arena Bill Kurelo staged a great pre-game ceremony. Weston Adams and Lynn Patrick came to Oshawa for the first game in our new building. It was a thrilling night for the local owners of the Generals who had joined me in bringing Major Junior A Hockey back to the City of Oshawa. Bill Kurelo and Bob Attersley co-published a history of the Oshawa Generals starting back from the very beginning, written by Mrs. Babe Brown, who did an excellent recall of all these exciting events. We now had our own new dressing room and I had a brand new office, which connected to the dressing room. Mrs. Marg Armstrong became my secretary with the Generals. Marg had been the secretary to Mr. O'Neil, Principal at the Oshawa Collegiate and Vocational Institute. Back in my school days, I was sometimes called up to his office (we called him "Pherp"). I first got to know Mrs. Armstrong, as we called her then, sitting in Mr. O'Neil's office waiting for him to call me in for a stern lecture. After Mr. O'Neil retired, we became very good friends. He was a great hockey fan, one of several of my former teachers who sent me a telegram in Oslo, Norway when we won the World Championship.

As the season of 1963-64 continued, Bobby Orr was becoming the talk of the hockey world. High level sports reporters from Toronto region and indeed all over Canada were calling to talk about the achievements of young Orr. One night when we were playing the St. Catharines Black Hawks in an OHA Major Junior A game, their General Manager, Jack Davison, walked down to the press box where I was sitting and said to me, "You're lucky you got Orr or we'd beat you guys every game." I'm sure that was correct. "Oh yea, but Jack we have him," I said. Jack stocked away in frustration.

Jack and I worked with Jim Gregory, General Manager of the Toronto Marlboros at that time, on many committees for the OHA Major Junior A League. At that time Jack was working in hockey in the winter only; he was an excellent Golf Professional at the Oakville Golf and Country Club in the summer months. Jim and I used to kid Jack that we were going to build a golf course and have Jack lay it out for us and set up the staff. While we were dreaming a bit, that's exactly what happened. A few years later Jimmy and I built the PineStone Inn and Country Club in 1974 and Jack acquired some stock in the company that owned the hotel called One-2-One Corporation. Jack and Ray Patterson laid out the entire course for PineStone, first nine holes and later expanded to a full 18 holes. The course is played heavily to this day at PineStone Resort and Conference Centre on #121 Highway between Minden and Haliburton.

Bobby Orr was not the only General catching attention from

the media that year. Wayne Cashman was really starting to come into his own, as was our goaltender, Ian Young. The Boston Bruins had some great young goaltending prospects — Bernie Parent and Doug Favell in Niagara Falls, and Ian Young in Oshawa, whom I always believed was every bit as good as Bernie Parent

DURING THE SUMMER OF 1965, Boston had asked me to consider replacing Jim Cherry as the coach of the Generals with a player who had played in the Bruins organization a few years back. Jim wasn't sure that he wanted to coach another year in Oshawa in any event, so in conversations with Lynn Patrick and Weston Adams, it was decided that I should approach "Bep" Guidolin about coaching the club. Years earlier, I had been instrumental in getting Bep to come down from his home in Timmins, Ontario to become playing-coach of the Belleville McFarlanes in the 1956-57 season. Bep had coaching experience in Belleville, prior to that in Timmins, and two or three other places, so he was well qualified to become the coach of the Generals. He was also a former Generals player back in the early 1940s. When he came to Oshawa at 15 years of age, the youngest player at that time to ever play junior, he only played one year for the Generals, if I recall properly, and then turned pro at 16 years of age with the Boston organization. Later Bobby Orr became the youngest player to play Major Junior A Hockey when he came to Oshawa to play for the Generals at 14 years of age in 1962.

We signed a few more top young players to go along with Bobby Orr, Wayne Cashman, Billy White, Danny O'Shea, Chris Roberts, Billy Little, Nick Beverley, George Babcock, who were all returning from the previous year. We added Billy Heindl, a good skating forward who had been playing Major Junior A in Winnipeg, and Barry Wilkens, who had been playing in Niagara Falls, as well as Chris Hayes, Danny Sanford, Peter Nevin, Brian Morenz, Jimmy

Whittaker, Ron Dussiamme, and Bobby Black. It looked like the Generals were ready for a battle for first place. We ended the regular season of 1965-66 only three points out of first place. Bobby again fought it out with Andre Lacroix for the league's most valuable player, and the Oshawa fans were in shock when Lacroix again was selected. Lacroix was the most valuable player by far to the Petes, because without him they could not have been in a playoff spot.

The first round of the playoffs saw the Generals playing their bitter rivals from St. Catharines in a best of seven series. "Peanuts" O'Flaherty, the coach of the Black Hawks, was a fiery competitor as a player and certainly as a coach Every game in the new Oshawa Civic Auditorium was a sell-out. Two games ended in a tie — in those days it as an eight-point series to win. The series stretched to a 7th and deciding game. The Generals were extremely fired up for the 7th game and trounced the Black Hawks 8-1 to win the series. In that series, however, young Brian Morenz, who played on the Generals "Kid" line, suffered a fractured skull. He was taken to a Toronto Hospital in serious condition but he soon recovered.

An extremely tired Oshawa club moved on to play the always highly talented Montreal Junior Canadiens. Scotty Bowman was coaching the young Canadiens in those days, but the tired Generals, still on cloud nine following their victory over St. Catharines, won the first game in Montreal 5-3. The series alternated when the Generals again won at the Forum 3-2, but then came home and lost 2-1. In the fourth game in Oshawa, the Generals took the series lead with a 4-0 win. Back in Montreal, the Generals played a tremendous game. Danny O'Shea, whose NHL rights were owned by Montreal, had one of the finest games of his junior career when the Gens beat the baby Habs by 3-2. Ian Young also played exceptionally well. On that Montreal team were Yvan Cournoyer, Andre Boudrias, Carol Vadnais, and Christain Bordeleau. It was the first time that a Generals team had beaten a Montreal team out in playoff activity since 1944.

Then it was on to play the first-place Kitchener Rangers for the League Championship. The Rangers had beaten out the Toronto Marlboros to gain the final against the Generals. Kitchener had a talent-laden club with players like Don Luce, Sheldon Kannegiesser, Walt Tkaczuk, and Keith McCreary. In the first game in Kitchener, the Generals won 4-1 with Ian Young playing brilliantly. The Generals went on to win the next two straight. In the next game, the coach of the Rangers surprised everybody when he replaced regular goaltender Gary Curt with John Voss. Voss had not played in nearly a month, but came up with a big game. But in the fifth game the Generals survived to squeak out a 3-2 win and take the series to win the OHA Major A Championship. The Generals received the John Ross Robertson Trophy, presented by OHA President Matt Leyden. Matt had been the General Manager of the Oshawa Generals back in their glory days of the late '30s and '40s. Mr. Leyden presented a trophy to Captain Bobby Orr. Coach Guidolin described his Generals as "a dozen and half crazed lions". He said in the end, he just opened the door and let them go. The Generals were greeted with a ticker tape parade throughout the City. From my point of view, after assembling the club from scratch four years ago, it was one of the most exciting nights of my life.

Following the OHA Championship, the Generals moved on to meet the NOHA champion North Bay Junior Trappers. The fired-up Generals defeated the Trappers in four straight games, winning by scores like 11-4, 11-2, 10-1, and 11-2. Next on the road to the Memorial Cup was the Shawinigan Falls Bruins, another Boston-sponsored team and the champions of the Quebec Junior League. Phil Myre was a top-rated goaltender for Shawinigan, but the Gens prevailed in the first game winning 7-2. Shawinigan stunned everybody by handing the Generals their first home lost in 13 games when they beat the Generals 5-4 back in Oshawa. The third game went back to Shawinigan and the Generals took the Eastern

Canada Hockey Crown with a 4-2 win. During that series, Bobby
Orr suffered his first of many knee injuries.

Having won the Eastern Canada Major Junior A Championship qualified the Generals to enter the Memorial Cup playoffs,
the first time since the 1943-44 season that a Generals team had
played for the cup. The opposition club were the champions of
Western Canada, the Edmonton Oil Kings. The Memorial Cup had
not been drawing well in the past few seasons, partly because at
that time in the East, all games were played in Toronto's Maple
Leaf Gardens. I called Bill Hunter, the General Manager of the Oil
Kings, just before they left to come East to see if we could create
more attention to the series by staging a press conference to do a
bit of bragging about each of our teams. I didn't realize what a
showman Bill Hunter was. I found out a little too late that his nickname was "Wild" Bill Hunter. We arrived at the press conference
and Bill suggested that since we were the host club that I should
speak first. I said that the East was getting a bit weary of the West
winning the Memorial Cup so often, and this was a year that things
were going to change. I extolled the merits of several of our players.
I said that Bobby Orr was probably the best Major Junior A Hockey
player in Canada. Then I talked about other stars on our club like
Wayne Cashman, Danny O'Shea, Ian Young, Bill Little, Barry
Wilkins and others, and that since the series would start the following night, Edmonton was going to find out what the East was all
about this year. When I finished, Wild Bill, with his flaming red
hair, came to the podium to speak. I have always fancied, especially
when I was younger, that I was a pretty flamboyant speaker, with
usually a great message to deliver. It soon became evident to me
that I was a rank amateur in the speaking department when Wild
Bill got up and started his oration. When he strode to the mike, he
paused dramatically, looked over the crowd, and stood there for a
moment for effect. A real MGM Hollywood performer. Suddenly, in

a loud voice, he sneered, "Who is this kid Orr? We've never heard of him in the West. But wait till you Eastern people see our star defenceman Al Hamilton, and you'll all forget about Orr." He made it sound like the Oshawa Generals were a Junior "B" Hockey Club by comparison. Our media conference certainly worked, because in the opening game we had close to 15,000 people in Maple Leaf Gardens, was almost double what the Memorial Cup games had drawn in recent years.

Little did I know at that time that the knee injury Bobby Orr picked up Shawinigan was going to bother him further, to the extent that he could hardly play at all in the Memorial Cup finals. Against the dictates of Weston Adams not to dress Bobby for the series for fear he might jump on the ice and further injure his knee, Bep and I went ahead and let him dress after meeting with his father, Doug. Bobby sat on the bench, dressed with our other players, and several times when "Bep" would go to the other end of the bench, and a player would come off, Bob would jump on the ice to try to play for a few seconds. Weston ranted and raved at me. Bep explained to me, "Wren, you know the competitor Bobby is, and how badly he is hurting because he can't play all-out because of his injury. If a player comes off during play, Bob jumps on. I sometimes am unable to see that, but what can I do?"

In those days, the Western Canada winners were allowed to add six players from the team they had defeated in the Western Canada Junior Finals. The team Edmonton defeated was Boston's sponsored team, the Estevan Bruins. Now, here we were, losing Bobby Orr, the best junior player in Canada, and they were adding six of the top players from the Estevan Bruins. It swayed the balance of competition tremendously. In the end, the 'Orrless' Oshawa Generals lost the Memorial Cup final to the Edmonton Oil Kings 4 games to 2. Most of our players gave everything they had for the proud history of the Generals and for the fans in the City of Oshawa.

As it turned out, that was my last year operating the Generals. The Generals have always been blessed with great management with the likes of Stew McTavish, Neil Hezzelwood, and Matt Leyden in the era before the arena burned to the ground. When the club returned in the 1962-63 season, I was determined to follow in their footsteps. Following my years, the Generals have had very strong management from Sherry Bassin, who now is one of the owners of the Erie Otters, followed by Wayne Daniels, who did a great job for the Generals. The Generals continue to play out of the Oshawa Civic Arena, and the club is now owned in large by John Humphreys, the son of his late father Russ Humphreys. John is a valued member of the OHL Board of Governors and a friend that I'm associated with on our OHL Board. The Generals have gone on to be involved in a couple of Memorial Cups in recent years, and won it again in 1990, led by the great Eric Lindros. Besides Eric Lindros and Bobby Orr, other great stars who have played Junior hockey for the Generals over the years are Jo Jo Grabowski, Billy "The Kid" Taylor, Bill Ezinicki, Ross Lowe, "Red" Tilson, Floyd "Busher" Curry, goaltender Les Colvin, Alex Delvecchio, Bobby Attersley, and Dick Gamble. One of the greatest thrills I ever had in my hockey life was bringing the legendary Generals back to my hometown, rivalled only by the Whitby Dunlops winning the World Championship in 1958 and my years with the Minnesota North Stars in the NHL.

PROFILE

Sam Pollock

SAM POLLOCK WAS THE BEST general manager I ever met in my hockey career. My first dealings with Sam came when he was involved with the Montreal Canadiens back in the 1950s. He called me one day when I was coaching and managing the Whitby Senior B team, before we were called the Dunlops, and he said: "Wren, you are involved with the Eastern Ontario Senior B League, are you not? The Montreal Junior Canadiens have withdrawn from the Ontario Major Junior A Hockey League in a bit of a battle with the OHA, and we are going to play exhibition games all year. We are proposing to play 20 games in the Quebec Senior League, 20 games in the Quebec Junior League, and we would like to play 20 games with your Eastern Ontario League. From what I gather, you have quite a bit of influence with the teams in that league. I was wondering, first of all, how you feel about this?"

"Sam, I would feel much better if these were not exhibition games. I would rather see those 20 games count in our league standings, and then they would not be exhibition games to us."

He thought that was a great idea, because, not only would the points count in our league, but it would provide more impetus for his players, knowing that the games actually meant something. I told him I would see what I could I do. At the next league meeting, however, I received nothing but negative comments from the members of the league when I proposed this plan. The other league members felt that the Junior Canadiens were a powerhouse and trounce our teams. The Junior Canadiens did have a power-packed lineup in those days with the likes of Bobby Rousseau, J.C. and Gilles

Tremblay, Ralph Backstrom, and Claude Ruel. I countered this objection by impressing on the team owners that we had to keep in mind that these players were boys and our players were men. I felt we could hold our own and even beat them from time to time. "Can you imagine the kind of crowds we'll draw by having the Junior Canadiens in the league?" We eventually agreed to Sam's proposal. Sam was delighted, and I don't think he ever forgot that favor.

In the 1959-60 season, Sam was the General Manager/Coach of the Hull-Ottawa Canadiens in the Eastern Professional Hockey League and they were in the first round of the playoffs against the Sudbury Wolves. Just before the playoffs were to begin, Sam phoned me. "Wren, we have a pile of injuries right now. Do you think you could get Harry Sinden and Bobby Attersley to play two or three or four games for me to help us out? I would pay them more than the going rate." Harry and Bobby agreed, though Bobby couldn't make the first game because of business commitments. Sam said he would need to put their names on Montreal's negotiation list in order to get clearance for them to play on a five-game tryout basis.

I drove Bobby to the second game in Sudbury, and because of highway construction, we arrived only 10 minutes before game time. I dropped Bob off at the main entrance to the arena and went off to park the car. When I entered the arena, I had trouble finding a place to see because the fans were lined up four deep. All of sudden the PA system came on and announced, "Hull-Ottawa goal, Attersley." Isn't that something, I thought to myself, the game's just started and that little bugger got a goal for Sam already. Harry and Bob played extremely well for Sam during that series.

The next year, I was hired by the Boston Bruins to run the Kingston Frontenac EPHL club. I began checking the reserve list of the various NHL clubs to see if there were any players available who could help our club. When I checked the Montreal list, I was astounded to find the names of Harry Sinden and Bob Attersley. I immediately phoned Sam in Ottawa. "I just signed a contract with Lynn Patrick in Boston," I told him. Sam and Lynn were very good friends, and I sometimes think Sam had something to do with Lynn hiring me.

"Gee Wren, that's great, welcome to the league," Sam said.

"Thanks very much, but you may not be too happy when I tell you why I called."

"What's that?"

"Well, you have to take Harry Sinden and Bob Atterlsey off of your negotiation list, so I can sign them for Kingston.

"Oh, jeez, Wren, I don't want to do that. I was kind of hoping I could get them."

"C'mon Sam, you only got them on your list, because I got them for you last year, to play in your playoffs on a five game trial."

"I guess, you're right. I'll take them off."

During that year, we had many EPHL meetings in Ottawa. We normally played Sunday afternoon games in Hull, and if there was a meeting the next day, I would stay overnight at the Albion Hotel. Sam lived at the Albion Hotel in Ottawa, permanently. Many times, Lynn would also stay in Ottawa. The three of us would go out for dinner and end up in the evening talking for hours and hours. One night Lynn said to me, "Wren, do have any idea what a great baseball man, Sam is?" Sam is a very shy man, and he usually was most reluctant to get into those discussions. Lynn turned to Sam. "Name some of the teams from years ago, their rosters, the MVPs, the batting champions." Well, Sam, eventually got talking, and I was absolutely amazed at his baseball knowledge. The next morning he explained to me, "For years before I got into hockey, I ran nothing but baseball teams in Montreal, and good baseball teams. Eventually, I got into hockey, but if I had been offered the chance to manage a major league baseball team, I'm not sure which I would have chosen. When people see that Sam Pollock is a member of the

Board of Directors of the Toronto Blue Jays and question what he knows about baseball, I have a ready answer. For years, Sam had a chauffeur who would drive him all over the U.S. to see Major League baseball games.

Over the years, I made many deals with Sam Pollock, both with the Bruins and later with the North Stars. When I was starting the Oshawa Generals, Montreal operated both the Peterborough Petes and the Montreal Junior Canadiens. Danny O'Shea, a player on their list, refused to play in Peterborough. Danny lived in Ajax, just down the road from Oshawa. I called Sam with a proposition. "If you keep Danny on your Canadiens list, to retain his pro rights, is there any reason you can't loan him to me to play for the Oshawa Generals?" Sam immediately arranged for Danny to play for us in Oshawa. Danny eventually played for me in Minnesota. Other players I acquired through deals with Sam were Claude Larose, Lou Kazowski, Danny Grant, Andre Boudrias, Jude Drouin Don Johns, Bobby Rousseau, Gump Worsley, Mike McMahon, and Billy Plager.

Since Sam left hockey to work for the Bronfman family and became involved with the Blue Jays, I haven't talked with him much. I will always relish our friendship, though. A few years ago, when I was nominated for admission to the NHL Hockey Hall of Fame, the five names on the nomination ballot were Milt Dunnell, the long-time Sports Editor of *The Toronto Star*; Harry Sinden, President of the Boston Bruins; Bob Atterlsey and Sandy Air, stars of the Whitby Dunlops; and Sam Pollock. I cherish the letters they sent on my behalf.

OSHAWA GENERALS O.H.A. JR."A"

1964-65

Oshawa Generals 1964-65 OHA Jr. A

Oshawa Generals 1965-66 OHA Jr. A Champions

Front Row (from left) — Billy White, Wayne Cashman, Bobby Orr (Captain), Wren Blair (General Manager), Russ Humphreys (President), "Bep" Guidolin (Coach), Billy Heindl, Danny O'Shea, Chris Roberts.

Middle Row — Chris Hayes, Jimmy Whittaker, Barry Wilkens, Ian Young, Nick Beverley, Ron Dussuaime, Paul Cadieux, Danny Sanford.

Back Row — Stan Waylett (Trainer), Billy Little, Brian Morenz, Peter Nevin, Bob Black, George Babcock, Gordie Myles (Assistant Trainer).

Wren Blair, General Manager of the Oshawa Generals, with Head Trainer Stan Waylett (left) and Assistant Trainer Gordie Myles (right). Myles had been a star player with the Whitby Dunlops.

Wren Blair with Bobby Orr. Blair signed Orr to a Boston Bruins contract, and Orr played four years of Major Junior A Hockey for Blair in Oshawa.

The Minnesota North Stars Join the NHL and the Death of Bill Masterton

8

IN FEBRUARY 1966, THE NHL expanded, right out of the blue, it seemed. I don't think any professional league has ever doubled its size in a single jump from six to 12 teams.

On the day that the expansion was announced, I went into Maple Leaf Gardens in Toronto to talk with Emile Francis, the General Manager and Coach of the New York Rangers, who were playing the Leafs that night. When I went down to the Rangers' dressing room, I asked Emile if he had been at the expansion meeting that day. "Yes, I just got in here about an hour ago," he responded.

"Do you know who got the Minnesota franchise," I asked?

He thought for a moment and then said, "Oh, your guys, you know Bush, McNulty, Ritz and a couple of others."

"I can't believe it, they're in the NHL!" I exclaimed.

The next day, I called Walter Bush to congratulate him on getting the franchise. This was still about a year and a half before the expansion teams started to play. Walter was on Cloud Nine. As our conversation progressed, Walter asked me, "Okay, we got into the league, what about you now?"

'Walter, what are you talking about?'

"We always said that when we got into the NHL, you were going to come and be our General Manager."

"Oh hell, Walter we were just kidding around."

"Well, we weren't," he said. "Bob, Gordie and I would like to

187

talk to you. You know that because we know Weston (Weston Adams, the Bruins' owner) we can't be seen talking to you because of the tampering rule." Tampering was a big thing back then, probably twice as serious as it is today. "What we'd like to do," he continued, "is to get off somewhere, away from everybody and talk. I'll call you in a day or two, after I've talked with Gordie and Bob on where we should meet."

A couple of days later, Walter asked me to meet them in Fargo, North Dakota. I couldn't think of any place right then that was farther off the beaten path than Fargo. It was either in late February or early March when I arrived. It was the coldest day I can ever remember. We talked all day Saturday and Sunday, and by the time I left I had signed a four-year contract as General Manager of the North Stars, with the option to coach if I wanted.

One of the conditions written into the agreement was that I had to get my own release from the Bruins to make this contract effective. I knew that was not going to be an easy task. Lynn Patrick had already left Boston to join the St. Louis Blues, another expansion team, and Hap Emms had been promoted from Niagara Falls to become the Bruins' General Manager. Hap had been the owner of the Niagara Falls team when I was running the Oshawa Generals. Because we were beating Niagara Falls fairly regularly, Hap wasn't my greatest friend. When he was appointed to Boston, I thought I had better think of getting out of here soon.

When we were preparing to meet the Kitchener Rangers in the league final, Hap called me and said, "I want to see all the games in the league final. I will be flying into Toronto, and want you to pick me up and then go with me to all the games." On one of these drives to Kitchener, Hap mentioned to me, "I see your name being bantered about quite a bit about becoming a General Manager for one of these new expansion teams. Is there anything to it?"

Well, I said, even though I had already signed with Minnesota,

"Nobody has talked to me. However, suppose someone did want to talk with me and did offer me a job, would I have permission from the Bruins to do so?"

"Why would you want to do that? Everybody knows that if you're hired by an expansion team, you're eventually going to get fired. I'm in my late 60s and not going to be around much longer. You could probably take over my job with the Bruins."

"Hap, I tried to get you to help me to join the NHL pension plan with Weston Adams a month ago and you couldn't even do that. How do you propose to get Weston to hire me as General Manager?" I then turned back to trying to secure his permission to talk to an expansion team.

He hesitated for a moment. "Well, I guess so. I think we'd be a pretty poor organization if we tried to hold you back." I then asked if he would give me a letter to that effect. I reminded him that he had always preached to me that your word is your bond so if you have already told me all this, then why couldn't I get a letter? He finally agreed, though it took two more meetings before Hap produced the release. When I told him that a team wanted to talk to me and that I thought I had a pretty good chance of becoming their GM, he looked at me and said, "That's crazy. Why wouldn't you stay with the Bruins? You are going to get fired — all the guys who take these jobs are going to get fired."

"That may be true, but one of the things that can never be denied if I land this job is that I will be the first-ever General Manager of this team. If you go way back to Conn Smythe, Lester Patrick, and Jack Adams, they were the first-ever General Managers of their teams, and I want that kind of history." With the letter in hand, I called Walter the next day to tell him that I was clear.

The new Minnesota owners came to the draft that year as members of the league, even though the team wouldn't start to play until the following year. Right after the draft, I flew out to Minnesota and the announcement was made that I was the new General Manager of the North Stars, with an option in my contract to coach if I wanted.

Now I had the job of creating an NHL caliber team. To prepare for the expansion draft in 1967, we had to scout all of the pro leagues across both Canada and the United States in the American Hockey League, the Central Professional Hockey League, and the Western Hockey League. One of my first moves was to hire Ted O'Connor as our head scout and my brother Gerald as his assistant. I had never seen the West Coast of Canada or the United States so I decided to scout the entire Western Hockey League on one trip starting in Victoria, British Columbia. The next night I went on to Vancouver, then down to Seattle, San Francisco, and Los Angeles to scout the Blades. In Los Angeles, I had made arrangements to spend two or three days in the Beverly Hills Hotel. I am a real movie buff and I just wanted to see this part of the country. I made a deal with Walter to pay the difference in price for the accommodations we usually have when we are scouting. I also wanted to spend some extra time visiting with Fernie Flaman, who was coaching the Blades and was an old friend of mine from the Bruin days.

When I was checking into the Beverly Hills Hotel, it was breathtaking. I had never seen palm trees before; the streets were clean, no snow, and the temperature was balmy. What I didn't know, as I was checking in, is that two of the desk clerks were Canadians, from the Montreal area, and when they saw my registration, they knew why I was in town. They were really excited about major league hockey coming to LA . One of these chaps was on duty when I registered.

"Wren Blair," he said aloud when I signed the register. "You're going to Minnesota as the new GM." As I was talking to him, Eddie Fisher walked right by me.

"Isn't that Eddie Fisher?"

"Oh, to hell with him, we see him all the time. But to see a hockey guy, this is big time."

When I got up to my room, it was full of gifts – champagne, a fruit basket, and chocolates — all gifts from these Canadian boys. I spent three beautiful days there, dining in the Polo Lounge and visiting many other places that I had read about in movie magazines.

From Los Angeles, I moved on to San Diego, another beautiful place where another old friend of mine, Max McNabb, was coach of the Gulls. I saw the Gulls play and the building was packed with 12,000 people. In LA, there had been 10,000 at the Blades' game. The American teams in the WHL always outdrew the Canadian cities. The Canadian fans knew that this was minor league hockey, while to the Americans it was big league.

The next morning I flew over to what has become my favorite place on earth, Phoenix, Arizona, truly was the Land of the Rising Sun. That night, as I was scouting the game with the Phoenix Roadrunners, Gary Hooker, one of the owners, invited me up to the team's private lounge for a bite to eat. Over the next few years, my wife, Elma, and I became very good friends with Gary and Sharon Hooker, and spent holidays in nearby Scottsdale. Sharon inherited her mother's home overlooking a golf course and let us stay there.

The draft was set up so the established teams could protect 11 players. The expansion team could claim one unprotected player, and then the established team could add one to their protected list. After the first round, the established teams had 12 players, the expansion team had one. And so on. It doesn't take a genius to figure out that this was anything but a liberal draft. It was the worst expansion draft in NHL history, with six teams taking players from six teams. In the next expansion, two teams were added, Vancouver and Buffalo, which meant there were two teams taking from 12.

About a month before the draft, I got a call from Sam Pollock of Montreal and he asked me if it mattered to me which team I claimed my first player from. I asked him what he had in mind. "Well, what I'm thinking about is that you agree to claim from Montreal first, I'll come down to your table just before you draft and tell you the one player you are not to claim. If you agree to this, then when the draft is over you come to my room and you can take the next five players off our list with no strings attached." I had done a lot of homework on this draft and found out that Montreal owned about 90 players going into the draft and the next team only owned about 65. I am a firm believer that out of quantity comes quality. I told Sam that I had no difficulty with this.

"Just let me get this straight — when we are both back to 18 players plus two goaltenders, I come to your room after the draft and take the next five players Montreal owns. Okay, you've got a deal."

Just before the draft started, Sam came to my table and slips me a note saying, "You can't claim Claude Larose." Obviously, Sam was trying to preserve the French-Canadian element on the Canadiens.

When Mr. Campbell called Minnesota as the next team to select, I stood up and said, "Minnesota claims Dave Balon from the Montreal Canadiens." Sam Pollock then announced that Montreal would fill with Claude Larose.

We took Balon first, Ray Cullen from Detroit second, Jean-Guy Talbot from Montreal third, and Bill Goldsworthy from Boston fourth. I also took Parker MacDonald right off the Detroit team.

The goaltenders were drafted separately. Los Angeles had drawn the first choice and took Terry Sawchuk. We had drawn third. We picked Cesare Maniago off the New York Rangers.

After the draft I went up to Sam Pollock's room and all his scouting staff – Scotty Bowman, Ron Caron, and Claude Ruel were there. I don't think Sam had told them of our pre-draft deal. 'Guys, I don't think I mentioned this before, but I made a deal with Wren that if he didn't take Claude Larose he could take the next five players off our list when we got back to 18." I don't think they were too thrilled, but no one said a word. The five players I claimed were Andre Boudrias, Mike McMahon, Billy Plager, Don Johns, and Leo Thiffault. Sam and I also agreed that if Sam was going to deal a player to an expansion team, I would get first right of refusal. That was a very important thing because I knew ahead of time the players he was thinking of moving.

Those five extra players were a godsend because, as part of the expansion agreement, each new team had to start a farm team in the minors. In the draft you only got 20 players, so what were you supposed to fill your farm team with? The universal junior draft had just started then, but part of the rules for that was that any player who had been owned by an NHL team was exempt. This meant the first player we would be able to get was probably rated about 160th. I had already found another way to stock out the team. Before the expansion draft, I paid a visit to Stafford Smythe. The Canadian National Team, under the directorship of Father David Bauer, was training out in Winnipeg and I had noticed, from the NHL protected lists, that the Leafs had about six pretty good players with that team. "You have a few players on that Winnipeg team," I proposed to Stafford, "who I would like to buy for cash. I would pay $30,000 to $35,000 for them."

"How many players do I have on that bloody team anyway?" I told him six. "I won't take the deal you propose, but what I will do is sell you all six off that team for $100,000. Go down the hall and talk to Punch and he'll draw up the papers."

Later Stafford and I were leaning against the wall in the pressroom following a Leaf's game when, he leaned over and said, "Don't think you're so smart buying those players for $100,000. You're not the first one to think of that."

"Well, how come you sold them to me, then?"

"Because you're the first guy who offered me a $100,000." And with that he walked out of the room, laughing.

Training camp that first year was held in Haliburton. I got thinking over the summer that because we were bringing in players from six different NHL organizations, there would be no camaraderie, no recent friendships, no real team spirit. I felt that we had to build that during training camp. All the players came into Toronto and we all stayed overnight at the Skyline Hotel in Toronto, then two buses transported us to a lodge called the Chateau Woodland in Haliburton, which was our training camp headquarters. I hired Lloyd Percival from Physical Fitness College in Toronto to work with our team.

I called a meeting with the team after we arrived at the Chateau Woodland. "Look guys, there is only one place in the village where you can drink, the Canadian Legion, and it is out of bounds. We are going to have a golf tournament, a shuffleboard tournament, a checkers tournament . . . a number of games. I want to find out who is competitive and who is not."

Later that evening, I left my cabin and went out for a walk. It was eerily silent around the grounds. I thought to myself, what is going on? I took a little drive and went into the Legion — and there were all of my players, drinking, playing darts, shooting pool — having a great time. I stayed in the background so that they didn't see me and I left. I returned to the lodge and parked in the shadows, about 100 feet back up the road. Around 1:00 a.m., I heard a couple of cabs pull up and guys started piling out, talking and joking and walking up the road towards their cabins. I waited until they got about 25 feet from me and pulled on my headlights. They were shielding their eyes, they couldn't see, they didn't know what was going on.

"Good evening, gentlemen. Have you all had a good time? I hope you did because this evening just cost you all $100 each." In those days, $100 was a lot of money.

"Goldie" (Bill Goldsworthy) stepped out and decided to be the spokesman. "A hundred bucks, are you nuts?"

"I would watch your tongue, Mr. Goldsworthy, it may soon be $200."

"That's stupid."

"It's now $200, Mr. Goldsworthy."

"How can you fine me $200, I haven't even made any money yet? What if I don't make the team?"

"The way you're carrying on right now, you may not." Years later, we used to laugh about this.

The next day I had a change of heart and let them go to the Legion because the local people loved it. We were going to play a couple of exhibition games there, so I rescinded the fines, but established a 10:30 curfew. I wanted to find out if they would respect this, and, not surprisingly, I had no real problems after that.

We played two exhibition games in Haliburton that year. The rink was jammed. Many people came daily to watch our practices. Among the players, gradually, you could see some camaraderie developing. When we broke camp, we traveled to Kingston for some more training and to play an exhibition game.

Over the course of the summer, I had sent contracts out to every player with the potential to become a North Star. Most had been signed and returned, but as we were preparing to leave Kingston, I knew that Andre Pronovost, whom I had drafted from Montreal, still hadn't signed his contract, so I summoned him to my room at the hotel. "Oh, no, Wren, there's no way I'm going to sign that contract."

"We're not too far from Montreal here, why don't you just go home and call me when you're ready to come back," I responded. So he went home, and stayed there for about a month, before he finally signed. By that time he was out of the swim of the team and was assigned to Memphis.

I had decided to coach the team. I wanted to get a feel for the real intestines of the team and the feeling for all of the players I had drafted. I also didn't feel it was fair to turn all the players on this team over to somebody else before I could be sure what kind of team I had drafted. I can remember lying in bed at night after that first draft, wondering if any team in history had ever gone 0-for-80.

We played our first four games on the road. That trip stands out in my mind. We were scheduled to open the season in St. Louis against the Blues. Scotty Bowman was coaching St. Louis and Lynn Patrick was the General Manager. All nine of our owners and their wives had flown in for the game. With just a minute to go in the game, we were leading 2-1. I called a timeout when there was a face-off just outside our blue line. I had Andre Boudrias at center, flanked by Wayne Connelly and Dave Balon on the forward line, and Elmer "Moose" Vasko and Mike McMahon on defence. I called them all over to the bench and said, "Look, guys, I don't want anybody trying anything. Try and get the draw, get the puck over the red line and fire it in. Don't try anything fancy." They all started to leave the boards and I said, "Come back here. What did I say?" They all repeated, almost verbatim, what I had said.

Boudrias won the draw and got the puck over to Balon on left wing. Davey's now skating down the boards and I yelled at him, "Way to go Davey, get over the red line and fire it in." Well, for some strange reason, just as he got to the red line he decided to skate sideways across the ice, he was checked and had the puck knocked off his stick at their blue line. St. Louis then passed the puck ahead and another Blues' player grabbed it and fired a shot right over Cesare Maniago's shoulder. The game ended tied 2-2.

I was steaming as I headed to the dressing room. I walked over to Balon." What's wrong with you? I told you what I wanted you to do, you repeated it, everybody understood what was to happen. We had that game won and then you decided to stickhandle, you jerk." I continued around the room, berating the players, kicking everything, and finally went into the trainer's room. Len Lunde, a centerman with us, came into the room. "Chief, we have a whole season to go, take it easy. You're going to have a heart attack."

'What! I know one thing. I doubt I'll have a heart attack, but I know one thing for sure, you never will." Len turned and went out of the room and I'm sure he thought, I'm not going to do that again. He ran into a buzzsaw.

Our next game in Oakland was hard-fought for two periods. Early in the third period, we were losing 1-0 when Parker MacDonald came out of our end with the puck. He elected to make a long cross-ice pass, a no-no. Larry Cahan, an Oakland defenceman, intercepted the pass and went in on Cesare and scored. That turned the whole game around and we eventually lost 6-0. I went into the dressing room, steaming, walked around the room, and finally stopped in front of McDonald. "

"Parker, you report to Memphis tomorrow." Parker was one of the few players that we had who had real NHL experience. I thought I had to set an example here, take control, and show the players that mistakes were not going to be tolerated. Hockey is a game of mistakes and the team that makes the most mistakes loses all the time. Parker looked up and said, in disbelief, "Memphis."

"Yeah, Parker, Memphis. Do you know where Memphis is? It's in the Deep South. You report to John Muckler there tomorrow." I turned around to John Mariucci, my assistant and say to him, "You get him to the airport tomorrow, get him a ticket and get him to Memphis."

I had hired John Muckler in the summer that year to coach Memphis with the understanding that when I quit coaching, John would move up and take over Minnesota. The day after I sent Parker MacDonald down, I called John to explain things. "John, I'm trying to make a point with the team here. The players are going to look at this and say: Jeez, Parker's got the most experience of anybody on the team and he makes one mistake and he's gone. What can the rest of us expect? I can't be without Parker very long, so after a couple of games I'll call you and you send him back." I brought Parker back within a couple of days and he went on to score 19 goals for us. He later went back to Memphis as the coach of that team when John finally took over the North Stars.

Coaches were a lot tougher on their players in those days than they are today. I can remember the coaches in junior who used to fight it out with their players; I've heard stories of coaches hanging their players up by their braces on coat hooks in the dressing room. I've always believed if you're tough on your children, it's because you love them. If you're not, it's because you don't love them enough. It's tough, it really is, to discipline your children. It's the same on a hockey club.

The third game we played in Long Beach, California, against the Kings, because the Forum hadn't been completed yet. In the first period, we are up 1-0 and they got a penalty late in the period. I had been telling Mike McMahon he had to learn that when he was backing in, he had to take the man to the boards and take him out. He was a very good defenceman, offensively, but had some defensive shortcomings. Anyway, we were on the power play and someone fired the puck to Wayne Rivers of LA and he skated like a streak down the boards. Mike backed over to the boards to take him out, but never really hit him. Rivers battled his way past McMahon and went in on Maniago and scored to tie it 1-1 just before the period ended. In the dressing room, I threw my topcoat at Mike as I berated him. However, as I threw the coat, I slipped on the orange peels on the floor, went straight up in the air, knocked over the big wastebasket in the center of the room, and landed flat on my back. I got up, still talking, and kicked the wastebasket. It was metal and I almost broke my foot. That little talk, obviously, didn't help. We still lost the game. On the plane the next day to Pittsburgh, I was sitting by myself, up near the front of the plane when our trainer, Stan

Waylett, came up and sat down beside me. "I came into the dressing room a little late last night because I was talking to a kid who had been to our hockey camp, and when I got in the room you were lying on the floor, flat on your back. Can you tell me, what kind of play you were trying to demonstrate?" One night when we were flying out of Minnesota, Cesare Maniago was walking back from the gate, probably because he was going to say goodbye to his wife, as I was walking towards the gate. The floors in the Minneapolis Airport were highly polished and very slippery. Just as I was passing Cesare, I slipped and almost fell. He stopped and looked at me. "Watch the orange peelings."

We played our fourth game in Pittsburgh and tied before going home to Minnesota to play our first home game against Oakland. Even though we won our home opener, there were only about 9,000 people in the stands. We had a tough time getting publicity in The Twin Cities because of the other big sports — basketball, baseball and football. Even the fans who attended our games were deathly silent. I was always thinking how I could create something, even if it was controversial to spur interest in the community, when an opportunity presented itself about three or four weeks into our season. A reporter came to me after a game and asked what I thought of the Minnesota fans. "Well, to tell you the truth they remind me of a bunch of phlegmatic Swedes." The next day a feature story ran under the heading: "Blair calls fans a bunch of phlegmatic Swedes."

The day after the story appeared, Jim Klobuchar, a well-known columnist in the Twin Cities, came out with a follow-up. He was a well-read writer, who wrote on politics, "I haven't met this fellow Blair, who is new in town, but I have already got a bone to pick with him. It makes me mad that he called the fans a bunch of phlegmatic Swedes. I've got news for Mr. Blair, there are just as many of us fans who are Polish, Czechoslovakian, Russian, Norwegian, who are just the same quality of fans as the Swedes are in our city." What he really meant is that he was on my side. I was soon interviewed on radio and TV to explain what I meant. I challenged our fans to become more vociferous, and it worked. Gradually, the crowds started to increase.

One night when a fan came to me and said, "I don't know much about hockey, but I only come to the games to watch you. I can't believe how hard you work up and down the bench. You're talking to your players all the time, you're yelling at the referees, the energy you display during the game is endless." John Mariucci told me, "You can't believe how many people tell me that they come for the same reason, to see you react." I always believed that if I lit a fire on the bench, the players would take it out onto the ice. That's why I was on the referees so much, to let the players know that I was on their side.

Our team was now starting to play extremely well and the fans were starting to identify with the players. Bill Goldsworthy was becoming a big hit with the fans because he had developed what we later called "The Goldie Shuffle" after every goal he scored. By Christmas that first year, we had a sellout — the first of the expansion teams ever to have a sellout. After that, we sold out every game for the next eight years. I can remember having friends of mine who wanted to come down from Canada, but even I couldn't get them tickets.

I am a great believer that if you have a player who can't play in the NHL, you are better off trading two or three players to get one who can. That's the only way you're going to build a team. During the draft, I had my eyes set on J.P. Parise, who had played for me in Kingston, but Oakland took him just before our next pick. Bert Olmstead, the Oakland coach, who was enamored with older players who had played with him, traded J.P. to Rochester in the American League for Gerry Ehman. Ehman and Olmstead had been teammates with the Toronto Maple Leafs. Rochester was always a power in the American League, but they had been just devastated in the expansion draft and were in last place. As soon as I heard about this trade, I phoned Joe Crozier in Rochester. "Joe, I have a solution for your problems there. I want to make a deal with you. I want to get J.P. Parise and maybe one other guy and I'll trade you five players, many of them you had there last year — Murray Hall, Duke Harris, Don Johns, and two other players for J.P. and Milan Marcetta." Joe agreed to the deal, but demanded that his new players arrive in Rochester the next day.

This was just before Christmas and that day we were having a skating party with all of our players, their wives, and children with hot chocolate and treats in the dressing room afterwards. I went down to the ice and called to John Mariucci and told him to ask Murray Hall to see me in my office. When I told Murray the news, he said, "Damn." I told him that I was sorry, and as he got up to leave, I asked him to send Duke Harris up. Then I asked Duke to send Len Lunde up. Later, while their kids were enjoying hot chocolate and hot dogs in the dressing room, the wives of the traded players came up to me to say, "Thanks a lot, Merry Christmas."

J.P. Parise became the guts of our team and I formed a line with "Goldie" and J.P. on the wings and Boudrias at center. J.P. worked vigorously in the corners and dug the puck out to "Goldie" in front of the net. J.P. and "Goldie" became great friends. Marcetta became a better player than I thought was possible.

We were really rolling along after that trade and reached first place on January 13 when we were at home to play the Oakland Seals. That night, Bill Masterton was checked by Ron Harris during the game, fell on the ice, and had to be taken off on a stretcher. The trainers brought Billy through the door on our bench en route to the first aid room. I was shocked when I saw Billy because he was foaming at the mouth. They had extracted his tongue so he couldn't swallow it. I couldn't believe that much injury could happen as the result of a fairly routine body check. Ron Harris was a capable defenceman for the Seals, and while he could deliver punishing body checks, this did not seem to be the reason in my mind for what was taking place.

I heard from our trainer, Stan Waylett, a few minutes later that they were taking Billy to the hospital. We finished the game — I cannot recall now the outcome of the game. I do know that we had to play in Boston the next night, so we had to get to the Minnesota International Airport for a late night charter as soon after the game as possible. I was in my office just after the game had finished when our Club Doctor Frank Seidel came in and closed the door. He sat down across from my desk. I was busily checking my travel bag to see that I had everything with me for the flight.

"How is Billy doing?" I asked.

The doctor looked at me for a number of seconds and said, "Let me put it this way. I think you better get another centerman anywhere you can as soon as possible." Frank knew that as an expansion team, we had only three centermen — Ray Cullen, Andre Boudrias, and Billy.

"God, is he hurt that bad that he'll be out for the rest of the season?"

The doctor looked at me for a few seconds. "No, I don't think Billy's going to make it!"

"What? You don't mean death, do you?"

"Yes that is exactly what I mean. As a matter of fact Billy is on life support now, and even if he recovers he would never be able to play hockey again." I was stunned. I couldn't believe an injury of this magnitude could have been caused by what had transpired on the ice. There wasn't even a penalty on the play. "Bob Reid will be at the hospital throughout tonight, all day tomorrow, and onward. Here is the hospital phone number and the room that Billy is in, and you can monitor his progress or lack of it by keeping in touch with Bob." Bob Reid was our Office Manager of the North Stars.

I looked at our doctor again. "I am sorry, but I have to run and get to the airport. We are flying to Boston in less than half an hour." When I got to the airport we were in the midst of a blinding snow-storm. Just before midnight we took off in the storm and headed for Boston. In just a little over an hour the Captain announced, "We can no longer continue tonight's flight. We will be forced to land in Chicago. If Mr. Blair would please come up to the Captain's cabin, I would like to speak with you." I proceeded up the aisle to the cock-pit and a stewardess opened the Captain's door for me. "Mr. Blair, your team will have to stay overnight in a hotel in Chicago and I have taken the liberty of booking rooms for the team at the Chicago Airport O'Hare Hotel. If your entire team can return to the airport by 7:00 a.m. tomorrow, we will try to proceed on to Boston as early in the day as possible."

When I finally got to my room, I called Bob Reid immediately for an update on Billy Masterton's condition. "There is no change Wren," Bob reported. "All I can tell you is to call me again tomor-row morning." We all spent a fitful night in the hotel. I felt sorry for our players because they were totally in shock about Billy's situation. I was also worried about Billy's wife Carol and their children. Early the next morning we were all back at the airport, but all flights were grounded. It was snowing very hard still, with high winds. The day wore on and the same conditions prevailed. I had thought of calling ahead to Boston to cancel the game, but I knew that if Weston Adams heard that the game might have to be cancelled, that he would go bonkers, so I waited to see if anything would break, weather wise. Just before noon hour, the dispatcher told me that they were going to let some flights go out of Chicago, but the best they could do was to place a few players on different flights from Chicago to Boston. In the end, our team had to travel on seven dif-ferent flights to get to Boston.

When we started the game that night, we had only eight players who had arrived to start the game. Weston insisted we start. Gradually as flights came in, three or four more players would arrive on the bench, and it was more than half way through the second period before our entire team was there. Our players were already emotionally upset because of Billy's situation, and with the disruption in our travel schedule, and the great team the Bruins had that year, we got slaughtered. I believe we lost 9-1 in that Sunday night game.

When I had arrived in Boston, I called Bob Reid again. "There is no question about this Wren," Bob told me, "he is not going to make it. The doctors have asked me to tell you that when the game is completed tonight, to talk to the entire team in the dressing room. They don't feel that the players or you should talk to any media people in Boston following the game." Immediately following the game, I called the players together in the dressing room. When it appeared that they were all dressed, I asked them to sit down. "Gentlemen, I don't know if I am going to do this right, or say it right, because to my knowledge this has never happened in the NHL before, so I have no precedent to draw from. The doctors have asked me to tell you and everyone else connected with our club that Billy is not going to make it. None of us are to talk to any reporters when we leave Boston Gardens here this evening. They want to make sure that we don't say anything that may be used in some adverse manner by the media later. We are to proceed right from the arena here to our hotel, and not talk to anyone."

The team sat there stunned and in silence for what seem like an eternity to me. Finally Ray Cullen, our player rep, spoke up. "Wren, is Billy still alive?"

"He is, but they are planning on removing the life support sometime during the night."

"Whatever happened to the old saying where there's life there's hope? Ray asked.

"I don't know. I'm only telling you people what I have been told to tell you. Let's not make it any more difficult for ourselves than it already is. Let's just get to the hotel."

I returned to my hotel suite and I called Bob Reid to leave him the number. I then called my assistant John Mariucci in his room. "John, do you have a bottle in your room? Bring your bottle and come on down to my suite because we've got to be on vigil all night because of Billy." Sitting up with "Maroosh" (John's nickname) was a nerve-wracking experience as he alternated between weeping and telling stories about Billy for the next several hours. At 4:00 a.m. the phone rang. I remember it like it was yesterday. I was sure of what I would hear. "Wren, Billy just passed away about 15 minutes ago," Bob told me. I took the receiver away from my ear and fired the phone right across the room. I never did complete my conversation with Bob that night. "Maroosh, you and I are staying here the rest of the night, and at 6:00 a.m. we are taking the rooming list of our players and going to every room to tell them personally that Billy is gone." Most players broke down. Most of these young men had never experienced a death in their own families, and yet here they were facing the loss of a team-mate.

When we returned to my suite, I gave John a long list of instructions. "We have got to be at the airport here in Boston at Logan Field to fly out at 8:45 a.m. You take the team back to the Twin Cities. Please call Carol (Billy's wife) express my sincere sympathy, and tell her I will call her when I get back to the Twin Cities. Please also try and find out John all the details regarding Billy such as where he will be resting, when the funeral is, the time etc. I will wait here in my suite until I hear back from you, because I then need to talk to Mr. Campbell (President of the NHL) and several other people. You should be back in the Twin Cities before 11:00 a.m. Minnesota time because you gain an hour from Boston. As soon as you can find this out, call me. I'll be waiting here beside the phone.

The phone rang before 11:00 a.m. When I answered, I was introduced to Jim Klobaucher from the *Minneapolis Star*. "I haven't met you yet," he said, "but I am hoping we can meet sometime shortly. In the meantime I have a couple of questions I would like to ask you regarding Billy Masterton. There's a story in this morning's *Minneapolis Tribune* by John Gilbert. He speaks of an interview he did with you — he makes it sound like he just did it this morning — talking about players in the NHL not wearing helmets. Could you tell me, Wren, when that interview was done?" I told him that it had been conducted in early November. I was surprised at the time that Gilbert elected not to use it. "Well he used it this morning in the wake of Billy Masterton's death, and as a fellow writer I am extremely upset about the manner in which he presented it." I asked Jim to read Gilbert's column to me. The more he read to me, the angrier I got. It sounded like I was standing over Billy's coffin saying that I don't believe in helmets. "Do you mind if I take Gilbert apart a little bit on this situation?" Jim asked. I invited him to be my guest. His column that evening began, "It is not normal for a fellow journalist to criticize any writer, let alone one from our sister newspaper here in Minneapolis, but I plan to do just that today. It concerns the column in this morning's *Minneapolis Tribune* by John Gilbert reporting an interview that he had with Wren Blair regarding helmets. I called Mr. Blair in Boston this morning, and upon questioning him found out that the interview that John Gilbert ran this morning was given by Mr. Blair to John Gilbert early in November. Gilbert makes it sound as though this interview was done this morning. The entire tone of it smacks of yellow journalism to this writer and I condemn Mr. Gilbert for the manner he presented this, the timing of it, at a time when the entire Twin Cities is in shock over the death of Billy Masterton."

About 11:30 a.m. Boston time, John called from Minnesota. He gave me the name of the funeral home where Billy was resting, and told me that the funeral was planned for Thursday afternoon. I knew that we were scheduled to play the Philadelphia Flyers at home Thursday night, so I called Mr. Campbell in Montreal. "Mr. Campbell, this is Wren Blair calling. I guess you have heard by now the terrible tragedy regarding our player Billy Masterton." Mr. Campbell expressed his shock. We are going to have to cancel our game on Wednesday night in Minnesota with Philadelphia," I continued.

To my great surprise, he said, "Wren, that game Wednesday night will go on as scheduled." I was dumbfounded.

"But Mr. Campbell, the funeral is in the afternoon. How can our players be expected to play that night after they have just buried a team-mate?

"Wren, to reschedule a game is very, very difficult, and if you do cancel, when do you replay it . . . the next day, the next week, the next month? It's impossible to do that, and even though it may sound cold to you, the game goes as scheduled."

So there we were, Thursday afternoon at Billy's funeral, the entire North Star Hockey Club and our wives on one side of the church, and the entire Philadelphia Flyers Hockey Club on the other side of the church. It goes without saying that our team proceeded to the game that evening with heavy, heavy hearts. We proved it, too, by getting soundly trounced by the Flyers in the game. I talked to Carol, Billy's wife, a few days later and told her how bad we all felt on the team at her great loss. I'll never forget what Carol said. "If it had to happen Wren, Billy would rather be involved in playing hockey than any other thing. Hockey was his life."

"Carol does that mean that you don't blame hockey for Billy's death or any type of play in that game?"

"No Wren I don't. It was a reasonably clean check."

Although I never discussed it with Carol, I don't believe Billy was killed because of this bodycheck. I remember that when Billy was on the bench in many games early in the season, his face would turn scarlet from time to time. I had even said to our trainer, Stan Waylett, on two or three occasions, "What's wrong with Billy? He looks like he's going to have a heart attack. His face turns red, he seems to be short of breath." For my part, I believe that Billy had a cerebral brain haemorrhage during that game and that seizure killed him almost immediately. My own mother had a cerebral brain haemorrhage while just talking on the telephone, and then died in the hospital that night. You read all the time about people having heart attacks and strokes while they are driving cars or just going about their daily business. I believe that's what took Billy.

Our team had been in first place in the six-team expansion division at the time we lost Billy. We then proceeded to lose the next several games. I just couldn't seem to get the team to rally past the point of their grief. Before a game in St. Louis, I felt that I had to jolt the team out of the doldrums if we were ever going to get rolling again, for we were now in danger of missing the playoffs.

"Does everybody know what we've gone through?" I asked in a thin whining voice as I walked around the dressing room before the game that night. "Oh goodness, we lost a teammate. Surely nobody expects us to win any more games. Poor us! Let me ask you guys something. At my age, a number of people came through the war. If you were in the trenches overseas, and one of your buddies took a bullet right between the eyes, would you leap up out of the trench and yell, 'Hold it! One of my buddies just got killed. Call off the war!' No! You bury your buddy and the war goes on, no matter how terrible you may feel. If a Sergeant or a Captain yells at you, 'Over the top boys,' do you turn around and say to the Captain, 'Are you crazy, they are shooting real bullets out there.' The war goes on. Some of you guys make me sick. Even Billy would be ashamed of you for the manner in which you are conducting yourself in the games we've played since his death. Life goes on. Get the hell out there tonight and get back in this race." We slaughtered the St. Louis Blues by a big score. The team returned to compete strongly during the balance of the schedule.

I was especially proud of the players for the way they handled Billy's death after the initial shock. A year or so later the National Hockey League established the Bill Masterton Trophy to be given to the player in hockey who displayed a tremendous amount of hard work on behalf of his team. Billy was not a gifted skater; he worked very hard for everything he got. I had acquired him from the Montreal Canadiens, from Sam Pollock. I had seen Billy play minor pro in Hull for the Hull-Ottawa Canadiens when I was General Manager and Coach of the Kingston Frontenacs in the EPHL. When I went to Minnesota, I felt that he might be able to help us on the North Stars. The Canadiens at that time had a powerhouse, and I didn't feel that he could play for the Canadiens, but I felt he could help us. I can't remember what I gave Sam Pollock for Billy, but I think it was cash, slightly more than waiver price. I always considered it a good deal for our club. Billy got his chance to play in the NHL, however briefly. I kind of think Carol thought that way too. We all still love you Carol, even though I haven't seen you or talked to you in many years, and I will always remember and love Billy.

I was also proud of the way this team played that first year. In our double home and away schedule with the established six teams, we were 2-2 with Detroit, 2-1-1 with Toronto, 2-1-1 with Chicago, 2-1-1 with Boston. The only established team we didn't beat that year was the New York Rangers. Our kids played over their heads.

We came down to the final week of the schedule and were clinging to fourth place, the final playoff spot. We could have possibly finished in third, but we lost a hard-fought game with St. Louis because I took a stupid bench penalty and they scored while we were short-handed. The referee had called a cheap penalty against

"Moose" Vasko and I had a towel in my hand and was wiping my brow when it happened. I went to throw it on the floor in disgust, but it flew over the boards onto the ice. I had tried to get the towel picked up, but by this time, Brent Casselman, the linesman, had spotted it. He skated over, picked it up, and fired it back over our bench, then headed towards the referee. "Casselman, if you tell the referee, I'm going to punch you right in the nose," I threatened. He goes right over to the referee, tells him and I get a bench penalty.

That loss sealed our fate and pitted us against the Los Angeles Kings in the playoffs. Red Kelly was coaching L.A. and Terry Sawchuk was in goal. We went into the sixth game in Minnesota trailing in the series, 3-2. After two periods we were down by a goal, but in the third period, Parker MacDonald scored the tying and winning goals and set the stage for the seventh game in L.A. It was tough to play in LA because of the warm weather, but we played like gangbusters and won 9-4, which put us in the division final against St. Louis.

We went into the St. Louis series at a distinct disadvantage. About halfway through the season, Walter Bush had called me into his office to ask, "Do you think we're going to make the playoffs? The reason I'm asking is that we will be fine for ice in the first round, but if we make the division final, we've got a chance to get the Ice Capades for about 10 days, which means a lot of revenue for our building. I hate to turn it down."

"Book it," I advised Walter. "I can't predict whether we'll make the playoffs or if we'll get by the first round. You can't afford to give up that kind of revenue."

Because the Ice Capades had taken over our building, we were only able to play two home games against St. Louis in what turned out to be a seven-game series. Four of the games in that series went into sudden-death overtime. The Leafs were not in the playoffs that year, so CBC chose to televise the series back in Canada. While we weren't the greatest teams in the world, I have never seen two more evenly matched teams. Cesare Maniago played brilliantly, as did Parker MacDonald, Mike McMahon, Wayne Connelly, Andre Boudrias, Ray Cullen, Dave Balon, Bill Goldsworthy, Bob Woytowich, J.P Parise, Billy Collins, and Milan Marcetta. All had shinning moments. We went to the 7th and final game in St. Louis and lost a bitterly fought 2-1 decision on St. Louis ice to the Blues. The game went in to the third period of sudden death overtime before Ron Schock scored the winning goal on a breakaway for St. Louis.

The Minnesota North Stars had acquitted themselves extremely well in our first year. Players who finished that season with the club were Cesare Maniago and Garry Bauman in goal. On defence we had Bob McCord, Mike McMahon, Bob Woytowich (our Team Captain) and Elmer (Moose) Vasko. Our forwards were Sandy Fitzpatrick, Ray Cullen, Andre Boudrias, Bill Goldsworthy, J.P. Parise, Wayne Connelly, David Balon, Billy Collins, and Parker MacDonald. Late in the season we had played Marshall Johnston on an eight game tryout. Mike McMahon, one of the players I had acquired in that deal with Sam Pollock, led all NHL defencemen, old or new division, in scoring. Andre Boudrias, another player acquired in that deal, also had a great year. Wayne Connelly scored over 30 goals. Parker MacDonald and J.P. Parise had outstanding years on left wing, as did Ray Cullen at center and Bill Goldsworthy on right wing.

We started slowly the second season in Minnesota, perhaps because I had driven the players so relentlessly that first season. They played over their heads and couldn't duplicate it. So I decided to take a different approach. I called in John Muckler from Memphis to coach, but the team floundered even worse. I believe at one stretch we went 13 games without a win.

Near the end of January, I was in the press box during a game when Walter Bush asked me to come to his office at the end of the second period. He looked at me and said, "Wren, we can't go on like this. We're starting to lose some of the crowds we had worked so hard to build up. We've got to make a change."

"Walter, where am I going to find a coach in late January?"

"Maybe, I'm looking at him."

I reluctantly agreed to coach again, which required that I release John Muckler. Walter and I agreed John could return to Memphis, but John was devastated by the news. When I consulted with Walter on how to solve this problem, he proposed, "What if we send John and Audrey (John's wife) on a cruise together to get away from here and get his perspective back together. At that time, the season will darn near be over."

I wanted John to stay on the payroll, even if he didn't go back to Memphis. We were contemplating moving our farm team to Cleveland in the American Hockey League, and I wanted John as General Manager and Coach there. Walter agreed. The next year we moved from Memphis to Waterloo, Iowa and John returned as the General Manager there, with Milan Marcetta as the Playing Coach. The next year we moved from Waterloo to Cleveland in the American Hockey League. John was the General Manager in Cleveland, and I made Parker MacDonald, my former player, the Head Coach. Eventually, John ended up in Edmonton in the NHL as the Assistant Coach to Glen Sather when they were on their Stanley Cup run. Later he became the Head Coach of the Oilers.

That year, we did not make the playoffs, a fact that made preparations for the 1969-70 season all that more pressing. In June I headed to Montreal to participate in the Annual NHL Meetings. Rumors began to fly. "Gump" Worsley was headed for the Blackhawks — he would become a North Star before the new season was over. "Punch" Imlach was coming to coach the North Stars – he eventually turned down my offer. When we got down to business, first on the agenda was the Intra League or minor league draft, where NHL teams select one player from another team's minor league roster. The North Stars first claimed forward Grant Erickson from the Boston organization, and Charlie Burns from Pittsburgh. Then came the amateur draft.

During the 1968-69 season, I had received a call from Eddie Redmond, a former captain and player of mine with the Whitby Dunlops. Eddie had two sons who were very good hockey players. Mickey Redmond, the oldest, had turned pro with the Montreal Canadiens and later was traded to the Detroit Red Wings, and a younger son Dick, was playing in Major Junior Hockey for the St. Catharines Blackhawks. Dick was coming up for draft in the amateur draft in June of 1969 in Montreal. When Eddie called me, he asked, "Have you seen young Dick play?" When I said I had seen him on several occasions, Eddie asked, "What do you think of him?"

"He's a pretty good player Eddie."

"Where have you got him rated in the amateur draft?"

"I'm not going to tell you that Eddie."

"I was talking to May the other night (Eddie's wife) and said to her I'd like young Dick to play for Wren. You know he's a good player Wren, but he is a bit of a wild young lad."

I kidded him by saying, "What you really mean then Eddie, is you want me to do some discipline with him that you failed to do as a father."

"Oh go to hell! Well, there might be a little bit of truth in that."

"Well in any event Eddie, we have him rated fairly high in the draft, and of course on draft day you never know which players are going to be available when you pick. But if Dick is still there, we would consider him for our first round pick." That pleased Eddie.

"Well I'll talk to you sometime later in the near future," Eddie concluded. Oh by the way, if you do take him, you'll have to pay him a lot more money than you paid me you know."

"Oh Eddie that wouldn't be any problem. He's a hell of a lot better hockey player than you were." And I kind of laughed.

"Goodbye! I know when I'm in over my head."

As it turned out, we did take Dick Redmond in the first round of the Amateur Draft in 1969, and following training camp, he joined the North Stars. We also took seven other players in the Amateur Draft, notably Dennis O'Brien, who also played defence for St. Catharines, and goaltender Gilles Gilbert from London. In late June I signed Danny Grant to a new four-year contract. Danny had won the NHL "Rookie of the Year Award" in 1968-69 with us. He was so excited because he got an outstanding raise in pay. Danny O'Shea, acquired from Montreal the season before, was also signed to a new contract, as was Claude Larose, putting an end to rumors that he was about to be returned to Montreal, and stalwart J. P. Parise. In August I signed two new defencemen to the North Stars, John Miszuk in a trade for defenceman Wayne Hillman, and Barry Gibbs. Only 20 years of age, "Gibbie" had already played minor pro hockey in Oklahoma City in the Central Professional Hockey League the year before. I had obtained Gibbie and Tommy Williams from Boston for a first round draft choice. "Gibbie" himself had been a first round draft choice the year before by Boston. Ray Cullen and Walt McKechnie were signed to new contracts. Cesare Maniago was already under contract for another year.

The team that had missed the playoffs the year before was being drastically overhauled. I even considered hiring a new coach, George "Punch" Imlach, who had been fired by the Toronto Maple Leafs at the end of the previous season. We had four meetings, and I was very close to getting Punch as my coach, but in the end, he decided to sit out the year and collect his thoughts before returning to hockey. Because he had a year to go on his contract with Toronto, he would be paid. In August a reporter talked to Punch who quoted him as saying, "Later, I almost called Wren back, because I felt I had made a mistake in not accepting his offer. I was getting bored sitting around home. I was sure I had made the wrong decision. My wife told me to quit brooding, pick up the phone and call Wren." But that call was never made.

In mid September we started our third training camp of the Minnesota North Stars for the 1969-70 Season. Once again training camp found us in Haliburton, Ontario. We played two exhibition games with the Chicago Blackhawks, one in Duluth Minnesota, and the other one at Met Center on home ice. The game in Duluth brought Tommy Williams back to his own hometown as we beat the Blackhawks 3-1. The next night we again beat the Blackhawks back in Minnesota 4-1. A few days later, we had a pre-season game against another old division team and beat the Detroit Red Wings 5-4 in Minnesota. Charlie Burns and Rick Dudley (a draft choice from a year earlier) had both played extremely well. Bobby Barlow, who had played pro in the Western Hockey League and was bidding to make the North Stars at training camp, also played very well.

We opened the regular season against the Philadelphia Flyers before a standing room only crowd of more than 15,000 at Metropolitan Sports Center. It was especially rewarding to see such a great turnout after our team had missed the playoffs the previous season. We had seven new players in our opening night line-up. That line-up saw Cesare Maniago in goal, with Lou Nanne, Leo Boivin, Barry Gibbs, John Miszuk, and Tom Polanic, a very big defencemen I had acquired from the minors, on defence. Our forwards were Danny Grant, Danny O'Shea, Claude Larose, Bobby Barlow, Charlie Burns, Billy Collins, J. P. Parise, Ray Cullen, Bill Goldsworthy, and Tommy Williams. Two new goaltenders were fighting for one open spot, Ken Broderick, who I had obtained from the Canadian Olympic Team, and Fern Rivard, who we had acquired in an earlier trade. Broderick beat the Detroit Red Wings in Detroit 3-2 in his National Hockey League debut. We got off to a great start that year and were in second pace by mid-December, just behind St. Louis.

Early in the year, I asked Charlie Burns, who had played with me in Whitby, if he wanted to assist me as playing coach. I was again feeling tremendous pressure trying to do both jobs as GM and coach. In mid January I named Charlie full-time coach for the balance of the year, so that I could concentrate on finding more players for the future of the club. Scouting new players meant that I had to travel a great deal. I was very relieved to get on with the very important chores of building the franchise, but team performance slipped, as it had the year before when I stepped back from coaching. By late February, we had slipped to fifth place in the standings.

We made one change and added one player in the effort to turn things around. Charlie returned to the ice as playing coach. The first game Charlie came back to play the North Stars beat the Toronto Maple Leafs 8-0. Then I acquired goaltender Lorne "Gump" Worsley from the Montreal Canadiens. Gump hadn't played for sometime after quitting Montreal and needed a period of time to get back in shape. He played his first game for the North Stars on March 4th against Philadelphia, and he played brilliantly. However, the team took four minor penalties in the last 30 seconds, which enabled Philadelphia to scratch out a 2-2 tie. Again Metropolitan Arena was sold out. After getting some well deserved rest, Cesare Maniago played a great game against Detroit to gain a 2-2 tie. There's no question in my mind that we had the best goaltending in the NHL at that time, with Cesare and Gump.

The North Stars had now moved up to fourth place in the standings, but had to fight it out the rest of the way with Oakland for the final playoff spot. On March 31st, Dan Stoneking, Staff Writer for the *Minneapolis Star*, penned a story with the headlines, "STARS ON THE ROPES — BUT STILL SWINGING." The Seals had 55 points and the North Stars 54 in the struggle for the West Division's final playoff spot. The Stars returned home to play the L.A.

Kings in another crucial game and won big time, 5-2. to take a one point lead in the standings on April 3rd. The North Stars now had two games remaining in the schedule, both on the road, Saturday afternoon in Philadelphia against the Flyers, and Sunday in Pittsburgh. The North Stars won a never-to-be-forgotten victory in Philadelphia, 1-0 against the Flyers, to put them in the playoffs. The only North Star goal was scored by defenceman Barry Gibbs, who flipped an 80-foot shot on a pass from Tommy Williams. The shot skipped and eluded Flyer goaltender Bernie Parent at 7:38 of the third period. Gump was outstanding. The next day we defeated the Penguins 5-1. The final standings saw St. Louis in 1st place in our division, followed by Pittsburgh, then the North Stars and Oakland, with Philadelphia and Los Angeles finishing out of the playoffs. This meant that the North Stars would go up against the first place St. Louis Blues in the first round of the playoffs.

Just before the series was to start, I got a letter from Canada: "To the Minnesota North Stars, Minneapolis, Minnesota. All the best in your quest for the Stanley Cup. From your Haliburton fans." The letter was signed by more than 200 fans from that small community were we held our training camp. A classy act.

In the first game in St. Louis, the North Stars took a lot of cheap penalties. The Blues took advantage and defeated the North Stars 6-2. They also beat us in the second game, 2-1. Now the series was back to Minnesota, where home ice was always sweet to our club. Cesare Maniago shut the door on the Blues during the third game, and the local team won 4-0. Cesare stopped 34 St. Louis shots in the shut-out victory. There was a turn-away sell-out crowd for the game. In game four, the North Stars defeated St. Louis 4-2 before another sell-out crowd. Bill Goldsworthy played an outstanding game scoring twice for the club. He was on a hot playoff scoring streak, trailing only Bobby Hull of Chicago in playoff scoring in the NHL after the first four games. As Dan Stoneking wrote in the *Minneapolis*

Star, "Maybe it was Bill Goldsworthy's special brand of annual spring fever, or could have been the three roses anonymously sent to our defenceman Tom Reid, or North Stars General Manager Wren Blair's hermitage. "Goldie" is hot once again in the spring playoffs, while Tom Reid has been outstanding on the North Stars defence, with crushing bodychecks and overall good defensive play, while Blair, ever superstitious, had locked himself in his office during both the weekend games (both won by the North Stars) at the Met. "That's where I'll be Thursday, when game six moves back to Minnesota. I listened on the radio in my office, alternately turning if off and then back on. I think I even kicked it (the radio) a couple of times, said Blair. Blair has so many superstitions it's hard to keep track of them."

Now it was back to St. Louis, for game five, with our veteran goaltender Gump Worsley going against St. Louis veteran goaltender Glenn Hall. In game five in St. Louis, the North Stars led on three occasions, but the team wilted in the third period, to see the Blues take a 6-3 victory. The sixth game back in the Twin Cities produced the largest crowd in the history of Met Center. The North Stars were jumpy and nervous, but the first period ended in a 1-1 tie. Defenceman Barry Gibbs had scored for the North Stars with assists going to J.P. Parise and Tommy Williams. St. Louis came back on a goal by Ab McDonald, assisted by Red Berenson and Frank St. Marseille, at 7:42. In the second period, St. Louis scored twice in a row, Ab McDonald again unassisted, and then Red Berenson assisted by Barclay Plager and Ab McDonald. Then Minnesota got one back when Ray Cullen scored from Billy Collins and Bobby Barlow at 14:54. The second period ended with St. Louis leading 3-2. In the third period, Larry Keenan scored, assisted by Red Berenson and Jean-Guy Talbot, and as they say in sports, "That's all she wrote." The North Stars season of 1969-70 was over.

PROFILE

Cesare Maniago, Gump Worsley & Bill Goldsworthy

IN JUNE 1967 AT THE FIRST NHL Expansion Draft, goaltenders were drafted a day ahead of the skating players draft. Each old division club could protect one goaltender and the six new clubs could select an unprotected goaltender. The order of the goaltender draft was based on a lottery. The Los Angeles Kings drew No. 1 ticket and took Terry Sawchuk from the Toronto Maple Leafs. The Philadelphia Flyers took Bernie Parent, just a kid from the Boston Bruins. Minnesota drew third choice. I took Cesare Maniago from the New York Rangers.

Cesare had played in OHA Senior A against the Whitby Dunlops, and when he turned pro with the Montreal Canadiens, he was assigned to play in the EPHL for the Hull-Ottawa Canadiens, against my Kingston Frontenacs. When the North Stars began play in the fall of 1967, Cesare was our No. 1 goaltender, with Gary Bauman as his backup. Cesare played at least 90%, of the North Star games in that first season, as he did in the 1968-69 season. As that second season moved on, I could tell that I had to get some backup help. One night after a game, trainer Stan Waylett asked me to look at Cesare. He was black and blue, from his toes to his shoulders, from stopping pucks. That did it for me. I had to do something.

I had just heard that Gump Worsley had quit the Montreal Canadiens, so I called Sam Pollock to see if there was any chance that I could purchase his rights from Montreal. "Sam, I just can't afford to trade you anymore draft choices, so I would like to do an outright purchase if you can possibly help me."

Gump was almost 40 years of age by this time, and so Sam said, "How much do you think you would pay me for Worsley?"

"Sam, what I'd like to do is pay the waiver price of $30,000"

"In all good conscience Wren, I can't do that. However, here's what I will do. Gump is telling everyone that he is retiring and not going to play anymore. You pay the Montreal Canadiens $40,000.00 for Worsley's rights, whether he plays or not. It becomes totally your responsibility to get him to play. If you agree to that, we'll sell him to Minnesota."

"Sam you've got a deal."

A few days later, I called Gump in Montreal where he lived. I chatted with him for a few minutes and then said, "I guess by now you know that we in Minnesota have purchased your rights from the Montreal Canadiens."

"Yes, I heard that."

"What do you think?"

"I think you made a bad deal . . . because I'm not going to play. I'm retiring."

"Do you think I could come up and we could have dinner and at least discuss it?"

"You buying?"

"Certainly I'm buying dinner."

"Fine, I can always use a free meal, but it isn't going to do you any good. I'm retiring."

A couple of days later, I flew to Montreal and we had dinner in the Mount Royal Hotel Dining Room, where I was staying. During the dinner I used all my persuasive powers and signing strategies, but I could tell I wasn't getting anywhere. Finally I said, "You know what bothers me Gump? I've got a copy of your contract of what you were being paid in Montreal, and I was surprised that you weren't making more money."

"Tell me about it!"

"I was planning to give you nearly a 35 percent increase."

He looked at me for a minute and said, "Are you nuts? I don't think anybody on the Montreal team including Richard or Beliveau make that much."

"I don't think they do either, but that's what I was planning to pay you."

He stuck out his hand out and said, "You've got a goalie!"

I quickly pointed out to Gump that his salary would be pro-rated because we were almost half way through the season. "I understand that," he said, "but there are a couple of things more that I need you to understand also, before we've got a completed deal. I'm not bringing my wife Doreen to Minnesota for the balance of this year. I want to live in that Sheraton Hotel right across the street from the Metropolitan Sports Arena. You know the one I mean? Also, I don't drink beer, I just drink rye whiskey, and who the hell am I going to drink with in the evenings? I'm almost twice the age of most of the kids on that team!"

"I'll come over and drink with you in the evenings when we're in town."

"Great, we're about the same age. You buy right? When do you want me in Minnesota?"

The Minnesota owners, players, and fans were excited by this acquisition of the legendary Gump Worsley. Gump and Cesare formed probably the strongest goaltending duo in the NHL. They seemed to play off each other. Cesare had played great for us from day one, but when Gump came, I think he played even better, if that was possible. For a while Gump was happier in Minnesota than he'd been in years.

One evening over our whiskeys at the Sheraton, Gump told me the story of when he was playing for Phil Watson, the coach of the Rangers, before he went to Montreal. In one stretch when Gump wasn't playing too well, Watson told the New York reporters that it was because of his beer gut. The next day, Gump told the same reporters, "Watson's nuts! He knows very well that I don't drink beer, I only drink Seagram's VO Rye Whiskey." Gump was a real character and so was Phil Watson.

A season or so later, Cesare came in one morning for practice. He usually got there long before practice to get his sticks and equipment ready. This particular morning he came right to my office and he asked my secretary, Marilyn Vaughan, if I was in. He wanted to talk to me. Cesare stepped into my office and sprawled out on a chair across from me. Cesare is about 6'3". We chatted for a couple of minutes before I asked, "What are you doing away from the rink these days?

"Well last night Mavis and I went to the Cooper Theater to see *Patton*." The movie was based on the career of General George Patton, a U.S. Army General during the Second World War who was known as a tough taskmaster

"Oh, we saw that picture, that was great. Did you enjoy it?"

"Ya, but a funny thing. I kept thinking about you all through the picture." I stared at him for a minute and then he got up, roaring like crazy with laughter and started out of my office.

I followed him and yelled as he was going out the door. "Thanks Cesare. I take that as a compliment."

"That's the way it was meant." I was known by the guys on the club as being pretty tough myself, but Cesare had given me the needle.

When Gump finished that first half season, I signed him to a new two year contract. He then brought Doreen down to Minnesota. Coming to the conclusion of the second year, Gump was already past 43 years of age. I began to read in the local papers from time to time that Gump was planning to retire at the end of the season."You know that fellow Blair, our General Manager, well when you see him, tell him I am definitely retiring at the end of this season." He had told me that he and Doreen would be going home in June, so by the end of May I structured another playing contract for Gump for one year as well as a contract for him to work as a scout for the North Stars for an additional four years.

"Gump, I've got another contract here ready for you to sign."

"Don't give me that stuff. You know, you've read it in the paper, I told the writers to let you know that I was going to retire."

"Ya, but Gump, I've got a five-year contract here for you. You don't want a five-year contract?"

"Are you nuts? I'll be nearly 50 years of age at the end of that."

"No, no Gump, you don't understand. It's one year to play and four more years to scout for the club, for a total of five years. You don't want to stay in hockey after you're done playing?"

He looked at me astounded. "You want me to stay in hockey after I'm done playing?"

"Yes I do! But first you must play one more year, and then you get that four more years for a total of five."

"You rat! I swore this was going to be my last year, but it's a pretty attractive deal, so where do I sign?" Gump stayed with the North Stars for 14 years until he was past 60 years of age, working for the club as a scout.

After Gump had retired from scouting in Minnesota and returned to his home in Montreal, I gave him a call one day when I was traveling to Kingston, where I was managing the Frontenacs OHL Major Junior A team. I talked to his wife Doreen for a few moments, and then I asked if Gump was there. "I'll get the old devil right now for you." Gump came on the phone. How the hell are you doing?"

We hadn't talked to each other for a while, so we had some catching up to do before I got to the point of my call. "I'm making a call to you for a reason not unlike the one when I called you back in 1969 to try to persuade you to come to Minnesota to play goal for the North Stars. I came up to Montreal and in the end we structured probably the best business deal you ever made. Now, we have purchased the Kingston Frontenacs Hockey Club in the OHL and I want you to come to Kingston three or four times a month as a goaltending coach for our kids. There isn't much money in it."

Gump quickly said in his usual way, "So what's new."

"Gump, we'll bring you and Doreen in from Montreal by train three or four times a month, put you up in a local hotel, pay all of your expenses, and pay you a modest fee for your services.

"Is this called 'putting something back into the game?'"

"Yes Gump, that's exactly what it is."

I'd probably enjoy that for awhile." And so for a couple of years Gump and I were back together again, through 1990-91 and 1991-92 seasons, as our goaltending coach in Kingston.

I also remember that for a week or so every summer during the years that he was scouting in Minnesota, Jimmy Gregory and I used to bring Gump and Doreen up to PineStone for a week and pay all their expenses. Gump would work in a public relations situation for us at the hotel. Anybody who ever was a hockey fan in Canada or the United States knew the "Gumper." One day he said to me, "Some guy came running up to me this morning and said to me, 'I saw a guy here at PineStone that I'm sure was Gump" Worsley.'" Gump teased him and said, "Na, Gump Worsley would never come to a dive like this." And as he told me he laughed his head off. Pine-Stone was a very beautiful spot that Gump and Doreen loved almost as much as Jim and I did.

When Cesare retired, he returned to his home near Vancouver. The last I heard, he owned a thriving wholesale sporting good business. I was privileged to have Cesare and Gump as my players and friends. I often think fondly of them to this day as I re-tell these stories to friends and acquaintances about our days together.

BILL GOLDSWORTHY WAS one of the first hockey players to start telling tales about me when Richard Rainbolt and Ralph Tutinen published *The Goldie Shuffle: The Bill Goldsworthy Story* (Minneapolis: T.S. Dennison and Co., 1972). Here is what Rainbolt, Tutinen, and Goldie had to say:

They were two things in life that Wren Blair had always been inflexible about. He could not tolerate losing and he would not accept mediocre performances from young men, who he knew were capable of much greater things. Known among hockey people as "The Bird," Blair had always been more hot than dumb in his approach to the game. If he erupted in anger, as he was prone to do, it was because he had a peculiar passion for winning. He spent the better part of his life scheming how to win hockey games. If there was a flaw in his strategy, he would evoke the wrath of the gods of hockey to drive his men to his victory by sheer determination or anger. He was also an astute hockey man, much respected, throughout his native Canada, and because of his accomplishments in 1958, he was named Hockey Executive of the Year.

While Blair did, of necessity, accept losing (but only in retrospect), he could not be so flexible in the matter of young men, who were not producing to their full capacity. He spent many years experimenting with techniques that would reach into the soul of a young man and drive him to achieve heights he, the young man, did not know he was capable of reaching. This did not always endear Blair to the particular young man he was driving, at first, and only years later, upon looking back to what happened, did many of his players come to recognize that at least part of their success had been due to "The Bird" being unable to accept less than their best.

There was a kid from Kitchener, Ont. – a tall blonde kid with wonderful sloping shoulders – and a temper every bit as explosive as that of Mr. Blair, who, particularly irked "The Bird" because he knew somewhere deep inside this firebrand were the ingredients of a very fine hockey player. "The Bird" devised various techniques to probe for these ingredients. There would be 15,000 loyal fans watching and the North Stars were not performing in a manner entirely satisfactory to them, or "The Bird." Blair was particularly annoyed with the big kid on right wing, but instead of sending out an entire new line, as most coaches in pro hockey do when they want to vent their wrath on one player, he would send out only one man, to right wing. There was no mistaking who the rebuke was intended for as the solitary figure skated toward the bench.

"You sit here, Goldie," said "The Bird," talking politely over the shoulder of the angry winger. "You're too tired to be out there and the other guys have to wait for you to catch up to them. I don't want to overwork you tonight." Goldie's line came off and was back on the ice for two or three more shifts without him, and by this time, he was seething, kicking the boards in anger, and talking straight ahead toward the ice, the words really intended for the curly-haired Blair behind him. Blair ignored the words unless there was something he could pick up and needle him with. When "The Bird" figured Goldie was really mad, he would lean over his shoulder once more. "Goldie, would it be too much if I asked you to play one more shift tonight? I know you're tired . . ." Goldie stormed over the boards, knocked down nine players and an official, walked in on the goalie, pulled him out of the net, and scored the game-winning goal. With a big smile of satisfaction on his face, he skated back to the bench. "You idiot," shouted Blair, turning his back on the big forward. The techniques had variations to them, but they were always spiced with the same kind of sarcasm.

"I put the needle to Goldie so bad that sometimes it comes out on the other side," said "The Bird." "I took the position that there was no way I was going to let this kid screw up, even I had to take him apart at the seams, which I did a few times. He was like a thoroughbred horse, some you can pat on the head, and some of them you have to put the whip too. You had to use the whip on Goldie.

"Sure, we've had our run-ins. If you really care for someone and you want him to be successful, you're going to be tougher on him than someone else. I believe that discipline is a very big part of love. It's hard to do. When you discipline someone very close to you, it hurts you as much as him. But if you love him enough, and he deserves it, then you better well do it, and fast.

"Goldie's temper is one of the things that has gotten him into trouble, but it has also been one of things that I liked about him. He has spirit, and that helps in hockey. His problem was that he didn't know how to harness his temper. He's learning, though, and this could make him a great hockey player."

In his first year with the North Stars, Blair began working his pyschology on Goldie.

"You know what really annoys me about you," said "The Bird" in a practice session. "You could be as good as Bobby Hull, if you wanted to be mad enough."

"Are you kidding," asked Goldie, smiling.

"No, I'm not kidding, I'm damn serious!" said Blair.

Their relationship would be stormy in years to come because Blair had never been known to be timid in applying the whip if that's what it took to get the most out of his horses, thoroughbred or not.

"One night," said The Bird, "I got mad at him and pulled him off the ice just before the end of the period. He was the last man on the bench and I was going to open the door, onto the ice, not knowing the buzzer was about to go off, ending the period. When it did, Goldie stood up quickly to go up the ramp and ran right into me. I bounced off and started back at him. Danny O'Shea grabbed me, and Stan Waylett, our trainer, was holding on to Goldie, and I was shouting around Danny.

"'Did you run into me on purpose?'

"Danny said to me, 'Come on, he didn't run into you on purpose.'

"I started up the stairs and turned around and said to Goldie, 'If you ever take a step at me . . .' You know he was standing above me, on skates, so it must have been comical.

"I went into my office and nothing further was said. When the game was over, I went into the dressing room and Goldie was bending over, taking off his skates.

"I said to him, kiddingly, 'Did I hurt you when I ran into you up there?'

"He looked up at me and said: 'Oh, Lord,' and rolled his eyes.

"Sometimes you do and say things for fun, to break tension, so I said, 'I'm sorry, Goldie, if I ever hit you hard . . .

"Then he started to laugh and everybody in the room broke up."

On the way out of the dressing room that night, Goldie crossed paths with Blair once again. "I don't think I tried to run into you," said Goldie.

"Oh, that doesn't matter, forget it," said Blair.

"Why is it always me? I'm always in trouble," said Goldie. . . .

"Even though we've had our ups and downs, Wren has really tried to help me," said Goldie. "I played for some good coaches, but I felt closer to Wren than the others because of the time we were together and he didn't give up on me. When he was coaching, he had that ability to get the adrenaline flowing in his players. Sure, he was stern but he was also honest and fair with the players and I respect him for that. I know he has had a great impact on my career," said Goldsworthy.

Minnesota North Stars 1967-68

Front Row (from left) — Ray Cullen, Wayne Connelly, Bill Plager, President Walter L. Bush, Jr., Captain Bob Woytowich, General Manager-Coach Wren Blair, Mike McMahon, Jean-Paul Parise, Andre Boudrais.

Back Row — Special Assistant to General Manager John Mariucci, Cesare Maniago, Sandy Fitzpatrick, Elmer Vasko, Milan Marcetta, Bob McCord, Bill Goldsworthy, Bill Collins, Dave Balon, Parker MacDonald, Garry Bauman, Clubhouse Boy Dan Blair, Trainer Stan Waylett.

Minnesota North Stars 1968-69

First Row (from left) — Danny Grant, Ray Cullen, General Manager-Coach Wren Blair, President Walter Bush, Jr., Special Assistant to the General Manager John Mariucci, Captain Elmer Vasko, Claude Larose.

Second Row — Fern Rivard, Leo Boivin, Danny Lawson, Cesare Maniago, Bill Orban, Joey Johnston, J.P. Parise, Garry Bauman.

Third Row — Trainer Stan Waylett, Walt McKechnie, Bob McCord, Wayne Hillman, Tom Reid, Bill Goldsworthy, Bill Collins, Danny O'Shea, Lou Nanne.

Minnesota North Stars 1969-70

Front Row (from left) — Cesare Maniago, Captain Claude Larose, General Manager Wren Blair, President Walter Bush Jr., Coach Charlie Burns, Special Assistant to the General Manager John Mariucci, Leo Boivin, Ken Broderick.

Second Row — Trainer Stan Waylett, J.P. Parise, Danny Lawson, Darryl Sly, Lou Nanne, Ray Cullen, Marshall Johnston, Danny Grant, Bob Barlow, Assistant Trainer Al Scheuneman.

Third Row — Bill Orban, Tom Williams, Danny O'Shea, Walt McKechnie, Tom Polanic, Tom Reid, John Miszuk, Bill Collins, Bill Goldsworthy, Barry Gibbs.

Minnesota North Stars 1970-71

First Row (from left) — Cesare Maniago, Captain Ted Harris, Coach Jack Gordon, President Walter L. Bush, Jr., General Manager Wren Blair, Charlie Burns, Gump Worsley.

Second Row — Trainer Stan Waylett, Bobby Rousseau, Lou Nanne, Buster Harvey, Barry Gibbs, Bill Goldworthy, Tom Reid, Gordy Labossiere, Dennis O'Brien, Doug Mohns, Murray Oliver, Assistant Trainer Dick Rose.

Third Row — Ted Hampson, Wayne Muloin, J.P. Parise, Gilles Gilbert, Jude Drouin, Danny Grant, Danny Lawson, Terry Caffery.

Minnesota North Stars 1971-72

First Row (from left) — Cesare Maniago, Captain Ted Harris, Coach Jack Gordon, President Walter L. Bush, Jr., General Manager Wren Blair, Charlie Burns, Gump Worsley.

Second Row — Trainer Stan Waylett, Dennis O'Brien, Lou Nanne, Barry Gibbs, Bill Goldsworthy, Tom Reid, Doug Mohns, Bob Nevin, Asst. Trainer Dick Rose.

Third Row — Ted Hampson, Jude Drouin, Murray Oliver, Danny Grant, Craig Cameron, Dennis Hextall, Dean Prentice, J.P. Parise.

The Rise and Fall of the Minnesota North Stars and Tommy Williams's Grief

9

EARLY IN THE SUMMER OF 1970, I had a very distasteful task to perform. As our playing coach, Charlie Burns had done a great job of leading our team into the playoffs, but NHL President Clarence Campbell was not in favor of playing-coaches. On several occasions the previous season, he had complained, but now he made a ruling. "Wren, this will not be acceptable to the league. We are not allowing playing-coaches anymore because of insurance problems and bench discipline, because if your coach is on the ice playing, there is no one on the bench to discipline the players if something happens. As a result of this, we are not going to allow playing-coaches any longer." Rather grudgingly, he allowed us to keep Charlie as playing-coach until the end of the 1969-70 season, with the understanding that it would not be continued in the future.

I met with Charlie and told him that we were going to hire a full-time bench coach because he meant too much to us as a player. I had no intention of dragging the league president into this discussion. Charlie was obviously disappointed but he also understood our position, and in the end he was a true professional, accepted the change and stayed with the club as one of our key players.

I then hired Jack Gordon to coach the North Stars. Jack had been around hockey for a long time, playing briefly for the New York Rangers, but most of his years were with the Cleveland Barons as a player and coach. Shortly after that we took our entire scouting staff to Las Vegas, along with Charlie Burns as a part of a reward for his outstanding work the previous season. We stayed at the Dunes Hotel for the best part of a week. Attending these meetings were Chief Scout Ted O'Connor, my brother Gerald Blair, John Mariucci, John Muckler, Parker MacDonald, and other "bird dog" scouts. We also brought all of their wives as well. The chief item on the agenda was the league expansion to Buffalo and Vancouver. We were only allowed to protect a specific number of players from our major league roster. At the end of our evaluation of personnel, we decided we could protect either Ray Cullen or Charlie Burns, but not both. Charlie was very important to our team defensively and had done a magnificent job the year before as playing-coach to get into the playoffs. Ray was our player representative and a very special player to me on our roster. But decisions must be made, and hockey is no game for the weak-hearted. We decided to protect Charlie and lost Ray to the Vancouver Canucks in the expansion draft.

Near the end of the 1969-70 season, I had been trying to get Murray Oliver from the Toronto Maple Leafs. It appeared that Toronto would not be able to protect Oliver in the upcoming expansion draft, but the Leafs wanted something in return. I acquired Oliver just two minutes before midnight on the trading deadline day and he was set to play for us the following season.

Before the draft meetings in Montreal later in June, the Montreal Canadiens advised us they wanted Claude Larose back after loaning him to us for several years. Sam Pollock, who was always more than fair with me, offered us Ted Harris, a very good defensive defenceman and a former captain of the Canadiens, and Bobby Rousseau, a very good forward, in exchange. Ted Harris became captain of our team, replacing Larose. Another prominent player I traded for was Jude Drouin. I knew Sam Pollock could not protect Drouin in the Expansion Draft if Jean Beliveau decided to play another year. Eventually Beliveau notified Pollock that he did intend to play one more year, leaving Drouin available. Drouin was probably the best minor league player at that time, and had he been with any other NHL team than Montreal, he would have been in the NHL the year before. I traded Billy Collins, who had scored 29 goals for us the year before, to Montreal for Drouin. In the 1970 Amateur Draft, I claimed Buster Harvey from Hamilton in the OHA. Buster made the North Stars that year, as did another draft pick, defenceman Fred Barrett. Part way through the year, we brought up Walt McKechnie from Cleveland and added young goal-tender Gilles Gilbert to the roster. I can remember a game Gilbert played in Montreal on October 21, 1970, where he stopped 46 shots as the North Stars defeated Montreal 3-1 right in the Forum. Coach Gordon instituted a defensive style of play, and Tom Reid, along with Fred Barrett and Dennis O'Brien, excelled.

With Vancouver and Buffalo coming into the league for the 1970-71 season, the league now had 14 teams, seven in each division. The two divisions were re-aligned with Minnesota grouped in the West with the Chicago Blackhawks, St. Louis Blues, Philadelphia Flyers, Los Angeles Kings, Pittsburgh Penguins, and California Seals. In the playoffs, four teams in each division qualified, with three out, which made it even tougher to grab a playoff berth. Going into December, the Blackhawks were leading the West Division followed by the Blues and the North Stars. Our team was improving rapidly.

In late November, tragedy struck the team again. Tommy Williams' wife died in an accident in their garage. I got a call from Tommy about 5:15 a.m. "Wren, Wren, you've got to come over," he cried.

"Tommy, Tommy, settle down, what's the matter?"

"Emmie's dead in the garage," he said.

"Are your kids there?"

"Yes."

"Tommy, Tommy, don't ever say anything in front of your children. Are the police there? Don't ever say anything to them. Don't say anything, I'm on my way."

I quickly got dressed and rushed over to Tommy's house. I'll never forget that scene. The whole neighborhood was out, with police cars and fire trucks on the street, their sirens silent, but their lights flashing. In the house, there was poor Tommy huddled with four or five of his children. When I asked him what happened, he said, "Emmie and I went out last night and came home real late. I immediately went up to bed and fell asleep. I don't know whether Emmie ever came up. For some reason, I woke up early, and Emmie wasn't in bed. I got up and started looking around the house, and eventually I opened the door to the connecting garage. I still can't believe the scene there. She was in the car, and the car was still running. The garage door was closed. I quickly opened it to let some fresh air in. It was terrible in there. I ran outside for a moment and then rushed back in to shut the car off. Emmie was in the car, and she was dead."

"Tommy, you don't know what happened. It could have been an accident. Did you have a fight?"

"Yes, we had an argument," he said.

"Well, she could have decided to go for a drive when you got home, and she was so sleepy she never got the door open, and was asphyxiated." I never asked the coroner for details of the autopsy on the real cause of death, but suffice it to say that she had died accidentally. I spent most of the day with Tommy, trying to get him organized. His parents to take some of the kids, and Emmie's parents, who were in Duluth, came to care for the rest.

The funeral was held a few days later, and three or four days after the funeral, Tommy returned to the team, but he was not able to rehabilitate himself on his own and started drinking rather heavily.

All through December and into January, he was creating many problems for Jack Gordon. We decided to drop Tommy from the line-up to stop the disruption. "Maybe Minnesota is the worst place for Tommy to try and turn his life around," I reasoned with Jack, "as this is his home state, and all his memories are here."

On February 23, I was able to conclude an excellent trade for Tommy. I traded him to Oakland for Ted Hampson, an experienced NHL centerman. The same day I traded Danny O'Shea to Chicago for Doug Mohns and rookie Terry Caffery. Mohns was a veteran NHL defenceman, who could also play left wing. I was very upset to have to trade Tommy because he was a great favorite of mine and I had first turned him pro in hockey in his home, in Duluth Minnesota when I worked for the Boston Bruins. He was assigned to me by the Bruins to their farm club in the Eastern Professional Hockey League at Kingston, Ontario. A lightning fast skater, Tommy was a great favorite of the fans in Kingston. Tommy and Emmie had also been married while he was playing for me in Kingston. Tommy was only 19 years of age at that time, and Emmie was only 17. He brought her to Kingston and she was a real sweet kid. I was able to get Tommy later in a trade with Boston. Tommy and I went a way back and were good friends.

Tommy went on to play two or three more good years in Oakland, but he was very bitter about the trade and tended to run off a bit at the mouth, blaming Jack Gordon for his problems. That summer at a golf tournament in Minnesota Tommy right off the tee when he saw me, came over to say hello, and started to cry. He put his arms around me and said, "I am so sorry, Wren, for anything I said. I played for you in Kingston and you were always great to me there and you have always been great with me here. I don't know what I was thinking when I said some of those things."

"Tommy, I understand that fully. You have been through a terrible tragedy and I understand everything you went through. You always were a bit mouthy, but it's over and done with now." Tommy kind of laughed.

When he finished playing, Tommy met another lady, got married, quit drinking, and moved his new wife and all five children back to Boston. He got a good job selling some underground piping to commercial companies and was doing really well. In the mid-1980s, my partner at PineStone Inn, Jim Gregory, and I were opening the second nine holes on our golf course and decided to hold a big tournament. We had made an arrangement to have George Knudson come and give a clinic and also play in the tournament. I mentioned to Jim that it would be good idea if he could get several foursomes from his hockey connections over the years, and I would do the same. Jimmy got Eddie Shack and Mike Walton, to mention a couple, and I got Lorne Worsley, Ray Cullen, Danny O'Shea, and Tommy Williams.

We had arranged to pay the player's transportation up and back and take care of their meals, accommodation, and expenses. The players were to pick up these checks when they left the next day. Tommy had brought his wife along and one of his children, and when he was leaving the next day for Duluth to visit his parents and Emmie's parents, he stopped to chat with me. We chatted a bit and I handed him an envelope with his expense money in it. "What's this," he asked?"

"It's to cover your expenses. You came all the way up here from Boston."

"I don't care, I'm not taking it," he said. No matter how hard I tried to convince him to take the money, he wouldn't hear of it.

I wrote him a nice letter a couple of days later, thanking him for his appearance and telling him how proud I was of him, the way he had straightened his life around and had reunited his family. He sent me back a wonderful letter a few weeks later. A couple of years later, I learned that he had died of a heart attack in Boston. Tommy was only in his 48th year. It is sad that he had to be taken so early in life, after all the tragedy he had been through. To this day, Tommy is never too far from my thoughts.

AS THE 1970-71 SEASON wore on, Jude Drouin was becoming a prime candidate for Rookie of the Year. Danny Grant had won this award the year before. It would be something for an expansion team to have two straight winners. On March 20th, the North Stars clinched a playoff spot, the earliest time that the North Stars had done so. We ended in fourth place in the West Division, one point behind the Philadelphia Flyers. Gump Worsley had been hurt quite a bit throughout the season, leaving Cesare Maniago to carry the load. He was voted the most valuable player on the team by his team-mates. Young Gilles Gilbert had played in goal for 17 games and showed clear signs that he was becoming our goaltender for the future. In the scoring department, Jude Drouin led the club, followed by Bill Goldsworthy, Danny Grant, Teddy Hampson, J. P. Parise, Murray Oliver, Charlie Burns, Bobby Rousseau, Buster Harvey, Doug Mohns, Tom Reid, Lou Nanne, Ted Harris, Wayne Muloin, Danny Lawson, Dennis O'Brien, and Terry Caffery.

Again the North Stars were taking on the St. Louis Blues, but this time we were victorious, winning the series 4-2.

Meanwhile the Montreal Canadiens had beaten out the Boston Bruins in the other division in a hard fought series, which meant that the North Stars were now going to play the Canadiens in the Stanley Cup final. What a thrill! The Montreal line-up was stellar: Ken Dryden was in goal; on defence was Jacques Laperriere, Terry Harper, J.C. Trembley, Guy Lapointe, and "Butch" Bouchard; and the forwards were Marc Tardif, Jean Believeau, Yvan Cournoyer, John Ferguson, Peter Mahovlich, and Claude Larose (who had returned to Montreal from our club).

In game one at the Montreal Forum, the North Stars scored first, but after that it was all Montreal, as the Canadiens scored a 7-2 victory. In the second game, we shocked the mighty Montreal club by beating them 6-3 right in Montreal. Cesare Maniago had a brilliant night. The North Stars jumped into a four goal lead in the first period on goals by Parise, Drouin, Hampson, and Lou Nanne unassisted. In the second period Montreal scored twice before Murray Oliver made it 5-2. In the third period big John Believeau made it 5-3 before Charlie Burns scored an unassisted goal for the 6-3 win. It was the first playoff win over an old division club in the newly expanded league. St. Louis Blues had met the Canadiens in the Stanly Cup final the year before, but went out 4 games to 0.

Following that game I got a very thoughtful telegram, which read, "Dear Wren, if it couldn't be done by us, we are glad it is you. Congratulations, now go ahead and win the Stanley Cup." It was signed by Jim Cullen, the Alternate Governor and Legal Council of the St. Louis Blues. Our entire expansion division was really excited. Another telegram said, "Wishing you good luck, we are all pulling for you in Whitby," signed by Madge and Don Wilson. Don had been the Secretary-Treasurer of the Whitby Dunlops a few years ago, and both Madge and Don had traveled to Oslo to see the "Dunnies" win the World Championship. A third telegram read, "Congratulations to you and the management and the team on their history making victory in Montreal last evening." It was signed by "All your friends at first Southdale National Bank, Edina Minnesota."

We returned to Minnesota for the next two games, losing 6-3 in game three and winning 5-2 in game four. Back in Montreal for game five, we lost 6-1. The sixth game on our home ice was controversial game. With the score 2-1 late in the third period, the North Stars scored a goal just as the buzzer went. Everybody on the North Stars swore that the goal went in before the blue light came on, but the referee ruled no goal. We lost the game and our bid for a Stanley Cup, but we had put a scare into the mighty Montreal Canadiens and proved that expansion teams were a force to be reckoned with in the future.

IN DECEMBER 1970, I had undergone lung surgery to remove the middle lobe of my right lung. Tests had shown that this lobe was not functioning properly, but a day or two after the doctors removed it, they told me that the middle lobe of the right lung had never grown from birth. The two other lobes, the upper and lower, had expanded to do the full duty. Had they known this they wouldn't have had to perform surgery.

As I lay in the hospital for more than a week, I did a great deal of thinking about our team. Even though I had put together our best roster ever, I saw the World Hockey Association on the horizon, bidding to implement a second major league in hockey. Players on all NHL clubs were being approached by WHA clubs, but most executives in the NHL felt it would never get off the ground. I wasn't so sure. I decided in my hospital bed that in the off season I would ask the owners of the North Stars to increase my player salary budget so we could retain as many players as possible.

In a meeting with the owners, I had asked them the question, "What's the most valuable asset you acquired when you purchased your franchise in the NHL?" I advanced the theory to them that the only real asset they had acquired was the right to draft 20 players from the six other NHL clubs four years ago. We even made a case with the IRS that these players were 90% of the value of the franchise, which can be depreciated over a number of years, the same as a corporation depreciates buildings as they get older, or a race horse, etc. In the meantime, we've improved this asset by signing better players while building a fairly strong club in the Twin City Area.

The players we own are the only real asset we have. We wouldn't get much for the used jock straps or used sticks or used equipment. Because it was so difficult to acquire players from the six old division teams, and because we are now getting some real value built up in the players, it would be most foolish for the North Stars – or for any of the owners of the six expansion clubs — to lose any of their players. Sure, it meant that ticket prices would have to be increased, but I was convinced that to stand by and lose our players then would be more damaging than the expense of increasing their salaries.

The owners of the club were good businessmen and saw the logic in this proposal. They increased my salary budget by more than 50%. I immediately set out to meet with every player on our roster. Until this time, NHL hockey players were seldom signed to more than a one-year contract. To give our organization security for the future, I was now talking about giving almost every player that we wanted to retain at least a three-year contract, at a substantial increase. Some of my fellow general managers in the league were critical of my approach, but I held my ground. Before our players left for that summer, I had met (sometimes on more than one occasion) with every player. I was able to sign most to new long-term contracts, though three or four wanted more time to consider the offer and did not sign until later in the summer. When the dust had cleared, we did not lose a single player to the WHA, which incidentally began play in that season.

Soon top stars from the NHL were signing with the WHA. The most notable, of course, was Bobby Hull, who would leave the Chicago Blackhawks the following summer to join the Winnipeg Jets of the WHA. As a result, the loss of some key players, especially from old division teams in the NHL, helped our team in Minnesota because we did not lose any players. In addition, I signed four new quality players to augment our line-up that year. We made a very good acquisition in obtaining Dennis Hextall from the Oakland

Seals. When I inquired about Hextall, the Seals indicated that they wanted youth in any trade they might make. I suggested two good youngsters, Walt McKechnie and Joey Johnston. Walt and Joey had played a few games with the North Stars. We completed that trade and added another power player to the club.

I had also been looking for a quality rightwinger for the club, and was surprised to be able to complete a deal with Emile Francis of the New York Rangers for Bobby Nevin. Bobby was 33 years of age at the time but had scored 20 goals or more for seven straight years. For Nevin we had to give New York a future draft choice. Another important transaction that we were able to make was to acquire from Sam Pollock of the Montreal Canadiens two players who were from the Minnesota area, Gary Gambucci, a quality forward who had played a couple of times with the U.S. Olympic Team, and defenceman Bob Paradise. We gave Montreal cash and re-arranged our draft choices with Montreal from past deals. As we moved towards the playing season of 1971-72, I felt that we now had the strongest line-up of quality players since the beginning of our franchise.

By halfway through the 1971-72 season, the North Stars were lodged in second place in the West Division, with only the Chicago Blackhawks from the old six teams ahead of us. We held second until the regular season was over and again faced our perennial rivals, the St. Louis Blues, in the first round of the playoffs. The series came down to overtime in the seventh game in Minnesota. Kevin O'Shea, the brother of our former player Danny O'Shea, scored the winning goal for the Blues. Danny was now playing for the Blues and set up his brother's goal. It was a tough defeat because I felt this was the strongest team that we had ever put together. A single shot in overtime turned the tide against us. That's what makes hockey such a great game. You just never can tell.

HEADING INTO THE NHL Intraleague Draft in 1972, we decided to protect Charlie Burns, Craig Cameron, Ted Hampson, Billy Heindl, Gordie Labossiere, Terry Caffery, Bob Paradise, Freddy Speck, as well as goaltenders Gilles Gilbert and Fern Rivard. But we still had Cesare Maniago and Gump Worsley on our roster to protect. If unprotected, we knew that any one of these goaltenders would be lost. To compound the problem, the WHA was now a threat: any player we chose not to protect would more than likely jump to the WHA. A WHA team had now been established on our home turf, the Minnesota Fighting Saints just across the river in St. Paul. Glen Sonmor, who had been involved in hockey for years around the Twin Cities, became the General Manager of the Fighting Saints. I would hear daily of some player from my team being wined and dined by that the St. Paul owners. Wayne Connelly, who had played for us in Minnesota before being lost to Vancouver in the second Expansion Draft, had apparently signed with the Fighting Saints, but this drew the threat of a lawsuit by Vancouver against this new WHA club. Every day you heard of new players jumping to the WHA. Johnny McKenzie, a Boston Bruins star, rattled a lot of chains in the NHL when he jumped to the WHA Cleveland franchise, along with Boston team-mate Gerry Cheevers. Our farm team Cleveland jumped from the American Hockey League to purchase a franchise in the WHA, with John Muckler as the general manager. Then Derek Sanderson signed with the Philadelphia Blazers, further decimating the Bruins. When Bobby Hull signed with the Winnipeg Jets for $3 million over 3 years, the NHL was more than rattled. This amazing contract forever changed the face of salary negotiations in the NHL.

Making things even tougher was the fact that the NHL was expanding by two more clubs for the 1972-73 season. We could only protect 15 skating players at the Expansion Draft, but to our good fortune, Gilles Gilbert and Fern Rivard were not selected, even though we had been forced to leave them unprotected in the early rounds. Others we couldn't protect were Craig Cameron, Billy Heindl, Gord Labossiere, Terry Caffery, Bob Paradise, and Ted Hampson. When Labossiere heard he wasn't protected, he jumped to the Houston franchise in the WHA. Ted Hampson was now being pursued by the Fighting Saints and eventually signed with them in August.

On July 19, 1972, I signed Bob Nevin to a new contract, the final player to complete our roster for the upcoming year. "A project that started more than six months ago, was completed today," the Minnesota papers reported, "when Minnesota General Manager, Wren Blair, announced the signing of right winger Bob Nevin. Blair said, 'The 34 year old National Hockey League forward acquired last year in a trade with the New York Rangers, signed a two-year contract. Nevin's signing means that we have signed every regular from last year's team,' Blair said, 'plus our four top minor league prospects, right winger Buster Harvey, defenceman Fred Barrett and goaltenders Gilles Gilbert and Fern Rivard." I was able to return to Coach Gordon the same roster he had the previous year when the club finished the season in good style.

As we headed into training camp and the exhibition pre-season, Team Canada was playing the now legendary challenge series against the Soviet Union. I was proud to see that Harry Sinden, my former player and coach, was hired to coach this team. The North Stars were also proud to have two players selected for Team Canada, J.P. Parise and Bill Goldsworthy. The spirited J.P. rose to the occasion, most notably in that unforgettable eighth game when he threatened the referee and turned the course of the game. When the team returned to Canada, Harry was appointed Managing Director, re-joining the Bruins organization after resigning as coach following their first Stanley Cup victory in 29 years. Harry was 39 years of age when he signed that contract. He remained the GM for 30 years before taking up the position of President of the club, a position he still holds.

We opened 1972-73 NHL season in Montreal with the following line-up: Jude Drouin, Danny Grant, Bob Nevin, "Buster" Harvey, Barry Gibbs, Dennis Hextall, Charlie Burns, Lou Nanne, Jerry Byers (our first draft choice from the amateur draft in June), Tom Reid, Ted Harris, Dean Prentice, Murray Oliver, Doug Mohns, J. P. Parise, and Bill Goldsworthy. In goal we started with three goaltenders again, Cesare Maniago, Gilles Gilbert and Gump Worsley. This appeared to be the best line-up we had iced since our franchise started. The North Stars started strongly, and by early December, we led the West Division, ahead of the once mighty Chicago Black-hawks. This was an exciting time for the players, our first run in first place, but by early February, we had slid back to third place. By early April, nearing the end of the schedule, the Stars had moved back into second place, a point ahead of Philadelphia, but when the schedule concluded, the North Stars and the Flyers were dead-locked. Dennis Hextall led the club in total points with 82, followed by J. P. Parise with 75 and Jude Drouin with 73.

The North Stars weren't a happy camp when they found out their first-round playoff opponents would be the "Broadway Bullies," the Philadelphia Flyers. The first game was played in Philadelphia. Cesare Maniago came up with a great effort as he shut the Flyers out 3-0. In the second game, the Flyers whipped the North Stars 4-1 to even the series. Bobby Clarke, the Flyers star centerman, played an outstanding game on home ice. Back in Minnesota, Maniago again shut out the Flyers 5-0 in the third game before more than 16,000 fans. We had slightly less than 15,000 seats at Met Center, so where we put all the fans for that game that night, still baffles me. Dave "Hammer" Schultz, one of the toughest players in the NHL at that time, started several fights. The Flyers came back in game four to win 3-0 over the Stars.

Another screaming crowd of close to 18,000 was on hand for the fifth game in Philadelphia. At the end of regulation time, the two teams were tied 2-2, but Gary Dornhoefer scored at 8:35 of the first sudden death overtime period to give the Flyers a 3-2 lead in the series. In the sixth game, Doug Favell had an outstanding game, stopping 37 shots. Bill Goldsworthy of the North Stars scored the first goal of the game, which also turned out to be the North Stars only goal, as the Flyers romped on to score four more, blanking the Minnesota club the rest of the way. We out shot the Flyers 38-23 in that game, but you couldn't get a pea past Favell after the first goal.

It was an unhappy North Stars group that trudged to the dressing room after the defeat. Bill Hengen, a prominent Sports Writer for the *Minneapolis Star*, added salt to the wounds in his column the next day. "It might be time for changes to be made in the club. . . . Now the only thing left is next year. It will be no surprise if several changes are made in player personnel. The North Stars have established themselves as a yearly contender for the playoffs. But playing for a place in the Stanley Cup finals, and reaching the goal, are opposite points. Jack Gordon, coach of the North Stars, has just completed his contract, and while he is expected to be signed to a new one, player personnel might need to be changed. The organization, under the capable direction of President Walter Bush Jr. and General Manager Wren Blair, has built the foundation. Now it's time to start building a complete winner. . . . When the time comes – if Blair should leave, there is the easy possibility that Jack Gordon would be named General Manager, and Parker MacDonald brought in as coach." I found that a strange comment by Mr. Hengen, and it bothered me a good deal. Little did I know how prophetic it was.

SHORTLY AFTER THE END of the 1972-73 season, I heard rumors that a new WHA franchise in Los Angeles was interested in signing

Gilles Gilbert, our young goaltender. His contract with us was about to expire, and we knew we could not match the LA offer. Their offer was much more money than we were paying Cesare and Gump. I knew that Harry Sinden in Boston needed a quality goaltender after losing Gerry Cheavers to the WHA. I decided to call Harry and discuss Gilbert with him.

He was indeed interested in trading for "Gillie." Harry asked who we might want from Boston, I replied, "I don't want a player who doesn't have more time on his contract, because I would then be fighting the WHA all over again with the player I get from you. I noticed part of last year that the Bruins weren't playing Freddy Stanfield too much, and I would be interested in him."

"I would likely make that deal Wren, but Stanfield has a no trade clause in his contract."

'Harry, could you talk to him and see if he would report to us in a trade, and call me back maybe tomorrow?" The next day Harry called to say Stanfield wouldn't report to Minnesota because he liked living in Boston and didn't want to play for an expansion team. Harry was clearly upset with Stanfield and apparently told him so. Now, we both had a problem. "Ok Harry, if we make this deal, you would have a problem, too, in trying to convince Gilbert not to go the WHA, but to report to Boston."

As we talked more about this problem, I said, "Harry, let's do something unheard of. Why don't you give me Stanfield's agent's name and phone number. I will see if I can get him to agree to meet with me and Freddy in Boston. I'll then give you Gilbert's agent's phone number and you try and arrange a meeting here in Minnesota with Gilbert and his agent." And with that we exchanged the player's agent's phone numbers.

Stanfield's agent, a lawyer, was very receptive to my proposal to meet with him and his client. Meanwhile I heard back from Harry that he also had arranged a meeting with Gilbert and his agent in Minneapolis. A couple of days later, I flew to Boston to meet with Stanfield and his agent. When I arrived at the agent's office, Freddy was already there. Freddy posed a very logical question to me. "Wren, I'm settled here in Boston. I have a home here in Boston. I have a contract with several more years to run with the Bruins, and a no trade clause in that contract. Why should I go to Minnesota?" I looked at him for a few seconds, because this was a tough question to answer. Everything Freddy said made sense, but as I looked at Freddy, I remembered that Harry was angry with Freddy. "Freddy," I said, "I would report to Minnesota, just because I know that Harry told you he didn't want you on his team and needed a goaltender. I wouldn't stay with anybody who didn't want me Freddy, if I were you."

Before Freddy could reply, his agent intervened. "You know Freddy, Mr. Blair makes a lot of sense with that statement." His agent then asked me if I would go out of his office for a few minutes while he and Freddy chatted. A few minutes later, I was invited back. "I have recommended to Freddy that he accept your offer to report to Minnesota with a few adjustments," his agent said. " I'm asking Freddy to leave here now, so I can confidentially discuss these proposed adjustments with you Mr. Blair." With that, Freddy and I shook hands and he left.

Freddy's agent suggested to me that he would report to Minnesota, if we gave him a reasonable increase in his salary and added two more years to the contract. I had studied my payroll budget at length before leaving for Boston. The proposed salary increase was not unreasonable. I instructed the agent to prepare the contract so I could take it with me back to Minneapolis. "I can't totally conclude the deal until I talk with Harry Sinden," I reminded him, "because of the player we're talking about trading to Boston for Stanfield. So I will take the contract, I will sign it, and you and I will hold it in escrow, pending a phone call back to you in the next couple of days, if we can indeed make it effective." He agreed, drew up the contract, and I returned to Minnesota. A couple of days later, Harry called me to say that he had been able to sign an agreement with Gilbert. Harry drew up the trade documents and we sent them to the Central Registry of the NHL. When this was done, I said to Harry, "Did you ever think that two NHL teams would make a deal by allowing each General Manager to go and talk to the other player's agents and players?"

"This has been amazing, but we got it done."

"I guess both of us can now talk about how two NHL GM's beat the WHA."

A few days later, Harry and I jointly announced the trade. In the St. Paul *Pioneer Press*, Sports Editor Patrick Reusse commented, "Despite his sentiments to the contrary, Wren Blair has made some good trades, and like everyone a few that didn't turn out, as the General Manager of the Minnesota North Stars. The 'Bird' however must be given credit for his latest trade. The Boston Bruins missed the playoffs last season and knew they needed a goaltender. Blair acquired high-class centerman Fred Stanfield for the unproven goaltender Gilles Gilbert."

That summer we also added to our roster Tony Featherstone, a player we drafted in the 1969 draft, and two good young players taken in the June draft that year in Blake Dunlop and Johnny Rogers. "This is a good time for the North Stars and Wren Blair," Sports Write Charley Hallman noted. "The past month has been almost sensational as the Stars have upgraded themselves tremendously in obtaining four new players. Players are Fred Stanfield, Tony Featherstone, Blake Dunlop and Johnny Rogers. In the meantime they lost only Gilles Gilbert in all of these transactions. 'We have had a good month,' Blair admitted in a conversation Friday. 'We think we have picked up some excellent hockey players, particularly Stanfield.'" Fred Stanfield played several seasons for the

North Stars. He was a decent guy and seemed to fit in with the North Star roster right away.

Meanwhile we prepared for the NHL player draft coming up in mid June in Montreal. We felt we would have difficulty in protecting players Charlie Burns, Doug Mohns, and Bob Nevin, whose careers would soon be coming to an end. At the time Burns was 37, Mohns was 39, and Nevin was 35. As always happens in the draft, other NHL clubs would have to drop one of their players to take any of them. When the draft took place on June 12, we lost Doug Mohns to Atlanta. In taking Mohns, the Flames had to drop a player. They dropped defenceman Billy Plager, whom I had drafted from Sam Pollock the day of the original expansion draft, but had been unable to protect in the expansion draft when Atlanta came in the league a couple of years earlier. When Atlanta claimed Mohns and dropped Plager, I went to the Atlanta table and asked Cliff Fletcher, the General Manager of the Atlanta club, if Billy was under contract for at least another year. When he said he was, I returned to our table and immediately claimed Plager. We lost a 39-year-old player Mohns and acquired a 27-year-old defenceman in Plager.

I was really worried about the possibility of losing Charlie Burns in the Intra-league Draft. To get around this, I talked to Larry Regan, the General Manager of the Los Angeles Kings at that time, and proposed to leave both Bob Nevin and Charlie Burns unprotected in that draft. If I left both of them unprotected, Larry would then claim them and then sell Charlie Burns back to me for $1.00. Los Angeles would get a good hockey player in Bob Nevin, whom they wouldn't have got otherwise because Larry knew that if he didn't agree to my proposal, I would protect both players. In the end it meant that I really only lost one player from the North Stars roster of three, that I couldn't protect, because we got Plager for Mohns, lost Bobby Nevin to the Kings, and re-purchased Charlie Burns.

Following the draft, an article by Charlie Hallman appeared in the St. Paul paper under the headline, "North Star Dealing Rated Tops in NHL." Charlie reported, "The Minnesota North Stars have escaped in the best shape possible. That conclusion was easily arrived at by National Hockey League people, after this weeks action in Montreal. . . . 'Wren Blair was really wheeling and dealing,' said club Public Relations Director Dick Dillman. 'Wren made the sharpest moves here, no doubt about it.'" Hallman then listed our line-up for training camp: "Centers – Dennis Hextall, Jude Drouin, Fred Stanfield, Charlie Burns, Blake Dunlop. Right Wingers – Bill Goldsworthy, Fred "Buster" Harvey, Tony Featherstone, Lou Nanne, Johnny Rogers, Terry Holbrook. Left wingers – J.P. Parise, Danny Grant, Jerry Byers, Dean Prentice, Gary Gambucci, Rod Norrish; Right defence – Barry Gibbs, Fred Barrett, Chris Ahrens, Billy Plager; Left defence — Ted Harris, Tom Reid, Dennis O'Brien, Jim McElmury, Ron Wilson; Goaltenders — Cesare Maniago, Lorne "Gump" Worsley, Fern Rivard, Lyle Carter.

Hallman concluded, "This certainly appears to be the strongest line-up in North Star history." In a later story as the season was about to open, Hallman added, "While nearly every NHL team has absorbed some losses to the WHA, the Stars have lost only a couple of fringe players. Meanwhile they have, through Blair's efforts, acquired some strong new bodies, and so coach Jack Gordon and General Manager Wren Blair, are ready for an exciting season."

We opened the schedule for the 1973-74 season at home against the Montreal Canadiens on October 9th. Opening against a team like Montreal is never easy – we lost 5-2 – and things didn't get any easier as the season progressed. After an especially disappointing road trip during November, ending in 5-0 loss to Boston, Jack Gordon let fly in the local newspaper: "It's a damn disgrace. We have no desire. When you're out shot 14-4 in the first period, you might as well give up." Jack and I were really concerned with the apparent lazy play of the team. We talked about doing something to shake up the club, and on November 10, we traded our Ted Harris, our captain, to the Detroit Red Wings for defenceman Gary Bergman, who had played on the Team Canada club.

A few days later the Stars defeated the Los Angeles Kings at home in Minnesota 5-2, and it looked like we might be coming out of our slow start in the early season, but we were already deep in the lower standings of the West Division in seventh place, only three points ahead of the lowly California Seals in the cellar. Then on November 19th, Jack Gordon suddenly resigned, citing health reasons. Jack told me that his nerves were so bad he couldn't even hold a cup to drink tea. I immediately called up Parker MacDonald from our farm club in New Haven, where he was the General Manager and Coach. I replaced Parker in New Haven with Charlie Burns, where he had been a player and assistant coach to MacDonald. Jack stayed on with the organization to scout in the Central Hockey League.

A month or so later, two journalists and one of our owners came to me and said, "If you tell anyone what I am going to tell you, I will deny it. But Walter Bush, President of the club, has told us that you are finished at the end of the season." I wrestled with the idea if I should go to Walter and confront him without naming any names and ask him to be honest with me in his reply. In the end I decided against that, because I felt that if Walter was indeed going to make a change where I was concerned, he would have the fortitude to come and tell me himself.

The club never really recovered that season following Jack's resignation. Parker worked very hard with the team – we had some good stretches, rising to fifth place at the All-Star break – but by mid February, we had slid back to seventh place. By March 15, we had moved a position higher, but it was tough slugging. Parker had the team fighting every way he could think of to gain a playoff spot.

On April 1, we had moved up another notch to fifth place, but that particular year, only the top four teams in each division would qualify for the playoffs. We trailed Atlanta by 7 points and with only four games remaining, which meant that we had to win all of our remaining games, while the Flames lost all of theirs. This miracle didn't happen. At the end of the schedule, we found ourselves out of the playoffs for the first time in many years. I suspected that my days with the North Stars were coming to an end.

A few days after our season ended, I suggested to Walter Bush that we get together to discuss the future of the club. When I walked into his office, I could sense immediately that something was wrong. Before I had a chance to sit down, Walter said, "Wren we are going to make a change." I knew immediately what he meant, but I wasn't going to make it any easier for him, especially after the rumors I had heard months before.

So I said to him, "Parker hasn't even had a full season of coaching yet. I think we should give him another chance."

Walter kind of hedged around a bit and then said, "Well uh uh, I don't mean Parker."

"Well, who are you going to get rid of . . . the trainers? That's really going to make an impact."

Walter fidgeted around a bit more, and then said, "Uh uh, no, you."

"Me! We missed the playoffs once in the last five or six years, and you go all the way to the General Manager?"

"Wren, this is no easier for me than it is for you."

"I doubt that Walter. As I understand it, I'm the one that is going to be let go."

"Yes, but it's not easy. You've done a great job here Wren, and nobody wants to see you get hurt in this. So if you would like to resign, I will see that you are protected with excellent comments from the North Stars, and so on."

"Walter, I'm from Canada, and I don't think Canadians are ones to quit that easily, so I'm not about to resign. Also there's a little thing about two more years left in my contract. So I guess the only thing left to do is to let you know where to send my check on the 15th and the 30th of the each month."

I knew Walter felt bad. We had been together a little over nine years, through good times and bad. "Walter, you hired me into the NHL. I will be forever grateful to you guys for that. Now the full pressure of this move is now going to fall on you, and the next go around it may be you getting fired as the President of this club. In any event, thank you for the memories."

Despite my bravado, I was pretty shook up as I made my way back to my office. When I walked in, my secretary for many years, Marilyn Vaughan, said, "You're back pretty early from the meeting."

I looked at her for a minute. "Marilyn, I just got fired."

"Don't start that stupid stuff, you're always putting me on."

"I'm telling you honestly. I can't be anymore serious. I'm finished here immediately."

"Well, if that's the case, than I'm through too." I could tell she was serious. In early October or 1967 I had hired Marilyn, and she stuck with me when I took over ownership of the Saginaw Gears and later when I became one of the owners of the Pittsburgh Penguins. One of the things that I had asked Marilyn to do shortly after she started was to keep a scrapbook of all games and transactions of each season. That scrapbook has proved invaluable in writing this book.

That night when I got home, I went downstairs to the rec room, mixed a drink, and another drink, which was followed by many more drinks. That year my brother Gerald had given me a record by Glen Campbell entitled 'Glen Sings Hank Williams.' I really loved it, all of Hank Williams biggest hits. Nobody I have ever heard before or since could sing those sad songs like Glen

Campbell. I had a few more drinks, and then turned on that recording. Then it all really hit me. I was getting a little bit woozy from the drinks, plus these sad songs, and I think I cried at that bar for hours off and on. It just hit me so hard. By the next day that was out of my system, and I was ready to get going. Life goes on, and it certainly did for me, because in less than a year, I became one of the owners of the Penguins. Incidentally, as soon as that happened, I called Walter and told him that I was relieving the North Stars of any further payments owed to me, although I still had more than a year left on my contract.

A local writer asked me what it felt like to be fired by the North Stars after so many years. "Obviously, it came as a big shock," I said, "but perhaps I should have seen it coming. I feel like a parent who adopts a child, and after nine years and you've pretty well raised them through their formative years, someone comes along and says, 'I'll take that child now.' You know how that would feel. That's how I feel about being fired, because the North Stars, for over nine years, were certainly my baby." I did suspect that the team had been stolen from me. When Jack Gordon had quit the North Stars that season, he told me he would never coach again, but then he was named the GM and Coach.

Jack began immediately to trade the players that I had worked so hard to acquire. J.P. Parise and Jude Drouin went to the New York Islanders, Danny Grant and Dennis Hextall to the Detroit Red Wings, "Buster" Harvey to Atlanta. J.P. and Jude became part of the powerhouse Islanders team that won the Stanley Cup. Danny Grant had a 50-goal season with Detroit. It really hurt me more than anything to see the team that I had built, dismantled in such a way.

Less than two years after I left, Gordie Ritz called me in Pittsburgh to tell me that they had fired Walter Bush and that he was now the President of the team. The team had missed the playoffs again and the crowds had dwindled down to 5,000 and 6,000 people. The owners of the club began losing big-time money. Not long after, the North Stars owners were forced to sell the team to the Gund Brothers, who owned the Cleveland team that had joined the NHL in the wake of the collapse of the WHL. The league allowed Cleveland and the North Stars amalgamate their best players onto one club. The day that meeting was held, I called Jim Gregory, who was the Vice-President of the NHL at this time, and asked him what had happened. "The Governors decided to amalgamate the players, Wren, to get the North Stars quality back to where you had it a few years ago." A few years later, I was at the draft meetings in Montreal, where I met a writer from the Minnesota days. "Wren, I want to tell you something confidentially. Recently I went to visit the majority owner of the North Stars in your days, and asked him what happened to the Minnesota club. He said, 'I can tell you , but you must promise you can never write this.' He told me, 'We only made two mistakes. One was when we let Wren Blair become the owner of the Saginaw Gears Hockey Club. The second was when we fired him.'"

Lou Nanne, one of the players I had acquired for the North Stars, was named the club's General Manager. With the best players of two clubs and Louie's leadership, the North Stars club returned to respectability, but the crowds never seemed to return. I was totally shocked when my beloved North Stars left Minnesota altogether to become the Dallas Stars. Minnesota is now back in the NHL, with a new rink, a new franchise, and new owners. The team is called the Minnesota Wild. I still talk to some of the players who played for me. Tom Reid contacted me a short while ago to invite me to a reunion. "Wren, there are 10 of us that still live in the Twin Cities area who played for you, and those guys have asked me if you come to see us when your book is published. We'd like to get together with the 'Bird' again."

PROFILE

Jim Finks, Billy Martin & Vice-President Hubert Humphrey

WHEN I WENT TO MINNESOTA in 1966, Billy Martin was a third base coach for the Minnesota Twins. The next year he moved up to become the Manager. As a result Billy and I would see each other a fair amount as speakers at Sports Celebrity Dinners and things of that nature. I also became a good friend of Jim Finks, who was the General Manager of the Minnesota Vikings NFL Team at that time.

From time to time Billy and I would go out for a couple of drinks, but it wasn't long before I told Billy that I wouldn't go out publicly with him to bars any longer. Billy was a fiery individual, and more often than not, would get into a scrap in the bar with someone who might have said the wrong thing to him, in his opinion. I liked Billy a great deal, and we became very close friends. I also spent some time with Jim Finks, and gradually the three of us decided to meet each Monday evening behind closed doors, over at the Holiday Inn on 494 West in Bloomington, Minnesota. We used to get a small conference room where we would have dinner and a few drinks, without encountering frustrated fans who would sometimes say things that were better left unsaid to us.

Not long after we began our Monday night ritual, a new manager had come on board at the Holiday Inn. One night he said to us, "Guys, let me set you up with a better room for your Monday dinners, complete with your own bartender in the room, and you can stay as long as you want. I just insist on one rule that we can agree on, and that is the Hotel will send you guys home in a limo, so you are not driving late at night after having a few drinks. Then we will deliver each of your cars the next morning to your home, and you will be set for your regular business day. The Hotel will make only a small nominal charge for this service, but it is safer for you guys and safer for the hotel." We all thought this was a great idea, and so for almost two years, until the Twins let Billy go, we did this.

Jim Finks had worked in the Canadian Football League with the Winnipeg Blue Bombers, where he introduced his sons to hockey. When Jim and his family moved to Minnesota, he bought a home in Edina, not too far from where my family lived. All of our kids went to the Edina High School. Later Edina built another high school: the old one was called Edina East and the new one became Edina West. Jim's kids went to Edina West. They had an excellent hockey program there and both of Jim's sons played on their teams.

One day Jim said to me, "Wren, how come both my kids want to be hockey players and not football players?" Football, of course, was Jim's profession.

"Jim, they must take after their mother, because they are smart kids and know that hockey is a better game than football." In fun Jimmy threw a little bit of lettuce from his salad across the table at me, and we laughed about that many times later.

Billy Martin piped up. "All your kids are nuts, baseball's the better game of all three." We had fun debating the merits of all these great games for the next couple of years.

On a couple of occasions, Jim Finks gave my family and a couple of our friends a private box at Met Stadium to see the Vikings play. They were high in the standings in the NFL at that time. Jim moved on to become the General Manager of the Chicago Bears, and then took over the job with the New Orleans Saints.

From Billy Martin and from Calvin Griffin, who owned the Minnesota Twins Baseball Club in those years, I received complimentary tickets to the Twins games. I always loved baseball. Years before, I had coached several very good softball teams.

After Billy left the Twin Cities, he took over as the manager of the Detroit Tigers before moving on to coach the New York Yankees. Billy had played for the Yankees during the era of Mickey Mantle and Whitey Ford, his two good friends. While managing the Yankees, Billy's way of playing ball often clashed with the plans of team owner George Steinbrenner. The scraps between Billy and George became legendary over the next few years. George fired and rehired him on three different occasions, I recall.

During one of those times when George and Billy were squabbling, we met Billy in Las Vegas by chance. We were staying at the Dunes Hotel, where a very good friend of mine, Charlie Speck, was the Pit Boss. Just as you come out of the casino, there's a small little curved bar to the side, and sitting there was one lonely figure, Billy Martin. I walked up quietly and said, "Martin, I don't think you're so damn tough."

These were fighting words to Billy, and he swung around with his eyes blazing, then let his guard down. "Wren, what are you doing here?"

"Better still, what are you doing here?"

"Wren, you won't believe this. Let me tell you what I am doing here. I'm still under contract to big George, and every year the Yankees run a special plane trip to Vegas for senior citizens. I was assigned to be the host of those people on this trip here." Billy and I spent another hour or so together talking about old times. He had to leave that night as their junket to Vegas was just concluding.

Several years later I was visiting with a partner of mine in Naples, Florida, Larry Needler. Larry was a partner in our hotel operation in Haliburton, Ontario. At the Naples Beach and Golf Club Resort where I was staying they offered a free cocktail and food on Sunday afternoons. I was standing in the line-up when I heard the two young lads right in front of me talking to each other. The one lad said, "See that line-up in the pool area?

They're waiting to get Billy Martin's autograph." I jumped lines and grabbed a scrap of paper. About 20 minutes later, I made it to the front of the line. People had been shoving a piece of paper in front of Billy and he had been signing his autograph without even looking up. I slid my piece of paper forward, and then leaned over and whispered in his ear, "Martin, I don't think you're nearly as tough as you think you are." Once again, he jerked his head up with his eyes blazing, and I started to grin at him. "Wren, is it ever good to see you," he said as he put his arms around my shoulder. Then he looked down the line at the fans and said, "That's all for today folks. My good friend and I are going to spend the rest of the evening together."

During the evening I told him I had read his book, *Number One*, and he asked if I had read his new book, *Billy Ball*. He said he would send me an autographed copy. One day in November that book appeared in my mailbox. I told my daughter to remind me to send a thank you letter to Billy. It's funny how life turns for all of us. I never got that letter written. On Christmas night, Billy was killed when his pickup truck went over a small cliff right near his home in Binghampton, New York. Billy and an old Detroit Tigers friend were going down to the local bar to have a drink. Billy was not driving the truck, but unfortunately he had failed to do up his seatbelt.

Jim Finks has passed away as well. Not too many days ever pass that I don't think of Jim and Billy and our good times together.

Another fond memory of my years in Minnesota came in the early 1970s when we had an NHL Meeting of the Governors and General Managers in New York, at the Waldorf-Astoria Hotel. At that meeting, the New York Rangers organization provided us with tickets to the first Ali-Fraser fight in the new Madison Square Gardens. We were also invited to a reception following the fight in

Room 200 of the Gardens. Representing the meeting on behalf of the North Stars besides me were three of our owners, Gordie Ritz, Bob McNulty, and Walter Bush.

We had great seats in the second tier. Right below us in the first tier were all of the VIPs — movie stars, celebrities, politicians, all dressed in evening attire. I spotted Frank Sinatra and Bing Crosby in this group. The fight was very close, but at the end of 15 rounds, the decision went in favor in Joe Fraser. Many of the fans booed loudly.

When the fight was over, we went to Room 200 for the cocktail party. Among the celebrities and politicians attending was Joe DiMaggio. Walter, Gordie, Bob, and I were in the throng enjoying hors d'oeuvres and cocktails when all of a sudden we felt an arm embracing all of us. "How are my Minnesota friends tonight?" We looked back and it was Vice-President Hubert Humphrey. I had met the Vice-President a year or so earlier when Walter Bush asked me to give him a tour around our dressing room and introduce him to the North Star players. Vice-President Humphrey was from Minnesota. He had served as the Mayor of Minneapolis and the Governor of Minnesota.

"I am having a late night dinner at Toots Shore's," Vice-President Humphrey continued, "and I would like my Minnesota friends to be my guests for dinner. My assistant will come to you after I am in my limousine downstairs, and bring you to my car." With that he excused himself. About 40 minutes later we proceeded to his limo, where I sat beside the Vice-President.

"Wren, what's wrong with our North Stars?" The team had not been playing well.

"Mr. Vice-President, I really don't know. We had a good year last year, but just can't seem to turn the corner to get moving again."

At that point Vice-President Humphrey said, "Wren, could we

just please make it Hubert and Wren the rest of the evening?"

"Mr. Vice-President, I don't know if I can do that. It's very difficult for me."

"Don't worry about it. All of my close friends call me Hubert, and I would like to feel that we are friends."

When we arrived at Toots, there was a red carpet strung from the door right out to the curb. Standing there was Toots himself, obviously an old friend of the the Vice-President, for he greeted him, playfully. "Where the hell have you been Hubert? You are a half hour late." Toots Shore's in those days was a prime hang-out for sports celebrities, a favorite of Jack Dempsey's before Jack built his own bar, as well as Joe DiMaggio, Mickey Mantle, many of the Rangers players.

Almost everyone in that restaurant came over to our table to talk to the Vice-President. They would all tell him their names, where they were from, and so on. No matter where they lived in all the far-flung regions of the United States, when they mentioned that community, the Vice-President would say things like, "Oh, Omaha Nebraska, do you know so and so there?" Next person would say, "From Louisville, Kentucky, do you know Joe Smith there and whatever business he was in?" All of them would say, "Oh yes, we don't know him personally, but we know his business." The Vice-President would say, "You tell Joe, or Bill, or Sam, that Hubert says hello."

I couldn't believe his memory — all those people in and all those communities. I leaned over to the Vice-President and said, "How do you remember all these names?"

"I took an extensive course in that subject, and it's been very helpful to me. Since I'm sure you meet tons of people in the hockey business, in many, many communities, I would recommend that course to you as well."

There is no politician I have admired more than Vice-President

Humphrey that night. I couldn't believe that a kid off the streets in Oshawa was sitting having dinner with the Vice-President of the United States. I am so grateful to the game of hockey for giving me the chance to meet such fine men. I received a Christmas card from Vice-President Humphrey every year until he died, simply signed, "Hubert and Muriel."

Wren Blair with his back to his players, leaning against the glass between the North Stars player bench and the fans, saying to his players: "Just tell me when the red light goes on behind our net. I can't stand to watch this any longer."

Wren Blair in the coach's office in Minnesota following a game: "What do the fans want from us anyway, we're in first place."

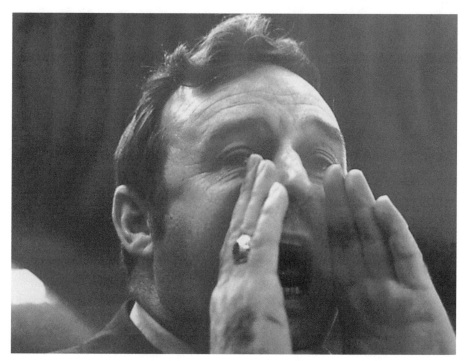

Wren Blair on the bench in Minnesota. Note the championship ring from the Whitby Dunlops 2nd Allan Cup Championship, 1958-59.

Wren Blair gave up his coaching duties mid way through the 1968-69 season, but returned to the bench later in the season, much to the delight of the Minnesota fans.

10

The Saginaw Gears and the IHL Championship

WHEN I WAS IN MINNESOTA, we played two exhibition games each year in Duluth, Minnesota, one against the Chicago Black-hawks and one against the Detroit Red Wings. We played the games over a span of three days and it was always a good trip for us. We always packed the new Duluth Arena for both games. The third year we played there I picked up our share of the gate from Bill Fifer, the Assistant Manager of the arena, and said, "Bill, I'll see you next year."

Bill hesitated for a moment. "No, you won't see me next year. I've signed a contract to manage the new arena in Saginaw, Michigan. The arena is still being built, so I won't be leaving here for six or eight months yet. By the way, that brings up another matter. Part of the criteria for my job is that I have to get an International Hockey League club to play out of the new arena in Saginaw. Do you know anyone who would like to put a team in Saginaw?"

I immediately thought of Tommy Ivan, the General Manager of the Chicago Blackhawks, who owned the Flint Generals with Frank Gallagher. Flint was a great franchise, only 37 miles from Saginaw, I had no doubt that Saginaw would be equally as good, especially since Saginaw was building a new facility. The new Saginaw Civic Center would seat at least 1500 more people than the Flint IMA Arena.

"Yeah, I know a guy who might be interested," I told Bill, "but I don't think it would be fair to him to bring up his name without dis-cussing this with him first. When you get down to Saginaw, why don't you call me and maybe I'll be able to come down and discuss it with you."

About six months later, Bill contacted me and I arranged to travel to Saginaw. Bill picked me up at the Tri-City Airport, and as we were driving into Saginaw, he asked, "Wren, when we talked before you said you could probably tell me who would, perhaps, like to operate a franchise in Saginaw."

"Yes, Bill, I can tell you now, but it is extremely confidential."

"Who, I won't say a word to anyone."

"Me."

"You?" Bill responded incredulously. "Do you think we could get some players from Minnesota placed here? We have a luncheon scheduled for today with the arena board and they asked me to bring you down. Mr. Paul Wendler will be chairing the luncheon. Do you think we could tell the arena board today that you might be interested in putting a team in Saginaw?"

"Let me think about that, Bill, until we get to the meeting. My problem is that in my contract with Minnesota, it says that I cannot take any other job, hockey or otherwise, without written permission from the North Stars. And I don't have that yet." I had thought about this problem all the way down to the meeting, but felt that I had to get started because it was my understanding that four other groups were also bidding to operate the franchise.

After lunch, Bill stood up and introduced me. "Gentlemen, I told Bill on the way here today that I am interested in putting a team in Saginaw."

Paul Wendler immediately rose to say, "Mr. Blair, I can't tell you how exciting that is for us." I explained my situation with the North Stars and instructed the board, "This must be kept completely under wraps. No one can breathe a word."

After the luncheon, Bill took me down to show me the new arena. Although it wasn't finished yet, I could tell it was going to be an outstanding facility. When it was finished, this rink had a seating capacity for 5,400 people. Attached to the rink was a beautiful reception facility, called Unity Hall, which could cater to banquets for more than 1,000 people. Within this facility, there was also a smaller room, called the Garden Room, for smaller meetings accommodating 50 to 100 people. Attached to that was a full-blown theatre, called the Heritage Theatre, with a full Broadway stage that could accommodate 2,600 people. I had never seen a facility like that, before or since, in a small community.

When I got back to Minnesota, I wrote a letter to Mr. Wendler explaining that I could stock the team with players from Minnesota and other NHL teams. I already had made contact with Jim Gregory of the Toronto Maple Leafs and George Maguire of the Los Angeles Kings. I pointed out to him that it would be virtually impossible to operate a minor-league team without contributions from NHL teams. I doubted if the other people bidding for the franchise had this to offer. Some time later Paul called me in a panic. "Wren, all hell is breaking loose here. There are rumors going around town that you are involved in bringing a team here. I don't know how they got started, but I have to make an announcement today, and we are prepared to grant you the franchise. However, because of this leak, we must make the announcement today."

"Jeez. I haven't even approached my boss, because I didn't know if I was going to get the franchise. Can you give me a number where I can reach you, and I will go and talk to the president of Minnesota right away and get back to you."

I went down the hall and walked into Walter Bush's office and explained the situation to him and offered him the chance to join me in this enterprise. "That might be interesting. We could put players in there, couldn't we? Well, I don't see anything wrong with that and everything here is hockey related."

One of the conditions I had to meet was to secure a franchise in the IHL within the next six months. I had to be fully capitalized with the bank on net worth statements. And I had to come up with an arena contract with the board that both parties could live with. The first thing I did was contact Bill Beagan, Commissioner of the IHL. Bill was a former linesman in the NHL and I had known him for years. He explained to me that the franchise fee for an IHL franchise was $50,000, with a payment of 20 percent down and the balance payable within one year. I asked for a meeting with the IHL board to make my pitch. I put up the $10,000 fee immediately and that went a long way to securing the franchise. I now had six months to pay off the balance. I then negotiated a four-year contract with the arena management, paying 12 percent the first year, 13 percent the second year, 14 the third, and 15 percent the final year of the four-year agreement.

As this was happening, I put up huge billboards all over Saginaw announcing the coming of IHL hockey. We held a contest to name the team – the winner would get a pair of season tickets — but even as we received over 6,000 letters, I knew in my heart the name we were going to use. General Motors had a huge business in Saginaw where they made all of the steering gears for cars. Eighty percent of the people in Saginaw worked at that plant. I knew I was going to call the team the Saginaw Gears. I had also decided that I was going to use the Miami Dolphin colors for the team – aqua blue, tangerine, and white – and arranged for the seats in the arena to be made with this color scheme. I hired Pat Shetler, a former NHL linesman, to work on marketing the team and Al Blade, a radio broadcaster for the Port Huron IHL team, to assist with the marketing efforts and to do play-by-play for the local radio station. I don't know anybody in the history of hockey that has been as good a salesman or as personable as Al was. In Minnesota, our play-by-play man was Al Shaver, and I added his son Wally to the Saginaw group to assist Al with the play-by-play. The sales staff did a great job, especially in promoting group nights. We had every school in Saginaw involved in school promotions. We had firemen nights; police nights; and season-ticket holder nights where they could bring another person to the game at a discounted ticket price. We had service club nights, and ladies night. We never had a game where we didn't have at least 20 promotions going on. In the first year, we had 22 sellouts, 5,463 people per game, and many nights we turned up to 1,000 people away.

The year 1972 was an Olympic year and Murray Williamson, a good friend of mine, had been named coach of the United States Olympic hockey team. They were heading overseas in February, and I invited the team to play an exhibition game in Saginaw. I made arrangements for a DC3 charter for them and agreed to pay $3,000. We hadn't put the Gears team together by that time, so I gathered a team of old pros and called them the Saginaw Stars. Parker MacDonald, Leo Boivin, and Bill Gadsby agreed to play, along with several other retired NHLers and a few players with Senior A experience.

The morning of the game arrived. It was a bitter cold January day. At 9:00 a.m. Murray called me from Minnesota to say that their DC3 charter plane was on the tarmac at the Minnesota Airport, but it was so cold they couldn't get the engines on the plane started. I panicked. "Murray," I said, "Please don't tell me that. We've got a sold-out arena here. More than that, all the equipment for the Saginaw Stars team, including sticks, is on board that plane." (I had borrowed equipment from North Stars trainer Stan Waylett to use.) I then told Murray that all the guys that were going to play for me were arriving early for a noon hour skate, but he told me it wouldn't be possible to make it to Saginaw for this skate.

By noon hour most of the guys who were going to play for the pick up Saginaw Stars had arrived. They had their skates with them, a few had sticks. When they took to the ice without equipment, they looked strange. As they skated around, there were two maintenance workers getting the building ready for the game. One of them said, "Hey man, I thought all of those hockey players had sticks."

The other one replied, "No, no, man, only some of them use sticks. Don't be so stupid." I was flabbergasted. Cripes, here I am bringing a hockey game to Saginaw and they don't know anymore about hockey than that. The charter arrived between 5:00 and 6:00 p.m. that evening, but the game wasn't much of a contest because our guys were old and out of shape. The spirit was willing, but the legs were weak. In the end we lost to the Olympic Team 9-2.

After the game, I threw a reception across the road from the arena at the Saginaw Club, a well-respected men's club. I invited the Mayor of Saginaw, the City Council, Federal and State Representatives, many prominent business people, the entire 1972 Olympic Team, and our 'Stars'. This event certainly improved our public relations in the community and showed that the people of Saginaw would support hockey, even if they weren't yet sure what and when to cheer.

I hired Don Perry, who had played in the old Eastern League for many years and later coached in the EHL, to coach the Saginaw Gears Hockey Club. For the 12 years I owned the club, Don was my only coach. In the summer of 1972, Don and I traveled all over the country signing up players to play in Saginaw. Jim Gregory gave us some players from the Leafs organization, and George Maguire optioned three players to me from LA. We added five players from Minnesota, three of whom we had taken in the draft that year. The club was comprised of the following players: Ray Belanger (goal) Juri Kudisovs, Stu Irving, Dennis Romaneski, Raynald Tessier, Cal Hammond (goal), Elgin McCann, Butch Morris, Marcel Comeau, Jim Maertz, Mike Hornby, Murray McNeil, Steve Lyon, Tom Thomson, Mike Legge, Bruce McIntosh, Dennis Desrosiers, and Russ Friesen. Our trainer was Gunner Garrett. Some of the teams in the league that first year were: Saginaw Gears, Port Huron Flags, Columbus Owls, Flint Generals, Kalamazoo Wings, Milwaukee Admirals, Dayton Gems, Toledo Blades, Des Moines, Iowa and Fort

Wayne Komets. When the season finished, we were in fifth place in the Eastern Division. We ended with 63 points, the same number as the Fort Wayne Comets, but missed the playoffs because the Comets had more wins than we did. The Gears would never miss the play-offs again while I was involved with the team.

That first season, we sold well over 2,000 season tickets. There is an old adage that says whatever your season ticket base is, your walkup crowd will match that. We had 22 sellouts and never under 4,500 at any game that year. Dennis Desrosiers led our team with 97 points, made up of 60 goals and 37 assists, over 74 games. At the same time, he drew 186 minutes in penalties.

The Saginaw Gears became an outstanding franchise for the IHL, for the city, for the arena, for the fans, and for me, personally. In the 1973-74 season, we finished in second place in the Northern Division behind the Muskegon Mohawks, but went on in the play-offs to meet Des Moines for the Turner Cup, emblematic of the IHL championship. We lost the seventh game in Des Moines. When we lost that final game — I breathed a tremendous sigh of relief.

Al Savill, who owned the Columbus Owls, and I had become good friends. Al came up for the final game and stood with me up on the catwalk to watch the game. "Wren, that's a damn shame. You should have won, you had the better team."

"Al, if you repeat what I'm going to say, I'll deny it, but I am so happy we lost." It's better sometimes early in history of a franchise to be the bridesmaid for a while, rather than the bride. If you win in a new franchise too early, you have nothing to sell but another win. If you don't, the fans become sour and it really hurts the franchise in the long term.

The team continued to play well in the next few years, with a line-ups that included Wayne Zuk, Dave Westner, D'Arcy Ryan, Marcel Comeau, Jim McMahon, Gordie Malinoski, Dave Miglia, Garry Sittler (brother of Darryl Sittler of the Toronto Maple Leafs),

Joe Leduc, Stu Irving, Mike Ruest, Marcel Comeau, Greg Hotham, Kevin Kemp, Jean-Marie Nicol, John Gravel, Paul Evans, Borden Smith (who had played for me in Clinton), Dennis Desrosiers, and Harvey Stewart. That year we may have had the best goaltending in the history of the IHL. Mario Lessard was placed with us by the L.A. Kings right out of the Quebec junior league, and part way through the season, we added Mike Palmateer from the Toronto Marlboros. Mario became a stand-out goalie for the Kings, as did Mike for the Maple Leafs several years later.

In 1975-76, we won the Turner Cup, led by Paul Evans, who scored 112 points, made up of 50 goals and 62 assists, followed by Dennis Desrosiers with 96 points and 255 minutes in penalties, second in that department to Gordie Malinoski, who racked up 280 minutes. One reason for our victory may have been our ability to kill penalties when the playoffs came!

At the end of the 1975-76 season, my contract with the Saginaw Civic Center board expired. They opened the discussion to renew the agreement by asking for 20 percent of the gate, which was a percentage unheard of in hockey in those days. Over a number of weeks of negotiations, I went as high as 16 percent, and they countered with 19 percent. By this time, we were well into August and I still had to get organized for the coming season. At our next meeting I erupted in frustration, "Gentlemen, let's adjourn this meeting and schedule one more. Only this time, we'll hold it at center ice at the Civic Center. I will install a table at center ice, suitably equipped with loud speakers hooked up, and invite all the season ticket holders to the meeting and serve them champagne and caviar."

One of the board members questioned, "Why would you do that?"

"I want the fans to see just how greedy and stupid you guys are and I don't think the fans will be too happy."

A few days after that, they requested another meeting. This time I invited my lawyer in Toronto, Terry Donnelly to join me. We got them to drop to 17 percent, but I was still adamant that I was not going to pay more than 16. Finally, I said, "Gentlemen, if we can't resolve this today, I am going to instruct Mr. Donnelly to sue you for restraint of trade."

A board member asked, "What does that mean?"

"It means that you are creating a situation where you have the only arena in this community and you are forcing the Saginaw Gears out of business."

At that point, the chairman asked if the board could be excused for a few minutes. When they came back in, they conceded, "Wren, here's the deal. We will go with 16 percent during the regular season, but move that up to 17 percent for the playoffs."

"Fine, we've got a deal."

We didn't have an office in the Civic Center at that time, but my office was just a few yards down the street. As Terry and I were walking back to my office, he said to me, "You know, Wren, you cannot sue a government body, nobody can."

"I know that, but I don't think they realized that. Anyway, it worked, so let's not worry about it." Terry and I have laughed for years over this.

In the 1977-78 season, we added Pierre Gagnon, Lorne Mollenkin (in goal), Bobby Gladney (another Toronto Marlboro who moved on to the NHL), Dan Eastman, and Warren Holmes, who played Major Junior A the year before in Ottawa and still lives in Saginaw today. Lorne Mollenkin eventually became the coach of the Chicago Blackhawks. In the 1978-79 season, new players joining the team were Doug Keans (a goaltender who eventually ended up in the NHL with the Bruins), Lynn Jorgenson, Tim Thomlinson, Keith Johnson, Larry Hopkins (a former Oshawa General), Mark Toffolo, Scott Jesse, Jean-Paul Fountas, and Claude Larochelle (one of our best acquisitions). We won the Turner Cup again in 1980-81.

At the beginning of the 1980-81 season, I had decided to sell the Gears to a group of eight businessmen in Saginaw. When it became time to draw up the official papers, the group surprised me by saying they would buy only 10 percent each and wanted me to retain 20 percent and stay on as General Manager for the next six years. A few years earlier, Jim Gregory and I had opened the Pine-Stone Inn and Country Club, a resort hotel, and by 1980 it was growing by leaps and bounds. We needed some more capital, so I wanted to transfer some of the equity I was going to get from the Gears into PineStone. After the group's proposal, I told them I wanted to think about it overnight, but I felt that if I turned them down, I might kill the entire sale. I also thought that if these owners were like owners I had worked with, I could probably make them sick of me pretty fast. And that's exactly what happened down the road.

Although the 1980-81 Gears team won the second Turner Cup for the City of Saginaw and we were expanding our fan support to Bay City and Midland, the franchise soon deteriorated. The new owners made many bad decisions against my will — I kept getting outvoted 7-3. One of the owners kept saying, "We asked Wren to stay on because we don't know anything about hockey, and yet you continue to ignore his advice."

The new owners first offended the local newspaper, *The Saginaw News*, and then the rest of the local media. My custom had been to send press releases to the newspaper the evening before a press conference so the report would appear the day of the conference and at the same time as they were broadcast on radio. I called the press conferences for 11 a.m., about the same time the *Saginaw News* hit the streets as an evening paper, so it was fair to all parties. The board voted to end this practice, 7-3.

They next challenged my practice of giving complimentary

tickets to the media. We customarily gave away 300 to 325 tickets, 50 to the visiting team (a league rule), 50 to the home team, two to each staff member, and about 70 to our sponsors. We also gave two tickets to any newspaper, radio, or television reporter or announcer if they agreed to mention the Gears on their show. There were 14 radio stations and three newspapers in the area. You can't buy that kind of publicity, but the board chose to stop this practice.

A few days after this decision was made public, 'Muddy' Waters, the weatherman for the local television station, called me. He came to every game, and when the Gears scored, he did this special little dance that the tv cameraman always captured for use on the news the next day. "You know, Wren, I guess we, in the media, didn't value you enough. I just want you to know, Wren, that as long as I live I will never set foot in the Saginaw Civic Center again to watch a Gears game."

To top things off, the board next offended our season ticket holders. One board member proposed to sell tickets for less than a buck to draw a crowd. "Wren, I've got a great idea, you're a pro-moter, so you can't be opposed to this," he said. "We're going to have a 98-cent night to get a big crowd. We'll have a sellout. You can't be opposed to that." When I disagreed with him, he wanted to know why.

"Well, let me give you an example. I'm a guy who bought two season tickets to the Gears games for me and for my wife. I paid about $520 — $260 each. Now, this other guy comes in and sits down beside me. 'Hey, this is great, I've never seen a Gears' game before.' I reply, "Yeh, that's why I have season tickets. How did you happen to come here tonight?" The 98-cent fans answers, 'Oh, they've got a big promotion tonight – 98-cent tickets – so I bought six of them. My whole family is here.'" As I pointed out to the board, "Do you think that season-ticket holder is going to buy sea-son tickets next year, after hearing that people are getting in for 98 cents and he's paid full price for tickets for every game?" I voted against the plan but I lost again.

The following year, the season ticket base dropped almost in half. I was getting nervous about my 20 percent stake in the company and called an emergency meeting to tender my shares. "Look, fellows," I said, "you can no longer afford me. I will discount the remaining four years on the purchase of this club. In the meantime, you will release me from my contract. They asked me if I would leave the room so they could discuss it. When I returned, they said we had a deal. I immediately left and headed back to Canada.

Despite these problems, I must say that the experience of owning the Saginaw Gears Hockey Club was one of the most exciting times I've had in hockey. The fans jammed the arena through most of my stay there. We had a Blue Line Club in the arena, and the fans used to come there for dinner, and then after the game, we would bring in various groups to play music until the traffic from the parking ramp slowed down. My daughter Jill used to sing in the Blue Line Club. The people in the City of Saginaw were great, not only to me, but also to the players. I later formed a corporation there called Wren Blair, Inc., and in 2002, I returned to Saginaw to lead a team from this good hockey town into the OHL Junior A League.

PROFILE

Jim Gregory

I HAD FIRST MET JIM GREGORY in 1962 while he was operating the Neil McNeil Maroons in the Major Junior A Metro League in Toronto and I was operating the Oshawa Generals. After one game we had a bit of a confrontation in the old pressroom at Maple Leaf

Gardens, just across from the visitors dressing room. I was upset because Jim had let the top eight or nine players on the Maroons go home for Christmas just before a game with Whitby. I asked Jim if we could play the Maroons minus the same eight players. He didn't like my suggestion. Sometimes friendships begin in an unfriendly way. That is the way it happened between Jim and me. We were working on many committees in the league and began to see a great deal of each other.

In 1964 my brother Lyle and I purchased some land on Koshlong Lake in Haliburton, Ontario, to build a Boys Camp that would give a full camp life to young lads — swimming, canoeing, water skiing, hiking, arts and craft, as well as three hours of hockey instruction each day. A few months later, my brother was transferred by his employer to Europe and didn't feel he could be much use to me as a partner, so I bought his interest in the land. Later that summer Jim Gregory was coming up to Minden to play golf with me. When we finished, we went to my cottage to barbecue steaks. When we finished dinner, I said, "I'd like to take you out to Koshlong Lake to see some land that I purchased." It was only seven or eight miles from my cottage. When we got out there, Jim looked around and finally said, "This is really beautiful." The property had over a 1,000 feet of clear running sand beach. Going away from the water were hundreds of beautiful birch trees. "What are you going to do with this land?" Jim asked. I told him about my plans for a boys camp and hockey school, and when he said he thought that was a good idea, I proposed that he become my partner.

"Why would you take in a partner? You have the land, you have the idea, why a partner?"

"First of all, I could use an investor to share the cost of the project, but even more so, there is no use of having a boys camp for hockey if it is not full. You probably have a list at Maple Leaf Gardens of every Pee-Wee, Bantam, and Midget age players in the city.

I think that would be a natural marketing tool. We could write to everyone of those kids and send them brochures." Before Jim left to go home to Toronto, we had agreed to form a limited company.

Shortly thereafter, I negotiated an agreement with the Haliburton Arena for summer ice. We began construction of the cabins, dining hall, recreation building, and administration office. A year later, everything was in place. We had mailed hundreds of letters to young aspiring hockey players all over the country. We rented office space from Jim's father-in-law in Toronto, and after we returned from our games late at night, we would both trudge up those stairs and work until two or three in the morning stuffing brochures and letters into envelopes for mailing.

We had a narrow road built off the main highway back to the camp, right through the forest and over high hills. Opening day came and it poured rain all day. Parents got stuck in the mud on the road. We tried to help push some of them out. Then they had trouble passing in-coming cars as they were leaving. Jim and I decided we had better take two walkie-talkies and go to each end of the trail so we could direct traffic, stopping in-coming cars while others were out-going, and vice versa. But we got mixed up on who was to go first. I radioed Jimmy and yelled, "What the hell are you doing dummy? This is all screwed up." Jimmy came back on and yelled, "Who are you calling dummy?" Finally, we got all the cars in and all the cars out. We were drenched, tired, and fed up. We went into our office and sat down and were not saying too much. At last I broke the silence. "Do you want to buy my stock, or will I buy yours?" We stared at each other for a moment, and finally burst out laughing.

The next day wasn't too much better. Jim and I had gone into the dining hall to have a bit of supper with the kids. We thought we had ordered adequate milk for the kids over the weekend, but we had miscalculated how much milk young lads can drink. They started banging their cups on the tables, yelling, "We want milk! We want milk! We want milk!" To Jim I said, "I never want to hear this chant again. Let's buy more milk than we think we need, even if some of it goes sour, we'll just throw it out." We survived the first session and the camp continued for many years.

Jim and I had purchased some property on another lake, where we built seven cottages so that all of our instructors could be in the same area. Since most of the instructors were either NHL or Major Junior A Players, we wanted to provide them with a nice spot so they wouldn't be tempted to go with some other camp or some hockey school. Over the years our hockey instructors included Red Kelly, Bill Gadsby, Parker MacDonald, Bill Goldsworthy, Mike Walton, Brit Selby, Ron Ellis, Bobby Orr, Johnny Bower, Dave Dryden, Murray Wilson, Larry Robinson, Ron Stackhouse, Walt McKechnie, Johnny McClellen, Jim Dorey, Bernie Parent, Brian Watson, and other players too numerous to list here. These instructors were led by Pat Flannery, our Head Instructor, who planned and directed the entire hockey part of our operation. We also had several different Camp Directors who only worked out at the camp, including Jack McKenzie, John Petroshack, Bob Sloan, Pat Shetler, and Gerald Blair. David Branch worked at the camp for us for eight years. The Haliburton Hockey Haven Boys Camp became so popular that the *Toronto Star* ran an eight- page insert feature on us. The front page of the article showed a big picture of Bill Gadsby and a bunch of the young kids on the bench. The heading read, "Bill Gadsby's On My Team."

We had hundreds of parents over the years coming from far away points in Canada, the United States, and even from Europe. When they got to Haliburton, most of them marveled at the beauty of the area. There are more than 700 lakes in the immediate Haliburton Highlands area. Many parents asked if we could help them find accommodations, and we almost became a booking agent for the local lodges. This got me thinking. One day I said to Jim, "We should build our own resort hotel." There were many lodges in Haliburton, but no resort hotel. In 1975 we filled that need by building "PineStone Inn and Country Club," right on Highway #121, between Minden and Haliburton. The original investors at Pine-Stone, besides Jim and I, were my cousins Lee and Glen Blair, Jack Davison, and Art Ward, who also owned Wigamog Inn in the area. We soon expanded and raised funds to do so by selling shares. Key investors were Larry Needler, the owner of Travelways Bus Corporation, Bob Attersley, the owner of Attersley Tire Corporation, Don Anderson, the owner of Anderson Haulage out of Stouffville, Ontario, Bob Smith, and Dick Wilson, who eventually bought the boys' camp from us in 1978. Many prominent business people in the Haliburton community also invested.

When we opened, PineStone had 36 rooms, one dining room, one lounge and a nine-hole golf course. Over the years this became 62 rooms, 8 two-bedroom chalets, 8 one-bedroom villas, 8 two-bedroom villas, a whole new building housing 24 new deluxe hotel rooms. We built a new separate building that connected with the main hotel by an overhead bridge across the main driveway. We called it "Our Bridge Over Troubled Water." The new building had six new conference rooms, another dining room, and a Pro Shop. At the far end of the main hotel we built a huge new ballroom, and a few years later expanded that nine-hole golf course to 18 holes. We owned the hotel and the golf course until 1993, when it was sold to a new group. Delta Hotel, I believe, is now part owner of PineStone.

In all, Jim Gregory and I have been partners for nearly 40 years and we have shared similar careers in hockey. We were both General Managers of Major Junior A Teams. He was the General Manager of the Toronto Marlboros, when I was the General Manager of the Oshawa Generals. Jim became the General Manager of the Toronto Maple Leafs, while I became the General Manager of the Minnesota North Stars. Today, Jim is Vice-President of the

National Hockey League. It's been a wonderful ride for both of us over the years. Each year when our hockey seasons are over, we still spend a good portion of our time together every summer in Haliburton. Jim, his wife Rosalie, and their children and their families live next door to our cottage in Haliburton. From time to time, he says to me, "You are almost like a brother to me," and I feel the same way.

Saginaw Gears 1972-73

Back Row (from left) — Murray McNeil, Steve Lyon, Tom Thomson, Mike Legge, Bruce McIntosh, Dennis Desrosiers, Russ Friesen.

Middle — Gunner Garrett, Elgin McCann, Butch Morris, Marcel Comeau, Jim Maertz, Mike Hornby, Don Perry.

Front — Ray Belanger, Juri Kudrasovs, Stu Irving, Dennis Romanesky, Raynald Tessier, Cal Hammond.

Saginaw Gears 1976-77

Back Row (from left) — Greg Hotham, Stu Irving, Jean Marie Nicol, Wayne Zuk, Gordon Malinoski, Kevin Kemp, Gary Sittler, Wren Blair (Owner).

Middle — Ken Garrett (Trainer), Michel DeGuise, Marcel Comeau, Marc Gaudreault, D'Arcy Ryan, Don Perry (Coach), Mike Ruest.

Front — Mario Lessard, Rick Chinnick, John Gravel, Dennis Desrosiers, Dave Westner, Paul Evans, Tom Mohr.

Saginaw Gears 1978-79

Back Row (from left) — Kevin Kemp, Bob Gladney, Paul McIntosh, Jon Paul Fontas, Claude Larochelle, Wren Blair (Owner).

Middle — Billy Osborne, Don Perry (Coach), Keith Johnson, Larry Hopkins, Warren Holmes, Mark Toffolo, Scott Jessee, Ken Garrett (Trainer).

Front — Tim Thomlinson, Marcel Comeau, Lynn Jorgenson, Stu Irving, Dave Westner, Doug Keans.

The Purchase of the Pittsburgh Penguins

11

IN THE SUMMER OF 1975, MUCH of the talk around hockey circles was that the Pittsburgh Penguins were about to fold. The day before the NHL draft that year, I went to see Brian O'Neill and John Ziegler. Ziegler wasn't the President of the NHL yet, though he was the understudy to Clarence Campbell. I asked them how serious the Pittsburgh situation was? O'Neill, who always drew up the NHL schedule, answered, "Well, I'll tell you how serious it is. I have already drawn up a 17-team league schedule (there were 18 teams in the NHL the year before) . . . Pittsburgh is gone."

The next morning, I ran into Al Savill, the owner of the Columbus Owls of the International Hockey League, and asked, "Al, do you want to do something stupid?"

"Wren, I've had more fun in life doing something stupid than anything else. What do you have in mind?"

I told him about my meeting with O'Neill and Ziegler. "Let's buy that team from bankruptcy and resurrect the Penguins."

"Isn't that funny," he said. "I've been thinking about that, too."

Al was a mortgage banker out of Indianapolis, but he also did tons of business out of Columbus and Pittsburgh. After we chatted a little while longer, he said he was going to contact his bank and find out who held the bankruptcy papers on the Penguins. We broke for lunch at our International Hockey League meetings, which were held in conjunction with the NHL meetings, and when Al returned from lunch he was grinning from ear to ear. "Can you believe this, my bank, Equibank, holds the whole deal and they are very upset because everyone in Pittsburgh feels they are to blame for the Penguins' fate, that they pulled the rug on the whole deal. Anyway, I told them about you and they want us to fly to Pittsburgh first thing tomorrow morning and meet with Mr. Canceliere, the president of the bank."

That night, Al and I were sitting in our room having a few drinks and reflecting on the marvelous future we had planned for ourselves. "You know I have a good friend of mine in Indianapolis, Nick Frenzell, who is Chairman of the Board of the Merchants Second National Bank of Indianapolis. Do you think I should call him and see if he might want to come on board with us in this venture?" When Al called Nick, he showed some interest. Nick then suggested that we all fly to Pittsburgh on his private jet. There was only Nick and the pilot on board when we took off for Pittsburgh, and we never even entered the terminal in Pittsburgh as there was this big black limo from the bank waiting for us. The limo whisked us off to the main corporate offices of Equibank on the 36th floor. It was like something out of a Harold Robbins' novel.

By 4 o'clock that afternoon, we had structured a deal with Equibank to put up the money to purchase the team in bankruptcy court and also gained a $1 million line of credit. We had not put up any money of our own at this point. The franchise fee in 1975 was $6 million, but this was for an existing team and we knew the league didn't want to lose the Pittsburgh team. After we finished with our deal with Equibank, we made an appointment to go to bankruptcy court in Pittsburgh the next morning. The bank had authorized us to make a bid of $3.2 million for the team, which was $2.8 million below the going rate for a franchise. We had no idea how far they were in debt or anything else because all of the records were locked up. Talk about buying a pig in a poke . . . and this was at the time when the players' salaries were starting to spiral out of control, because of the WHA.

When the judge came to the Pittsburgh Penguins' franchise on the docket, he commented that he understood there was an offer forthcoming for this team. Al stood up to confirm this. "What is your offer," the judge asked?

Al answered, "$3.2 million."

And with no hesitation, the judge pounded his gavel and said, "Offer denied."

We sat there and looked at each other, along with the other bankers present and then got up and left. When we got outside the courtroom, the bankers advised us to go back on the docket later in the day and offer $3.8 million. So we went back into court that afternoon and went through the whole scenario again. When it came time for our second offer, the judge called Al once again and said, "What are you prepared to offer?"

Al said, '$3.8 million.'

"Accepted," said the judge as he struck his gavel once again.

I was appointed General Manager and Chief Executive Officer of the team. Just before we were ready to start the season of 1975-76, Al Eagelson, the Director of the NHL Players Association, called with a concern about the Penguins coach. "Wren, I have six players on the Penguins team that I represent. All of them are very unhappy with Boileau. I feel I must tell you that if you keep Boileau, none of my clients will be playing there this year."

"Al, the Penguins had a pretty good season last year. We can't purchase this team and immediately fire the coach coming off a good year. However, I am familiar with a couple of incidents involving Boileau and the players you represent. I can assure you, that if this were to happen again, he will not continue as our coach. If you would agree to work with us on this, we will monitor Boileau very closely, and do everything we can to repair this relationship between him and your clients."

"Ok Wren, I understand what you are saying. It is already a

difficult enough job to try and keep the Penguins a float, so let's see how things proceed."

Early in the season the team was not playing well. Al Savill was very unhappy with Boileau and the performance of the team. He asked me to replace Marc at mid-season, and when he asked me who I might have in mind to become the new coach, I suggested Ken Schinkel to fill in on an interim basis. If it goes well, we could make it permanent a bit later on. I talked to "Schink" and he agreed to do this.

Some of the players on that club that year (and I will not name all of them) were Davie Burrows, Colin Campbell (who is now a Vice-President in charge of discipline in the NHL), Ron Stack-house, Syl Apps Jr., Jean Pronovst, Vic Hadfield, Ron Schock, and Pierre Laroche. Supporting team operations was a cast of able staff members. Judy Berg worked in sales, promotions, and public relations. Beverly Schmidt worked in my office, as did Diane Dubis, Peggy Mullvihill, and Jo Anne Holewa. Tom Woods was our Box Office Manager, Paul Sandrock was our Controller, Terry Schiffhauer was head of our publicity department. Carla Hensler was our receptionist, and Marilyn Vaughan, who had come with me from Minnesota, was my Administrative Assistant and the Office Manager in Pittsburgh. The Mayor of Pittsburgh, Pete Flaherty, was behind us all the way.

In 1975-76, we made the playoffs, just barely, but it was a very difficult year. Aside from coaching problems, after the bankruptcy of the previous owners, we had trouble restoring the total confidence of the public. In addition to that, this was an era when the City of Pittsburgh had an outstanding baseball club in the Pittsburgh Pirates and an even greater NFL team in the Pittsburgh Steelers. Those two teams got most of the media attention.

That first year we lost about $1.5 million, more than our $1 million line of credit, which made the banks nervous, but they stuck with us for a second season before we sold our interest. But about halfway through the '76-77 season, I did a cash flow projection and called Al to tell him that according to my projections we would not be able to meet the January 15th payroll. "I'm not surprised," he said. I stressed that I did not think it was a good idea for us to put up any of our own money to salvage the franchise. We decided to meet with Nick in Indianapolis to consider our options. During the meeting, we considered bringing in more partners to raise more money, going back to the bank for more money, folding the team, or putting more money in ourselves. I insisted I was not putting any more money in.

A few days later back in Pittsburgh, Al and Nick met with me. "We are paying you a pretty good salary as President, GM and CEO of the club," they reasoned, "but you are not going to put any more money in. Nick and I have decided to put some more money in, and we feel that if you are not going to put any more money in, is it fair as an employee that you continue to take money out when you are not contributing."

"No, it is not fair." I had hired Baz Bastien as Assistant Manager a little bit before that and told them that he could move in as GM. I would stay behind the scenes and help out any way I could. "Before I do that," I told Al and Nick, "I want to tell you guys that you are nuts." Each of them owned 40 percent of the team and I owned 20. They then asked me if I would turn over my 20 percent to them. "Absolutely," I said, "as long as I get out and am free and clear of any debt." After we agreed to this, they told me that they were going to bring in Eddie DeBartolo as a third partner and that they would split the team three ways, a third, a third, and a third.

A few days later, I resigned; Baz took over as General Manager; Eddie came in as the third partner and they carried on the rest of the year. When the season ended, Al called me and asked if I was going to the NHL draft meetings. Even though I was out of the

National League, I still owned the Saginaw Gears in the IHL. We had dinner during the draft meetings in Montreal and during our conversation, I asked how things were going with the Penguins. "I really don't know," he said. "You don't know? When the season ended this year, Nick and I walked into Eddie Debartolo's office and told him that we were getting out . . . that we were going to turn our stock over to him, and that we were finished. He accepted the fact that we were leaving; however, just as we were getting ready to leave his office, he said, 'There is still a little matter of money here. We lost $2.1 million dollars this year, and by my calculations that works out to $700,000 for each of us. When you each write me a cheque for $700,000, then I'll accept your stock.' Well, that's exactly what we had to do . . . we each had to pay him $700,000 to leave. So, both Nick and I are no longer associated with the Penguins. Now, in looking back, I wish I'd listened to you when you got out."

Shortly after that, Al, his wife Becky, and their daughter moved to Florida permanently. Al died some years later. I feel sorry for Becky and their little daughter Kelly, who came late in life for Al, but he adored her. I often think of the great times that Al and I had together, first back in the IHL, when I owned the Saginaw Gears and Al owned the Columbus Owls. Al's coach in Columbus, Moe Bartoli, and I became good friends. Moe and his wife Beverly now live in Sudbury, Ontario. I have kind of lost track of Nick Frenzell, our other partner. I think that Al, Nick, and I can be proud of saving the Pittsburgh Penguins. Ed DeBartolo kept the team going over the years, until the great Mario Lemieux arrived in Pittsburgh, one of the greatest players in the history of the NHL. Mario and some other business associates own the Penguins today, although the team still struggles with some financial problems.

Our family also has fond memories of Pittsburgh. When I left the North Stars in 1974, I spent quite a bit of time in Saginaw, but Elma and the kids (Danny and Jill) remained in Minnesota, so that

Jill could graduate from high school. When we bought the Penguins in 1975, Jill graduated from high school and returned to Canada to live and Danny moved to Saginaw to work in the box office. We sold our home in Minnesota and settled in the Pittsburgh suburb of Fox Chapel, on a beautiful street and in a home with a full-size swimming pool. We joined the Fox Chapel Golf Club and thoroughly enjoyed living in this community.

PROFILE

Stan Waylett

I FIRST BECAME AWARE OF Stan Waylett when he was working full time in the maintenance department of General Motors in Oshawa and serving as the trainer for a couple of softball and baseball teams in the Oshawa area. When I secured a franchise in the OHA in Senior B hockey, I asked Stan to be the head trainer. We worked out a small financial deal at that time. Stan followed me through Senior B into Senior A, traveling with us to Europe for the World Championship in 1958. When I brought the Oshawa Generals back to Oshawa in 1962, Stan became the head trainer until the completion of the 1965-66 season when we went to the Memorial Cup final. I invited Stan to come with me to the Minnesota North Stars. I asked Stan what he thought about retiring from General Motors to become the head trainer of the Minnesota North Stars. Because he had been with GM for years, Stan was eligible for retirement with a fairly good pension. He asked me what kind of money I thought I could pay, and when I told him the amount I had in my budget, he was overjoyed. "With that salary and my pension from GM, I would be making more that I am now."

Stan joined the North Stars without another moment's hesitation.

I moved to Minnesota the year before the team started to play in order to get things set up. Elma and the kids stayed back in Oshawa that year, and I decided to get a small apartment. We had a lot of new equipment to buy, and I knew Stan would be a big help to me. I asked him if he would like to share the apartment with me and come to work in Minnesota a year earlier as well. Stan jumped at the chance, though he was sad to leave his wife Peggy in Oshawa with his son Donald. We rented a small apartment in Bloomington Minnesota, not very far from the new Metropolitan Sports Arena. That was fun as Stan and I did our own cooking, washed our own laundry, and kept the place clean. Stan was a big jovial guy, who had lost his hair years ago, and he loved practical jokes. I took him with me everywhere and introduced him to all the people I was meeting while I was trying to get exposure for the North Stars in the Twin Cities.

Once the season began, I told Stan to hire an assistant trainer. He hired "Doc" Rose, and they worked together for many years. When I left Minnesota in the late summer of 1975 to take over my new duties as the President, CEO, and General Manager of the Penguins, Stan remained the head trainer of the North Stars. He retired some years later but stayed in the Twin Cities. I used to keep in touch with him by telephone on a regular basis, but by this time Stan was in his late 70s, and seemed to be talking strange when I would get him on the phone. His wife Peggy had died two or three years before, and he was living alone in a small seniors building with his own apartment. The North Stars club doctor told me that Stan was in the early stages of Alzheimer's disease. Not long after this, Stan was denied the right to drive, and the doctors had told his son Donald that he should take the car away from Stan. I recall that near the end, I phoned him one day and he said to me, "Wren, in the end do you know who your worst enemies are? It's your own kids. That son Donald of mine betrayed me and stole my car from me." I knew this wasn't true. What Donald had done was for Stan's own good. I called Donald to assure him he had done the right thing.

Shortly after that, I got word that Stan had passed away. It was a sad day for me because we had spent over 30 years together. The players all thought the world of him. To me, Stan Waylett was part of my immediate hockey family.

DURING THE MANY YEARS THAT I have been in the hockey business, I've had my brother Gerald at my side. When I formed my first team back in 1949, he was only 14, but he started traveling with me and continued to do so for the next 17 years, all the way to Oslo, Norway when the Dunnies won the World Championship. When I signed on with the Minnesota North Stars, I had to put together a new scouting staff. I had hired Ted O'Connor, who had played for me on the Whitby Dunlops, as chief scout, and then I added my brother Gerald to his staff. Gerald had a natural-born insight into recognizing good hockey players. I hired him, not because he was my brother, but because he had the ability to become a quality NHL scout. Many other people in the hockey business share that opinion of Gerald today. He works for the NHL Central Scouting under our old friend Frank Bonello, the Director of Central Scouting.

Gerald scouted for me in Pittsburgh and worked with our box-office staff in Saginaw. Jim Gregory hired him to work in Central Scouting, but was somewhat distressed when a couple of years later, Cliff Fletcher, then the General Manager of the Calgary Flames, called Jim to inquire about obtaining Gerald as his Director of Player Personnel. Gerald took the job with the Flames and was responsible for helping to acquire the players who led them to a Stanley Cup victory. When Cliff Fletcher was leaving Calgary to join the Toronto Maple Leafs, he showed his high regard for Gerald by signing him to a new three-year contract with the Flames, thereby giving Gerald a good deal of security for sometime.

Gerald has always been a valued member of my natural family and my hockey family. He has been extremely important in my life. And although my other brother never followed Gerald and me into a hockey career, Lyle Blair has certainly succeeded in the business world.

One time when we were playing road hockey in our driveway with a few kids in the neighbourhood — I was about 12 years of age at that time and Lyle was about seven — we didn't have too many players for the game, so I told Lyle, "You're going in the net and play goal for the other team." He protested, "I am not." I insisted, "Oh, yes you are." And with that I grabbed him by the jacket and placed him in the net. Picture the next scene in this game. I was playing brilliantly – at least, in my opinion – stick handling through all of the opposition players, and was now bearing down on goal against my brother Lyle. As I got near the net, he stepped out of the net, leaving a wide-open goal for me. Now with no challenge from a goaltender whatsoever, I stopped dead and said to him, "Get back in the net. He said, "No." I said, "Get in the net!" Again he said, "No." As I made a move toward him, he took off running. I never did get to score that beautiful goal. That's when I realized Lyle was not going to pursue a career in hockey.

Lyle did pursue an education, though, graduating from Western University with a degree in Business. He was snapped up by the Proctor and Gamble Corporation, where he worked on the introduction of Duncan Hines Chocolate Cake Mix to the market. He was promoted to work at the company headquarters for Proctor and Gamble in England, and not long after that, he was promoted to the position of General Manager of the entire Proctor and Gamble Scandinavian operation. When he returned to Canada, he became

President of Pepsi Canada and Vice-President of Pepsi International. In those days he used to sit in board meeting with directors like movie star Joan Crawford. Some time later, he sold all his interest in the bottling industry for several million dollars and purchased the Steel Furniture Manufacturing Company in Pembroke, Ontario. Eventually he sold off his interest in Storewall, and today is a land developer on Georgian Bay and Lake Huron.

I often think how proud Mom and Dad would be to see the contributions their three sons have made to Canadian and international business, hockey and otherwise. Our sister Merle might have been the brightest one of all, but she died in 1960 of cancer. Lyle, Gerald, and I get together about twice a year for what we call "Our Brothers' Luncheons." We have a great time. A short while ago I said to Lyle, "We should have these luncheons more than twice a year." To which he replied, "I don't think so. It takes me six months now to get over the laughs and the fun and the shenanigans of the last one." I think maybe he's right.

Developing Player Personnel for the Los Angeles Kings

12

SHORTLY AFTER I SOLD MY SHARE in the Pittsburgh Penguins, I got a call from George Maguire, the General Manager of the Los Angeles Kings. He asked if I was clear of all obligations to the Penguins, then asked, "How would you like to come with me in Los Angeles as my Director of Player Personnel?"

I wasn't wildly enthused by the offer since I was still active in Saginaw and I was also President and CEO of PineStone Inn & Country Club in Haliburton. We were expanding like crazy, so I had all sorts of things on my plate. When I hesitated, George, who has a gruff mannerism, said, "Huh, that's something, eh. I used to work for you and now you won't come and work for me. You just say no . . . " I interrupted George to say I needed a little time to think about his offer. He went on to explain his situation. "Look, I'm away out here on the West Coast and when I come in around 9 o'clock and try to get somebody in the East, it's already noon there and they have gone to lunch. By the time I get back from lunch, and try and get somebody in the East, it's now after 5 and they've all gone home. The time change is brutal. . . . You've got all of this experience, more than I have, in signing players. Most of the agents are in the East, so you could be a big help to me in signing players and in management work. I would also like you to operate our American League farm team in New Haven, which isn't too far from where you're located. Let's get together in Montreal at the draft meetings to talk some more. You don't have to give me an answer today."

In June at the meetings, he talked, and talked, and talked. I always liked George, from the time when he worked for me as an area scout in Ottawa Valley for the Boston organization. George was also General Manager of both the Ottawa Senior and Junior Montagard Teams in those days and sent me some good players for my Clinton team. Finally, I gave in and agreed to do the job for one year, maybe two. Ted O'Connor, who had been my chief scout in Minnesota, was now George's chief scout in LA, so that put Ted and I back together again.

L.A. had three first-round draft choices that year. We drafted young Jimmy Fox from the Ottawa 67s and Larry Murphy, who played many years with the Kings before moving on to Toronto and Detroit, where he won a Stanley Cup. George had some trouble with the agent who represented "Murph" and asked me if I would go into Toronto and see if I could do anything to get Larry signed. I called his father and told him I wanted to talk with the family before speaking with the agent. I think that George had frightened "Murph" at the time because he was so gruff. I made friends with the family and offered a little more money than George had to close the deal. During that first year I also met Larry Kelly, an Ottawa-based agent, who represented Jimmy Fox. Since then, I've had many dealings with Larry as he represented kids out of Ottawa who had been drafted by the Kingston Frontenacs. Larry is a fair agent, who understands the benefits of junior hockey as a training ground for the players.

During my six years with the Kings, from 1979 to 1985, we signed other great players — Marcel Dione, Charlie Simmer, Dave Taylor (the General Manager of the Kings today) "Rogie" Vachon, Mike Murphy, and many others.

The Kings trained in Victoria, B.C., in those days, which was a great place for training camp. Ted and I used to go out and shop for all sorts of finger foods to eat in our rooms at night. George and Ted were what we used to call "Black Irishmen" and they used to get into some terrible arguments at night — with me as referee — but they always remained the best of friends.

By this time, Jack Kent Cooke had sold the Kings, the Lakers, and the Forum to Jerry Buss, a young entrepreneur who came out of nowhere. I really liked Jerry Buss and we talked quite a bit during training camps. Jerry had bought an estate known as PickFair in Beverly Hills. Being a movie buff, I had heard many stories of the big parties that Douglas Fairbanks, Jr. and Mary Pickford had held at PickFair while they were married. PickFair is right on the top of the hill overlooking the Beverley Hills Hotel. I told Jerry during one of our training camps in Victoria that I would love to see PickFair some day.

Jerry Buss was a man in his late 40s at that time and dressed differently than any hockey man I have ever known — very casual, jeans, open-necked shirts, trendy L.A. styles at that time. He didn't like anybody who got all dolled up all the time. In my younger years, I was a very natty dresser, but when I went to L.A., I used to wear jeans and open-necked shirts to 'suit' Jerry.

Under Jerry's ownership, the Kings began to struggle. He let Don Perry go as coach and then he moved George Maguire. I had heard rumors that George was about to be let go, so I phoned him. His wife Doris answered in a strange kind of happy mood. "Oh, Georgie got fired today and you're going to get fired . . . everybody's going to get fired." She had told me that George had just taken the dog for a walk, but before we finished our conversation, George returned. Well, George came on the phone and I could tell he had had a little bit of cheer to try and pick himself up. I could hardly understand him, so I said, "Why don't I call you in the morning?"

I got a hold of him around noon, L.A. time, the next day. "I've got the worst hangover this morning," he groaned. "I don't know whether you've heard or not, but I got fired as General Manager last night."

"But I heard that you moved up to be President."

"Well, you know how Buss is. He's a good guy, so rather than let me go altogether, he moved me up to President. What the hell do I know about being a President?"

"Well, George, who is going to be the General Manager?"

"Are you standing or sitting? Well, I suggest you sit down."

"Cripes, it can't be that bad, is it?

"You might not think so, but I kind of think so — Rogatien Vachon."

Rogie had been a popular goaltender with the Kings, but he had never even been a coach, let alone a manager.

I've always told you, George, that if you quit or got fired, I was finished. So, I want to tell you right now, I'm resigning."

"No, wait a minute. Don't do anything until I talk to Buss. He's out in Hawaii and I have to call him tonight, so I'll call you in the morning."

I agreed. I didn't dislike Rogie, but he was young. I could remember scouting him in bantam hockey. I didn't think we could be comfortable together, with me, a former GM in both Pittsburgh and Minnesota, looking over his shoulder.

The next morning George called me and said that Buss wanted to me fly out to L.A. to meet me face-to-face. "He said you've always wanted to see PickFair. So, he wants me to pick you up at the airport, take you to a hotel, and the next day pick you up and take you out to PickFair for lunch with him."

"Okay, I'd love to see PickFair."

When I arrived, Jerry showed me all through PickFair. I was amazed at how big and old it was. I asked him to tell me his motivation for buying it. "Well," he said, "Wren, it was such a bargain at $8 million that I couldn't pass it up." After our tour, we ended up in this huge dining room and he asked his butler to serve lunch. He sat at one end of a long table and I sat at the other end. I was so far away I had trouble hearing what he was saying.

"You know, Wren, I bought this hockey club to have a little fun. Well, it certainly hasn't been any fun. I had to fire Don Perry, I had to fire George, who I love, and now, he tells me that you want to quit. How could you call this fun?"

"Jerry, it's always been this way. When you get down to the real tough things in hockey, like firing a coach or trading players, it's never going to be easy."

"You want to leave, right?"

"Jerry, you've been wonderful to me. I think highly of you and I am very indebted to the Kings, but I told George, I would only stay two years and it's now six. It has been a beautiful experience, but I just don't feel that Rogie Vachon, at his age, and me, at my age . . . it just isn't going to be comfortable with me on his staff. And to be truthful, with our difference in age, I wouldn't be comfortable either."

"I understand exactly what you're saying, Wren. I've been there, too. However, there is a little matter of you having two years left on your contract."

"I know that, but if I resign then that's over."

"Oh, no. You've been in hockey for so many years, you can do the odd little thing for me. I want to pay you the remaining two years on your contract. I will keep you in the California Sports Pension Plan, the NHL pension plan, and the California health benefit plan."

"Jerry, that's more than fair, you don't have to do that."

"Well, I want to be fair. I'm sick and tired of these dirty jobs."

Just after that he got a phone call and had to leave. As I was waiting for George to come back to pick me up, I looked around this gorgeous mansion and thought to myself, probably I will never be in the National Hockey League again. I never was. Isn't it strange that a young man who started his career by coaching hockey in the cold winter in Oshawa, Ontario ends his NHL career in Beverly Hills, California, at PickFair, on a hot, hot day.

PROFILE

Jack Kent Cooke

MEETING THE LEGENDARY OWNER of the Los Angeles Kings, Jack Kent Cooke, was a highlight of my hockey career. Jack Kent Cooke was the only Canadian who gained U.S. citizenship in one day, so the story goes. Apparently, he spoke personally to the President of the United States and asked him point blank if he were to move all his assets, which were sizeable, to the United States, could he get instant citizenship.

Jack had started from nothing. He started out selling vacuum cleaners, but somehow or other, he befriended Lord Thomson of Fleet Street, who owned newspapers in the British Empire, Canada, and the United States. Jack sold advertising for *Liberty Magazine* (and later bought it outright) and other Thomson newspapers. He also developed one of the largest radio stations in Toronto, CKEY. He hired one of the best newscasters in radio, Lorne Greene. Years later, Lorne Greene went to Hollywood and we will all remember him as the father figure on *Bonanza*. Lorne was often seen in the crowd at the L.A. Kings games. He had bought some shares in the Kings. It was great to see all of these Canadians still together in business in Los Angeles.

Jack Kent Cooke had also bought the Toronto Maple Leafs AAA baseball team in the International League, long before the Blue Jays came to Toronto. They were a farm club in those days of the Brooklyn Dodgers. For years he owned 25 percent of the Washington Redskins NFL team, and in later years, became the sole owner. Of course, he owned the L.A. Kings, the Los Angeles Lakers, and the beautiful Los Angeles Forum.

In the early years of expansion, I had spent a lot of time with

Jack. Jack would call me in Minnesota regularly to discuss his team and what I was trying to do to improve mine. He knew that I was a good friend of Sam Pollock, and he was quick to realize that in those days, Sam Pollock was the best NHL General Manager in the business. Jack made as many deals with Sam as I did.

Jack Kent Cooke was one of the brightest men I have ever met. He was eccentric but he was a genius. I first met Jack in 1966 at the NHL Draft meetings in June of that year. The GMs of the expansion teams were sitting around chatting and socializing a little bit when Lynn Patrick piped up, "You know guys, we'd probably be smarter to go outlaw and start a new league. The players we get from the old division teams will be a joke." Lynn was really only kidding — there never was any real thought of going outlaw.

The next day the GMs met, with Jack Riley, GM of the new Pittsburgh entry presiding as the chairman of the meeting. Besides Jack and me, there was Bud Poile from Philadelphia, Lynn Patrick from of the St. Louis Blues, Rudy Pilous, the first GM in Oakland who was later replaced by Bert Olmstead, and Jack Kent Cooke from Los Angeles. He had yet to name a GM, so he attended the meeting. The first item on Jack Riley's agenda was an open forum where we would each speak of our plans and discuss the structure of the NHL expansion draft. Each of us spoke in order. Jack Riley first, followed by Poile, Patrick, Pilous, Blair, and then Jack Kent Cooke.

I will never forget Jack Kent Cooke that day. He had been sitting quietly almost ignoring us and looking completely bored at the proceedings. Then Jack Riley asked him, "Do you wish to speak for Los Angeles, Mr. Cooke?" Jack, like an actor, made a great "ta do" about getting up to speak. The rest of us had spoken just sitting in our seats. When Jack arose, he looked around the room sternly at each of us, and then in a booming theatrical voice said, "When I arrived here last night, I was appalled to hear from my good friend Stafford Smythe and my dear friend David Molson (representing

Toronto and Montreal, respectively) that some of our General Managers had a meeting last night and dared to breath the word *"Outlaw."* Gentlemen, do you people not realize that you can't intimidate people with threats such as that?" He paused, looked at all of us sternly again and then sat down. Jack was sitting next to me and there was dead silence. I don't think our guys had ever met anyone like Jack Kent Cooke before. I was a little ticked off. Who did Mr. Cooke think he was to come in and lecture the General Managers of all the other clubs?

"Mr. Cooke," I rose to respond, "anyone in the National Hockey League who says that anyone in this room breathed the word *Outlaw* in anything other than jest is a damn liar." Jack looked up at me. I sat down.

Then he rose to speak again, in a booming voice. "Wren, I will tell my good friend Stafford, and my dear friend David, that anyone who suggests that our General Managers breathed the word *Outlaw* in anything other than jest is a damn liar!" Well, at this point, all our guys broke right up because Jack was so serious.

The next meeting of the expansion team GMs was called a couple of weeks later in Minneapolis. We were at the Sheraton Hotel, and in the meeting, one of our general managers said, "Wren and Lynn know Sam Pollock really well, and it's very clear that Sam is going to be the architect of the expansion draft. I suggest that we have Wren and Lynn go and visit with Sammy to see if they can convince him to give us a decent and fair draft." At that point, Mr. Bill Putman, President of the Philadelphia Flyers and chair of this meeting, cut in to say, "No, no gentlemen. I do not agree with that. We should observe proper protocol and have one of our owners from our division meet with Sam." With that, Jack Kent Cooke, who had been sitting quietly, almost looking bored, again erupted. "Protocol be dammed," he said. "If we feel Wren and Sam are the right people to meet with Sam, protocol be damned."

I looked at Jack and said, "Jack, you are the most inconsistent man I think I have ever met. The last meeting you were crawling all over us, protecting your good friend Stafford and your dear friend David, members of the old division. Now, you are reversing completely by saying 'Protocol be damned.'"

Jack looked at me as he had in the last meeting. "Wren consistency is the hobgoblin of small minds. You remind me of a General leading his troops who were out-numbered and being beaten badly and kept on saying, 'Forward, Forward, Forward. Never once did he think of saying, 'Retreat, Retreat.'" Well, when Jack finished this pronouncement, all the guys in the room just howled. Lynn Patrick fell right off his chair laughing. For the rest of the year, all those guys nicked named me "Hob" from Jack's telling me that consistency was the hobgoblin of small minds. How do you figure a guy like Jack?

At that time, George Maguire was the assistant GM for Jack. Jack had become embroiled in a bitter divorce fight with his wife Jeannie, who was out to skin him. California divorce laws are probably the most liberal in favour of the women in the world. So Jack moved to Los Vegas to live and became something of a recluse for a year or so, like Howard Hughes had been in roughly the same era. Every week George told me he had to fly to Los Vegas to get all his instructions from Jack regarding the operation of the hockey club. Eventually, Jack and his lawyers made some sort of a settlement with Jeannie, and he returned to California.

Eventually, Jack hired Larry Regan as his General Manager of the Kings. Larry had been an outstanding player with the Toronto Maple Leafs and a couple of other NHL teams before he got into management. Today, he is the head of the NHL Alumni Association. Larry always called me 'The Bird' and in those days would call me at least three times a week. He'd always say something like, "Bird, you can't believe what he wants me to do now." Of course, he meant Jack. Dealing with Jack everyday, as Larry had to do, must have been a trying experience. Jack was a perfectionist who seemed to be living a bit in the twilight zone.

During some of those same years, we had another colorful owner in the league, Charlie Finley. Mr. Finley owned the Oakland Seals in the NHL and the Oakland A's baseball team that won several World Series in the era. We became good friends. I can still hear Charlie interrupting Clarence Campbell as he was outlining something that he thought the league should do. Charlie would stand up and say "Clarence, we would never do that in baseball." And Clarence would reply, "But Charlie, this is not baseball."

The sport of hockey sure does attract some odd characters, myself excluded, of course.

The Return of the Kingston Frontenacs and the Art of the Draft

13

IN APRIL 1989, BOB ATTERSLEY and I were talking in his office and he said to me, "Have you heard what's going on in Kingston with its Junior hockey club?" I said, yes, I've read a bit about it. "It seems this guy Lou Kazowski says Kingston is 'a lousy hockey town' and he is going to try and move the club to Owen Sound. I wonder if we should consider buying that team," Bob mused.

I was reluctant to get back into hockey because I was very involved in running PineStone, but the next day Bob invited me to meet with him and Don Anderson, one of our old friends. Bob and Don had decided to put in a bid for the Kingston team and wanted me to join with them. I indicated to them that Lou Kazowski had played for me a few years before when I was running the North Stars and we had our farm team in Memphis in the Central Hockey League. He was one of two or three players on loan from Sam Pollock of the Montreal Canadiens. In the deal, Kazowksi had been assigned from a first-place team in Omaha to a last-place team in Memphis, something that probably didn't sit well with him. I suggested to Bob that perhaps he would be better to go forward with his name only. I didn't know how Kazowski would react if I was involved.

Bob approached Lou Kazowski's attorney, who set out the terms of any purchase. The deal would involve a share purchase, and there were to be no negotiations on the price. Bob and I were both a little nervous on the share purchase element, because it means that if there are debts associated with the purchase, the new owners are responsible for them. We called Don and talked this over. I recommended that if there were not over $100,000 in debts, coupled with the purchase price, it was a good buy. We agreed to their terms and then called David Branch, the OHL Commissioner, to request a hearing. David convened an emergency meeting in Toronto in three days, on a Saturday. Our group was approved unanimously to take over the Kingston Raiders franchise.

One of the first things we did was to consider changing the name. When the team first joined the OHL, it was a farm team of the Montreal Canadiens and took on the name Kingston Canadiens. The name we wanted had deeper roots in the community. Bob had played for me during the early '60s with the EPHL team in Kingston called the Frontenacs. Kingston is the seat for Frontenac County, and Count Frontenac built Fort Frontenac on the waterfront back in the 17th century. We applied to the OHL Board of Governors for permission to rename the team the Frontenacs.

Following a press conference to announce our return to Kingston, we began a season-ticket sales campaign. There were less than 500 season-ticket holders the previous season. Without a good season-ticket base you can't operate. The crowds the year before were extremely small, largely because Kazowski had never really endeared himself and the team to the community. We were astounded at the complete turnaround in season tickets and in that first year — we went from 450 to over 1,300. The folks who remembered Bob and I when we were both with the Frontenacs in the Eastern Pro League came back to support us.

When I took on the role of General Manager on behalf of my partners, there were a few things that had to be taken care of right away, notably the coaching status of Larry Mavety. "Mav" had been dismissed by Kazowksi sometime in March and hadn't been paid since, even though he still had three years remaining on a four-year contract. Kazowski had declared that the contract was no good and that was that. I reversed this decision and told Larry and his agent that we would honor the agreement. We were all pleased to have Mav as our coach. His contract became active again around May 1, and I was happy with that since Mav knew all the players from the previous year and he would be a helpful at the forthcoming draft.

During the time we were re-instating discussing Larry's contract, I received a phone call from an agent asking me if we were going to keep Mavety, and if we were, then Drake Berehowsky would not return as a player because he did not get along with Mav. Drake was a highly skilled defenceman, and Mavety was counting on him to lead our club that year. This really upset me because what the agent was doing was illegal; besides, he was telling us how to run the team.

I consulted with Bob and Don before I spoke to Berehowsky's agent again. When I told him that we stood behind Mavety as our coach, he said, "Fine, then Drake Berehowsky won't play."

"Let me tell you something," I replied, "for a player or an agent to interfere with Larry Mavety's livelihood is a dangerous proposition. However, I will agree to talk to this player at length if you have him call Larry Mavety personally and explain why he doesn't want to play for him. Then we will meet with Drake and take it from there." When the agent said Drake would not call Larry, I continued. "He's going to have to call Larry at some point, because if he doesn't and if he doesn't report to training camp, then I am going to call a media conference and disclose what you have told me and what Drake has said. That will be very embarrassing for both of you. I would suggest that you immediately call Drake and tell him that he had better pull his horns in." Despite his agent's bluster, Drake did report. I met with Drake and his parents before the season began and detected no animosity towards Mav. Unfortunately, Drake was injured nine games into the season and missed almost the entire season.

The OHL entry draft that year was scheduled for June at the North York Arena. We were somewhat concerned because we had never worked with the Kingston scouts, though Bob and I did know Chief Scout Floyd Crawford from years ago when we played against him in Belleville. As it turned out, Floyd was pretty well prepared for the draft, and we came out of there in reasonably good shape. A good number of quality players returned for the 1989-90 season, and the season turned out to be a very good one for us. The Frontenacs missed finishing in first place by a single point, just behind my old team, the Oshawa Generals. Just after New Years, Oshawa won the 'Eric Lindros Sweepstakes' when Eric was traded from Sault Ste. Marie, where he had refused to play. Mav and I proposed a trade that we felt was even better than what Oshawa offered, but Eric chose to play in Oshawa.

At that time you were not allowed to trade your first-round draft until the end of the first year, but because Eric had refused to report to the Greyhounds and because OHL Commissioner David Branch wanted to get Eric in the league, we changed that rule so that teams could trade their first-round selection between January 1 and 10. That rule still stands today. We call it the 'Lindros Rule'.

In the first round of playoffs, we lost to the Belleville Bulls in seven games. We were within a whisker of putting Belleville out in the sixth game of the series when we lost in overtime. I can remember driving down from Haliburton for that game, and as I pulled into the parking lot a few minutes late for the game, I heard on the radio that we had just scored. Now, I am very superstitious, and I thought, since we scored without me in the arena, I'm not going to set foot in the building unless we fall behind. I circled the Belleville Arena for two hours and 20 minutes. We were now heading in the final two minutes of play when our radio announcer said, "It looks like the Frontenacs have this series won, but it's still unclear who they'll meet in the next round." I immediately started yelling in my car, "Shut up, don't start that stuff. That's bad luck . . . no hockey game is over until the final whistle." Just about then, Belleville scored to tie the game and send us into overtime. The game was in the fourth overtime period before Belleville scored to win and forced a seventh game back in Kingston. Back in Kingston, we were completely sold out and turned hundreds of fans away. It was a tremendous game, up and down, but in the end we lost 2-1 and were eliminated in the first round.

We knew the next season would be tougher since we were losing 12 or 13 players to graduation. Just before the 1990-91 draft, I began to hear the odd rumor that Larry Mavety, who still had two years left on his contract, might be opting to return to Belleville. I later learned that Bob Vaughn, the owner of Belleville, had indeed approached Mav, which bothered me because I believed Vaughn and Mavety should have been up-front with me. If contracts mean anything, then this amounted to tampering.

Then one day, David Branch, the league commissioner, called to say that Mav had contacted him to report that he had a personal problem about returning to Kingston. He didn't know how to approach me because he was under contract. Apparently David told him, "I know Wren fairly well and I think the only proper way to do this is to go to him and explain your situation. He is not an unreasonable person, but I think he would be very angry if he heard it from someone else." At the draft meeting, Mav came to see me one night to discuss the situation. When we first purchased the Frontenacs, I had heard that Mav was living in Belleville and commuted back and forth, which disturbed me because I feel a coach should be close to his players, especially junior players who are just teenagers and need close supervision. I had asked Mav to move to Kingston. "Wren, one of the criteria you had outlined for me," Larry explained, "was that I would have to move to Kingston this year. I don't think that is an unreasonable request, but my wife absolutely refuses to move to Kingston because we are settled in Belleville with our home and kids. This has placed me in a very difficult position. In addition to that, Bob Vaughn has offered me a small percentage of ownership in the Belleville Bulls, if I return to Belleville. So, with all things considered, I find it very difficult to fulfill my contract with you and ask you if you will release me from my contract."

I was very disappointed — I liked Mav as a coach and a person — but every one has a life to live and I understood his predicament. After meeting with Mav and his wife one more time, I reluctantly gave him a written release from his contract with a proviso that no other employee of ours could go and work for Belleville. Rhonda Sheridan, our box office manager, had worked for Mav in Belleville and I didn't want to lose her.

Now, we were facing a year without a coach and with a team that was losing 13 players to graduation. Bob Attersley had mentioned to me that Rick Gay, the owner of the Niagara Falls team, had mentioned they had an assistant coach there named Randy Hall who might meet our needs. Since I didn't know Randy, I wasn't too enthused about this proposal, but I went along with Bob's thinking. We interviewed Randy in Toronto and the interview went well enough for us to hire him.

Our first selection in the 1990-91 draft was Keli Corpse of London, Ontario, who still holds the franchise record as the career scoring leader, surpassing Tony McKegney. Keli wasn't a big player but he had tons of talent. He finished his junior career with 135 goals, 285 assists and 420 points. He played under three coaches in Kingston – Randy Hall, Paul Cook, and David Allison – eventually during a tenure in pro hockey when he was reunited with Allison in Grand Rapids, Michigan, in the International Hockey League. He also won the CHL's Humanitarian Award in his third season with the Frontenacs.

When you lose 13 players in one season, it's almost a foregone conclusion that you are not going to make the playoffs the next year and you might also miss them the following year as well because you are faced with such a tremendous rebuilding job.

Drake Berehowsky, even though he had missed almost all of the previous season, was drafted by the Toronto Maple Leafs and started the season in the NHL, but he was returned to us in late November. His knee injury had certainly slowed him down. Shortly after that, he was invited to try out for the Canadian National Team to compete in the upcoming World Hockey Championships. He went to that camp in early December, but was cut after only four or five days. He returned to the Frontenacs as a very dejected young man. Just after Christmas, I took Drake out to lunch. "Drake, I don't feel that you are a very happy camper with us."

"Wren, I'm not unhappy with you or the hockey club or the Kingston fans, but I have had two or three setbacks lately and I am really down."

"Would it help you if I traded you?"

"Wren, I think it would. But if you do trade me, could I ask that you trade me to a team that has a chance of winning."

"Well, actually the only team that we would consider trading you to is a team that has a chance of winning, because they would give us more. I have to rebuild this team for the future."

Eventually, I was able to trade Drake to Bert Templeton, the coach of the North Bay Centennials, and he offered me three players, John Vary, who had been a first-round selection with North Bay, Jason Beaton, a big guy, plus a fourth-round draft choice. John played very well for us on defence, and Jason played both defence and forward for us. Unfortunately, late in the season, Jason got into a stick-swinging incident and was suspended from the OHL for life. We were able to get the suspension lifted so he could play Tier II in the Maritimes, and eventually got the life sentence rescinded, but it was too late for him to play Junior as he was in his final year of junior eligibility at that time. As it turned out, that fourth-round draft choice was very important to us. We drafted goaltender Marc Lamothe, who was outstanding for the next three years. Late in the season, I traded Tony Iob, reluctantly, to the Sault Ste. Marie Greyhounds for Kevin King and a fifth-round draft choice. When you are down like we were, it only makes sense to trade for draft choices and build for the future. You often have to trade your better players in order to rebuild. You have to trade an Ace, a King, a Queen, or a Jack in order to get something in return. You are not going to gain much if you are trading deuces and threes.

One of the players we had drafted that year was Nathan Lafayette, a very good player out of Tier II. When the season got rolling, we were losing lots of games, as we expected given our young line-up, but as the season progressed, I noticed that Randy wasn't playing Nathan Lafayette. One night Nathan's father, David Lafayette, a very nice gentleman, came to me and said, "It is not my intention to ever be an interfering parent wherever Nathan's hockey career is concerned, but it is beginning to bother me that Nathan is not playing at all. Have you any idea why that is?" I asked Randy why Nathan wasn't getting much ice time, but he didn't give me a clear answer, and when I discussed this problem with Nathan, he had no idea why he had fallen out of favor with his coach. At that point, Randy became very upset, claiming that we should not be questioning his tactics. As the season wore on and it became evident that we were not going to make the playoffs, I called Randy in and told him that I would like him to forget about coaching for the rest of the year and go out in the field as a scout.

Now I had to find a coaching replacement for the rest of the season. I called Danny McLeod, who had coached the Junior B Frontenacs when I was in Kingston running the pro team, and asked him if he could assist with the coaching if I got two or three guys involved. He said he would be delighted. Then I called Dick

Cherry, who had played for me in the EPHL days, and asked him if he would assist Danny. He, too, agreed and then asked me to consider Bob Collins, who had played senior hockey with Dick and was a close friend. Bob also agreed to help out. After that I called each one of them into my office individually to discuss what kind of a financial agreement we'd have to make with them. I was most surprised when all of them agreed unanimously that they wanted no financial remuneration. I went to my partners and we agreed that as long as we owned this team, the three of them would receive a pair of season tickets for helping out.

In the 1991-92 draft, we had the third pick over-all. The top-rated player that year was Chris Gratton, but we were drafting behind Detroit, an expansion team that year, and Owen Sound. I had talked with Jim Rutherford, the Detroit General Manager, a few weeks before the draft, and he was debating whether to take Chris Gratton or Todd Harvey. I asked if he would call me when he had decided, so we could see what direction we were going to take in the draft. A few days later he called me and said that he was unable to convince the Gratton family to allow Chris to go to Detroit because they didn't want him continuing his education in the United States. They were going to take Todd Harvey. That took one of the teams in front of us out of the way, but we still had to convince Owen Sound to pass on Gratton if we were going to get him. I talked with Joe Holody, the owner of the Owen Sound team, and also to Rob Holody, his son, who was the manager of the team. Robbie was adamant that if Gratton was still there after Detroit picked, that he was going to take him.

His stand never wavered from our first meeting until the night before the draft in Kitchener that year. We had a small conference room off my room at the hotel, where I arranged a meeting with both Joe and Rob Holody in hopes of getting them to change their mind. Chris' father had told Rob and me that if Owen Sound drafted him, he would go to a U.S. college rather than report to the Platers, and while this angered Rob, he still wanted to take a chance. Our meeting broke up shortly after midnight. We had given up hope of landing Chris until about 4:00 a.m. when the phone rang in my room. It was Rob Holody.

"Wren, are you awake?"

"I am now."

"Do you have a cold beer in your room?" We agreed that the Frontenacs would give the Platers the rights to Joel Washurak, a draft choice, and another player to be named later if they bypassed Gratton. I had to meet my scouting staff for breakfast at 7:30 and the draft started at 9 a.m., so I certainly didn't get much sleep that night.

When the draft began, Jimmy Rutherford claimed Todd Harvey, as expected, Owen Sound took a youngster by the name of Smith from Trenton, to nearly everyone's surprise, and we took Gratton. All day long, teams kept coming to our table asking me how I got Owen Sound to pass on Gratton. I said I had no idea, maybe they saw something they didn't like, maybe they felt they needed a defenceman more than a centerman. I never let on that we had made a deal in the wee hours of the morning.

Chris stepped right up, even though he was an underage pick, and became a power player for us. However, he only played two years for the Frontenacs, as he was selected by the Tampa Bay Lightning, an expansion team, in the NHL draft and they turned him pro immediately.

Our second round pick in 1991 was David Ling, a young 17-year-old from Charlottetown, Prince Edward Island, who turned out to be one of the most popular players ever to play Major Junior A hockey in Kingston. He was a small guy, only about 5'8", but he was a firebrand . . . and he was tough. What David could do better than anyone else was to irritate other players on the ice. He used to skate by a player on the other team and say, "You touch the puck in the next two minutes and I'm going to beat the hell out of you." The next thing you know the other teams start chasing him all over the ice. There was a song on the charts when David was playing with us called "My Ding-a-ling," and I can remember them playing it one night in Oshawa before our game. The fans were all singing and David went over in front of them and started directing them. He had a great sense of humor and used to the drive opposition teams and their fans nuts.

In David's rookie year after we lost to Peterborough in the playoffs, I will never forget Dick Todd, the Peterborough coach, coming up to me after the game. He had a bit of a smile on his face. "You know, Wren, I'd give anything to have a kid like that David Ling on my team. After all the players had finished shaking hands at center ice at the end of the series, David came over to our bench and stuck out his hand to me and said, 'Mr. Todd, congratulations.' I said, thank you, David. Then, he said, 'I also came over here for another reason. Next year, I'm going to be a year older and I want you to tell your players I'm going to kick the hell out of every player on your team.'" In the 1994-95 season, David scored 61 goals and was named the most valuable player in both the Ontario Hockey League and the Canadian Hockey League.

I had not been at all enamored with Randy Hall's coaching the previous season, so after we participated in the OHL draft, I advised Randy that we were going to make a coaching change. I then turned to Paul Cook, who had been doing a fair amount of scouting for us and had coached at the university level. He was also an assistant coach with the London Knights of the OHL. Paul had a very good teaching position in London and I advised him not to take the job unless he could get a leave of absence from teaching for one year. He was able to do so and moved to Kingston for the 1992-93 season.

At the start of the third year, we had too many overage players, and it looked like Kingston-born Tony Cimarello might not make our team. With his permission, I traded Tony to the Detroit Junior Red Wings, but I got a call from Jimmy Rutherford, the GM of Detroit, who asked me, "If Tony won't report here, does that mean that the deal is still final and I owe you the draft choices we agreed to?"

"What do you mean . . . what is going on?

"Well, he told me this morning that he wouldn't report."

I smelled a skunk in the woodpile somewhere and said, "What does he want to do? He can't play here."

"He said he wants to continue at Queen's University and play in Belleville with the Bulls."

I suspected that Larry Mavety had talked to Tony after we had made the trade. So, I immediately called Mav, who seemed a little surprised when I said, "Okay, let's get to it, what do you want? I'm talking about Tony Cimarello. I traded him yesterday to Detroit and Jimmy Rutherford called me this morning and said he wanted to play in Belleville and continue going to Queen's, so I think your fine hand is behind this somewhere." Mav continued to protest that he had nothing to do with this, but then said he would like to trade for Tony. Mav gave me a fourth-round draft choice for Tony, plus the rights to Mike Yacknuk and Aaron Sussex. With that draft choice, we took goaltender Tyler Moss, who along with Marc Lamothe gave us the best one-two goaltending punch in the league.

In our third year, with Paul Cook as coach, our team played better, but in the end, we missed the playoffs again. Paul returned to teaching full-time, though he did some scouting for us. Shortly after that, I got a call from Pat Morris of Newport Sports asking me if I would be interested in David Allison as coach of the Frontenacs. David had been coaching in the American Hockey League and the East Coast Hockey League, but he wanted to move to the OHL to get a better build on his future. I was keenly interested in this proposal and drove to Richmond, Virginia where David was coaching.

He seemed like my kind of guy, with my passion for hockey, a good sense of humor, and a thorough knowledge of hockey. Almost then and there, we made a deal, subject to Bob meeting him, too.

After missing the playoffs the previous two seasons, our fortunes seemed to be looking up with the hiring of David as our coach for the 1992-93 season. Our first-round draft choice that year was Eric Lindros' brother, Brett Lindros, who had played with St. Michael's the year before in Tier II hockey. He was a big kid, only 16 years of age, and rated second over-all in the final Central Scouting List. A month or so before the draft, I received a call from Bonnie Lindros, Brett's mother, asking me whom I intended to take in the OHL draft. She was canvassing all of the teams.

"I'm glad you called. We hope to take Brett, if he is still available."

"That's foolish," she said. "He's not going to play in the OHL, he's going to play with the University of Michigan and you will just be wasting a draft choice."

"Bonnie, I'm still going to take him. If he doesn't report, then at least he won't be playing against me. The only way I can rebuild this team is by taking the best players available and that's what I intend to do." The night before the draft, Bonnie called me again and we replayed the same question and answer. And true to my word, we did draft him the next day.

I spent most of that summer meeting with Bonnie and Carl Lindros, not with Brett. His parents seemed to want to keep him away from me. Carl worked for an accounting firm in Toronto that had a little conference room where we would meet. After one of those meetings, Carl told me this later, Bonnie said to him, "Do you know, Carl, I'm starting to get to like that fella." Just before training camp started, I was able to set up a meeting with Bonnie, Carl, and Brett at Horseshoe Valley Inn, which was located not too far from their cottage. Bonnie was still adamant that Brett was not coming to

Kingston, but as we nattered back and forth, I heard Brett say, "I want to play in the OHL."

I immediately produced an OHL playing card and said to Brett, "Sign this." Bonnie objected for a moment before asking Carl if he agreed with Brett. "Yes, I think it will be all right," he said.

After that, when people asked me what I did for the summer, I'd say, "I spent my summer with Bonnie and Carl Lindros." I liked Bonnie Lindros. She wanted the best for her boys. Over the next few years, we became good friends, and on the day of the NHL draft when Brett was selected by the New York Islanders, they invited me to join them at their home with the rest of the family to celebrate.

After the NHL draft, the Islanders were determined to sign Brett and play him. Don Maloney, the coach of the Islanders, called me a couple of times to talk about Brett. I told him that Brett was a good kid and that he was playing better each game and developing nicely. I stressed that he needed another year of junior. I thought he might even become as good as Eric. Despite what I had said, the Islanders moved him into the NHL the next season. Brett's a big kid, everybody knows that, but he had suffered a concussion while playing for the Olympic team. There are tons of guys in the NHL as big as Brett, though, and it wasn't long before he suffered a few more concussions. These head injuries finished his career . . . far, far too early. In my opinion, he left junior hockey before he was physically ready to play in the NHL.

Besides Brett Lindros and goaltender Tyler Moss, we selected Duncan Fader, a young lad from Dartmouth, Nova Scotia, defenceman Jason Disher, who had played for Aylmer Junior Bs the previous year, and Todd White of Kanata, who was rated among the top prospects available. We took him in the 13th round on what we like to call "a flyer" because he wanted to play college hockey in the United States. I was never able to convince him to come to Kingston. He went on to play in the NHL with the

Chicago Blackhawks. We added this group of rookies to our complement of veterans — Keli Corpse, David Stewart, Nathan Lafayette, Chris Gratton, and Craig Rivet. Chris and Craig went on to star in the NHL. We had great goaltending in Marc Lamothe and Tyler Moss, who both went on to the NHL.

In David Allison's rookie year as an OHL coach, we finished with 36 wins, 19 losses and 11 ties for 83 points – good enough for second in the Leyden Division.

In the playoffs that year we opened against North Bay and won the final game of the series 5-4, to eliminate the Centennials in five games. In the second round, we eliminated Oshawa in six games. That win moved us into the Leyden Division final against the Peterborough Petes, who had finished first in the final league standings. The Petes eliminated us in six games. Despite this loss, the 1992-93 year had been a resounding success: we not only returned the team to respectability, but climbed all the way to second place after having missed the playoffs the previous two seasons. We had packed the Kingston Memorial Centre for the playoffs. We were geared up to sell season tickets on the strength of this performance on the ice, and we sold the highest number of season tickets ever – over 1,700 in a 3,000-seat arena. More than half of the patrons for 1993-94 were season ticket holders.

Heading into the June draft for that season, we had the 15th pick over-all because of our high finish in the standings the previous year, but we still managed to grab another big-time player with our first pick in centerman Chad Kilger from Cornwall. Like Todd White, Chad had told everyone in the OHL that he was not going to play in the OHL but rather was going to go to a U.S. college. His father Bob had played for me with the Oshawa Generals for a couple of years and I knew him well. Bob was now the Member of Parliament for the riding of Stormont-Dundas. On draft day, I didn't think it was time for the faint hearted to take over. Although Chad

324 | The Bird

was rated No. 1 on most teams draft lists, when it became time for us to draft, he was still available, and I was eventually able to persuade him to sign with the Frontenacs.

When I called Bob to see if Chad was sincere about playing NCAA hockey in the United States, he replied, "That's the way he is leaning and the family is not going to interfere with his decision, so it seems that he will not be playing in the OHL."

"I can't believe that as a member of the Canadian government you would allow your boy to go to the United States to play." I asked Bob where he was going to be on draft day, so I got the phone number and told him I'd be in touch.

We had the 15th position in the draft that year, but Chad had been so convincing that he wouldn't play in the OHL that all the teams ahead of us passed on him. When the 14th player was selected, we called for a time-out, and I told Ross Ainsworth, our chief scout, that I wanted him to select Chad Kilger. All of our other scouts looked at me in amazement. Ross said, "Don't tell me we're going to go through another summer like last summer. You lucked out with Brett Lindros, but don't count on it happening again." When we selected Chad, there was a great murmur throughout the building.

We had about an hour before our next selection, so I went out to my car and phoned Bob Kilger. "Bob, it's Wren, we got him."

"You're like a bloody dog with a bone. You never quit."

"Do me one favor. Give me 30 days to talk to you, your wife, and Chad before you do anything else."

"Okay, I'll do that, but I still don't think he's going to play."

Over the next 30 days, I talked to them several times before we met at the Holiday Inn in Trenton. Chad and his parents agreed that he would sign to play in Kingston.

Like Chris Gratton and Brett Lindros before him, Chad was drafted at 18 by an NHL team, the Anaheim Mighty Ducks, another expansion team. They turned Chad pro shortly after the draft, and he, too, was elevated to the NHL with junior eligibility still in front of him. If these three had played their full number of eligible years with the Frontnacs, they would have been on the same team. To this day, the Frontenacs are still the only Major Junior A team in Canada to have lost three underage players, for three straight years, to the NHL.

That year, we also drafted Brian Scott, Ken Boone, Cail McLean, and bantam-aged defenceman Marc Moro, the son of Tony Moro, a football player in the Canadian Football League. Marc eventually became captain of the Frontenacs.

We looked like a championship team, but we finished fifth in the Leyden Division that year. We met the Belleville Bulls in the opening round of the playoffs. It was a strange series indeed: we lost all three games at home and the series 4-2.

When the season ended, David Allison was extremely disappointed. "You know, Wren, I came here, to Junior A, to groom myself for a pro career, to work with kids who are heading for the National League. I've had two years here and it's been great, but I've got a couple of offers to move into pro hockey." Reluctantly, David and I parted company, but I still keep in touch with him regularly. After a brief stint as head coach of the Ottawa Senators in the NHL, he went behind the bench with Milwaukee in the American Hockey League.

After David left, I had heard rumors that Gary Agnew was not going to be retained by the London Knights, where he had coached for several years. Gary and I were able to structure a contract for him to join the Frontenacs. In the draft of that season, we took Chris Allen, a big, tall, gangly kid who had the hardest shot from the point of any player in the league. We also selected Rob Mailloux and John Hultberg, who had played goal in Tier II with Oshawa. John was from Chicago. He had had a bout with cancer and had missed a big portion of the year in Oshawa, but now had a clean bill of health and was anxious to report. We then claimed Colin Chaulk from Mississauga, David Bourque from Gloucester, and Jason Sands, a centerman from the small village of Battersea, just north of Kingston. Our first six picks from that year all made the team, which meant that our scouting staff had really done their jobs.

This was the best team we ever had in Kingston. We finished first in the Eastern Division, the only team in the history of the Kingston franchise to accomplish that feat. To win the title, we had to fight tooth and nail with Oshawa. Heading into the final game of the season with Oshawa, we were tied in the standings. In the second minute of play, Larry Courville of Oshawa slashed David Ling over the hand, breaking his thumb. There was no penalty called on the play. The refereeing for that game was some of the worst I had ever seen. Ling had finished second in the league scoring race to Oshawa's Marc Savard, Despite losing our star player, we rallied together that day and won to finish first.

In the first round of the playoffs, we took a bye that year, and then met our archrivals, the Belleville Bulls, in the second round. With Ling only operating with one good hand, we fell in six games to the Bulls to put an end to what was a most exciting season. Equipped with a playing cast, David Ling still led our team in post-season scoring.

At the June draft in 1995, we selected Matt Price and Matt Bradley, a right winger from Stittsville. Matt Price didn't see a lot of ice time in his first year, and I really feel that hampered his progress. He never developed to the full potential that we saw in him when we drafted him. Late in his career, we traded Matt to Sarnia.

Matt Bradley was leaning towards playing with a U.S. college team until I was able to sit down with his father, Paul, just prior to training camp. Under NCAA rules, a player is allowed to attend an OHL training camp for 48 hours before losing his eligibility. I told Paul Bradley, who was the Mayor of Stittsville at the time, that I would not keep his son beyond the 48 hours if he chose to leave. I remember teasing him that in a democracy, his son should have the chance to choose where he played. "I think you've made your point," he responded. "We will come to training camp."

I spent the first two days at the camp with Matt's dad explaining the education process we had in Kingston. Finally, Paul said, "Let's bring Matt into your office and let Matt make his own decision." When Matt came in, his father explained, "Matt, I have talked to your mother and she is far more against you playing in the OHL than I am, but we both agreed that at least it's your life, and you should make the decision." Without a bit of hesitation, Matt said, "I want to play in the OHL."

With that his dad said, "Then this discussion is over. Get back out on the ice." He made our team and eventually the San Jose Sharks in the NHL as well.

Our third pick that season was had been the talk of hockey the year before – Mike Olivera. Mike had played Junior B hockey in Sarnia when he was only 14 years of age and had burned up the league, but he was still not eligible for the OHL draft the following year because he was still too young, and he sort of sulked his way through the next season. If he had he performed in his second year in Sarnia as he did in his first, he would have certainly been a first-round choice. With the Frontenacs, he had some brilliant games, but he never ever regained the edge he had as a 14-year-old.

Following Olivera, we selected Mike Tillson of Pickering, the grandson of one of our scouts, John Trempe, Justin Davis from Ottawa, goaltender Bujar Amidovski, and Bill Minkhorst, a winger from the Brockville area.

All our selections in the first seven rounds made the team, but we had lost a ton of players to graduation. In the final standings that year, we finished fifth and made the playoffs, but lost in six games to the Peterborough Petes in the first series.

In the 1996-97 draft, our first round selection was Kevin Grimes, a big, rugged defenceman from Ottawa, who later became a first-round pick of the Colorado Avalanche. I had a tough time getting Kevin signed. We met several times over the summer, but made little or no headway until I sent a fax to his agent, Larry Kelly, late in the summer with our final offer and with an ultimatum that if it wasn't accepted within 48 hours, the offer would be withdrawn. The 48-hour time period passed, and I notified Kelly that the offer had indeed been withdrawn. The next day, I received a call from Larry saying that Kevin had come into his office that day and now wanted to sign. "You wouldn't give us a day's grace?" he asked. I stipulated that the signed contract had to be in my office within 12 hours. I received the contract with time to spare.

Our other selections from that draft who made the team were Jonathon Schill, goaltender Curtis Cruickshank, Kevin Malcolm, and Greg Willers. Although we made the playoffs with a fourth-place finish, for the second straight year, we were matched against the Peterborough Petes, who eliminated the Frontenacs in five games.

At the end of this season, Gary Agnew left the team, despite having a year remaining on his contract, to return to the London Knights. In this world of revolving coaches, we had the good fortune to re-hire Larry Mavety for the 1997-98 season. Our first draft choice was Jamie Young, an underage player from Thunder Bay. That year we had scouted the all-Ontario Bantam final in North Bay to look over the top-rated draft prospects. There were several prospects on the Thunder Bay team, who went on to win the championship, including Jamie Young. I checked the Central scouting list and he was rated in the No. 7 position. Late in the season that year, Jamie Young suffered a serious knee injury that finished his junior career. We were forced to release him the next season. The same year, the Sudbury Wolves selected Taylor Pyatt from the Thunder Bay team. He is now a member of the Buffalo Sabres, having turned pro with still another year of junior eligibility remaining.

We selected another underage player in Mike Zigomanis, a center who played in Wexford the year before. Zigomanis had indicated that he would only play in the Toronto area, but we drafted him nevertheless. "Ziggy" was another player who took all summer to sign, and in the end he was still unsigned when we opened training camp. I was staying at the Ambassador Hotel in Kingston and had made arrangements for the Zigomanis family to stay there as well. On the second day of training camp, after several meetings, I was able to convince them to sign with Kingston. "Ziggy" became team captain in the 2000-2001 season and was drafted by the Sabres. Zigomanis was injured at the end of two seasons he played in Kingston, and without him, it was very difficult for the team to advance.

We then selected Sean Griffin, a big defenceman from the Ottawa area, D.J. Maracle, a rugged winger from Deseronto, who had played for the Quinte Hawks, Danny Gould, a goaltender from Brampton, Colin Scotland, a Maritimer who had also played with the Quinte Hawks, and Eric Braff, a big rugged defenceman.

We made the playoffs again that year, and for the first time since David Allison's first year as coach, managed to get by the first round as we eliminated the Oshawa Generals in a series that went the full seven games. In the second round, we met Gary Agnew's London Knights, who eliminated us in five games.

In the summer of 1998, we had sold the hockey club in a five-year buyout plan to the Springer family of Kingston. Norm Springer wanted the club for his two sons, Doug and Michael. Doug was a real hockey nut and he asked me if I would groom him over the next couple of years in the inner workings of hockey ownership and operation.

I remember telling him early in our relationship that there was only one university that gave a course in hockey ownership and the art of being a general manager.

"I didn't think there was any university that offered that course," Doug commented.

"Oh, yes there's one. It's called the Wren Blair Institute and I can tell you that it is very difficult to pass that course."

In the 1998-99 draft, we selected Brett Clouthier, a tough left winger from Arnprior. Clouthier played on our No. 1 line with Mike Zigomanis and was drafted by the New Jersey Devils. We also drafted right winger Morgan McCormick from Guelph, underage centerman Darryl Thompson from Barrie, Nathan Tennant, a bantam-age defenceman from Chalk River, Shayne Kanyo, a right winger from Georgetown, and left winger Andrew Ianiero, a superb pick from Hamilton. We made the playoffs in the final game of the regular season when we hammered the Peterborough Petes 8-0. That meant a playoff meeting with the first-place Barrie Colts, who eliminated us in five games.

In the 1999-2000 draft, we selected Cory Stillman from Lindsay. We had seen Stillman go head-to-head with Jay McClement, another highly-rated player who had played with the Kingston Voyageurs, and in that particular game I felt that Stillman had outplayed McClement. When I said this out loud at the game to Paul Cook, a woman sitting right in front of us, turned around to interject, "I couldn't help but overhear some of your conversation. Are you scouting for the OHL?" We said yes. "Did I hear you say that you really liked Cory Stillman? Well, that's nice to hear because I am Cory Stillman's mother."

"I was born in Lindsay," I told her, "so us Lindsay people have to stick together." Shortly after that, I called Cory's father and talked with him about the possibility of signing Cory if we drafted him. I explained that if he didn't get a pro contract when he graduated from junior, we would also look after his university education for four years, as all OHL teams do. Based on that information, Cory's father told us to go ahead and draft him. Cory soon became one of the leaders on the Frontenacs team.

That year, we also drafted Brad Horan, J.F. Seguin, Matt Junkins, goalie Mike Smith, and goalie Glenn Ridler. While we drafted these promising young goalies, we knew we needed another with experience. We knew that Bert Templeton had goalies in their final years and he certainly wouldn't go into the season with both of them. Bert was not sure on which one he would keep, either Andrew Raycroft or Mike Gorman. We said it didn't matter to us. As it turned out, he dealt Raycroft to us. That turned out to be one of the best deals Mav and I ever made. Raycroft was selected as Goaltender of the Year in the OHL and went on to vie for national honors in the Canadian Hockey League. He turned pro with the Boston Bruins. We finished the season in third place in our division and fifth in the conference. We drew the Sudbury Wolves in the first round of the playoffs and lost in five games.

For the 2000-01 season, we drafted Justin McCutcheon, a 17-year-old, and two bantam-age players, Brody Todd and Sean Langdon. McCutcheon and Todd both made the team, while Langdon split his time between Tier II and the Frontenacs. Late in the season, our top player, Mike Zigomanis, dislocated his shoulder and was unable to play in the playoffs. Once again, we met those lucky Belleville Bulls, who always seem to catch us when the injury bug has our team, and we were eliminated in the first round.

The years of operating the Kingston Frontenac Major Junior A Hockey Club were especially rewarding. To my delight, Bob Attersley and I were re-united in a hockey ownership situation, together with our mutually good friend Don Anderson. Among the highlights of those years was seeing Keli Corpse win the Humanitarian Award in the Ontario Hockey League in his final year of junior. It was thrilling in 1997 to win the Eastern Division Championship of the OHL with Gary Agnew as our coach, the first time that a Kingston junior club had ever won this championship. It was exciting to see David Ling, a second round draft choice, win the OHL and CHL Player of the Year Award in his final year. It was also exciting to see Andrew Raycroft win the OHL and CHL Player of the Year Award. Mav and I had traded with Sudbury for Raycroft and he had an outstanding year for us in Kingston the next year. A number of other good goaltenders played for the Frontenacs during those years, notably Marc Lamothe and Tyler Moss.

We were the only operation that I know of in the CHL that had three players drafted in a row by the NHL at 18 years of age. First was Chris Gratton, followed the next year by Brett Lindros, and then the next year by Chad Kilger. These players were big losses to the Frontenacs because all three were eligible to play another year with our club. I sometimes think what a great team we might have had if these three lads had not gone to the NHL at 18 years of age. No amount of money paid by the NHL for underage players can match this loss in potential for winning and box-office income. Other memorable players during these Kingston years were Mike Zigomanis, Sean Avery, Brett Cloutier, Matt Bradley, Nathan Lafayette, and Cory Stillman.

I had extremely good relations with most, if not all, of our coaches in those Kingston years. Larry Mavety and I always worked very closely and very well together. I also had an outstanding and still have a very lasting relationship with David Allison. David and I talk two or three times a year and always have a few good laughs. I also still talk from time to time with Gary Agnew, who at this time is the coach of the Syracuse Crunch in the American Hockey League.

I also enjoyed working with our scouting staff in those years, first with Floyd Crawford, then with Ross Ainsworth, Paul Cook, and

Wayne Smith. In the later years, I added John Trempe to our scouting staff. John had scouted for years with Bert Templeton in North Bay. Yes, they were good years.

PROFILE

David Branch

I FIRST SAW DAVID BRANCH AS a hockey player with Toronto Marlboros Midgets at the George Bell Park Arena. He was a pretty good defenceman. After scouting David that year, I received a list of the counselors we had hired for the Haliburton Hockey Camp our first year of operation. I was delightfully surprised to see David Branch's name on that list. David was a CIT (counselor-in-training) his first year. The kids liked him; the staff liked him; and our chief cook, Bernice Stewart, was fond of David and vice-versa.

A couple of weeks after the camp first opened, I had to go to Minnesota for a week of meetings. When I came back to the camp, I couldn't help but notice this old wreck of a car in the parking lot. Was this a joke or did someone actually own this car? I thought. I asked Jim Gregory, my partner, about the car, and he laughed, "Oh, some of the counselors and counselors-in-training bought it."

"Jim, do these fellows have insurance on this car?" He said he didn't really know, but assumed that they did. I then asked him if he could round up the counselors involved and bring them into the conference room so I could have a chat with them.

A few minutes later, one by one, they trudged in and sat down at our round conference table. "Mr. Gregory tells me that you gentlemen are the proud owners of that relic of a car that is sitting in our parking lot." They nodded in agreement. "Boys, I have a few questions. Do you have insurance on the car?" Oh yeah, they said. "Well, what is the name of the company?" They said they couldn't remember the company name. So I continued. "Do your parents know that you all own this car?" Oh yeah, they all know. "I'm concerned about this car," I said. "There must be insurance on it, because if anything happens to you boys while you're driving it without insurance, Mr. Gregory and I would be responsible. What I would like to do is investigate a little further and contact some of your parents to make sure they are fully aware of the purchase of this car and the ramifications that go with it."

One of the counselors spoke up and said I wouldn't be able get a hold of his parents because they were away on vacation. Everyone else in the room said the same thing. "Now look boys, let's level with one another. First of all, I don't believe your parents know that you have this car to drive back and forth on this dangerous camp road. Secondly, I doubt very much you have insurance on that car. And thirdly, you were not brought here to own a car and go back and forth to town, but rather to work with the kids. You get one day a week off and I believe you would be wise to spend it around camp in any event. Finally, I doubt whether Mr. Gregory and I are going to permit you fellows to have that car around camp, whether it is insured or not or whether your parents know about it or not. It is simply too much exposure for us and you are all too young for this responsibility. I would like you to now put your car keys up on the table for me."

At this point, David Branch became the spokesman of the group. "I don't believe you can tell us whether or not we can have this car," he said.

"David, you are absolutely right. As long as you *don't* work here, I can't tell you that. However, as long as you work here, I can tell you, so get those keys up on the table." After I warned them that I was going to sell the car back to the dealer, and that they would likely lose money on this transaction, I repeated my demand. "Look boys, I'm not kidding. Either turn those car keys over to me or quit your jobs and get that car out of here." They continued to stare at me for a few more moments, but gradually, one by one the keys arrived on the table. I then called the dealer, Lloyd Coneybeare, and he came and picked up the car. I never found out whether or not they got the full amount of money back or not, but I believe that was one of the first lessons David and the rest of them had in growing up in the real world. David and several of the other boys stayed on for many years. David worked his way all the way up to assistant camp director before he left. He was a great asset.

When David 'graduated' from our camp, he asked Jim Gregory to assist him in applying for a job as the assistant to Bill Hanley, the Secretary-Manager of the Ontario Hockey Association. Jim advised David that he would discuss the matter with me, and if I thought he would be a good candidate for the job, we would talk to Bill Hanley. Jim and I knew Bill quite well because of positions as General Managers with the Toronto Marlboros and Oshawa Generals in the Junior A league. The OHA office was directly across the street from Jim's office in Maple Leaf Gardens, so we simply walked across the street and recommended David for the job. Although Bill had already spoken to a number of applicants, he agreed to interview David. He was impressed with David and subsequently hired him. That's how David got his start in hockey administration.

David worked with Bill for a few years until another job came up. Gordon Juckes, the Secretary-Manager of the Canadian Amateur Hockey Association, headquartered in Ottawa, retired. With a strong recommendation from Bill Hanley, David succeeded Juckes. About two years later, the Major Junior A League broke away from the OHA and formed a own separate division, the Ontario Hockey League (OHL). The league was still under the CAHA umbrella, as it is today, but the teams operated independently with their own rules and regulations. Bill Beagan, a former Commissioner of the International Hockey League, was the first OHL Commissioner, but he had to leave that post after seven or eight months. David decided to apply to the OHL Board of Governors for the position, and after a couple of interviews, he was selected unanimously to take over as the Commissioner of the OHL, a position he still holds today. In addition to that post, he is also President of the Canadian Hockey League, which is comprised of the three Major Junior A hockey leagues in the nation – the Western League, the Quebec League, and the Ontario Hockey League. During my years with the Kingston Frontenacs Junior A team, I have served on the OHL Board of Governors and have watched David manage the expansion of the league and the transfer of several franchises with great skill. A few years ago, when the NHL Board of Governors was searching for a new league president, they interviewed David for job, but they decided to hire Gary Bettman instead. David now lives in Whitby with his wife Charlene and their three sons.

David Branch is one of the finest hockey administrators in the world. I am honored to call him my friend. I even let him drive his own car now.

The Saginaw Spirit Joins the OHL Junior A League

14

A LITTLE OVER A YEAR AGO, SOME business people in Saginaw, led by former mayor Paul Wendler, commented to me that there had been no hockey team in the Greater Saginaw area for more than three years. They also pointed out that the Saginaw Civic Center was in a poor financial situation, and that the City of Saginaw had declared that any losses from the operation of the Civic Center would not be funded after December 31, 2000. We discussed this problem with Marc McGill, CEO for the County of Saginaw, and nearly everyone felt that it really should be the County, not the City, that operated the Civic Center. Saginaw County embraces nine townships and a couple of smaller cities around the city.

The Saginaw Civic Center includes a beautiful arena, seating over 5,000 people, attached to that a banquet area called Unity Hall, with a couple of extra small meeting rooms where a banquet for over 1200 people could be held, and attached to that is the beautiful Heritage Theater, with a full size Broadway stage and over 2,000 seats for such productions. I don't know any other small community in either Canada or the United States that has such a beautiful building embracing all levels of entertainment.

Eventually, a committee was formed to explore the possibility of the County funding the Civic Center, and the County held a vote in May 2001 to see if the taxpayers would agree to less than a 1 percent mill rate increase to operate the Civic Center properly. Many people felt that vote wouldn't carry, but being an ever-positive person, I passed on the sentiment that it would carry. On May 8, 2001, the vote was held. Many voters from the outlying townships voted against the proposal, but as the votes from the townships close to the City of Saginaw and the City of Saginaw itself were tallied, the result was 19,000 in favor versus 16,000 opposed.

After securing County support for the Civic Center, now re-named the Saginaw County Event Center, Mr. Wendler asked me about trying to start another high-calibre hockey club. I was thrilled to take on this challenge, especially so out of respect for the hockey fans who had supported my Saginaw Gears club so well back in the 1970s and 1980s. I told Mr. Wendler and Mr. McGill that there were two things I would not do this time around. Previously, I was the sole owner of the hockey club, but made it clear that this time around I would not own the team because of my advancing years. I also said the only league where I would operate a team was the OHL Junior A League.

A successful automobile dealer and well-respected family man, Mr. Dick Garber, showed an interest in owning a hockey team, but in my early meetings he had said that his father had always told him to operate only a business that he was familiar with. "Wren I am an automobile salesman, first and foremost," he said. I prevailed, keep-ing in touch with him for nearly seven months until finally he agreed to become the owner of an OHL team in Saginaw, providing we could get an expansion franchise in the OHL. In early November 2001, we put a bid into the OHL for an expansion club in Saginaw to begin play in the 2002 OHL hockey season. The Board of Governors of the OHL turned down our request.

It became clear that the only route available to us would be to purchase another OHL club operating in the league. Shortly there-after, we learned that the North Bay Centennials Club was looking to sell their franchise. In December, the owners of the Centennials, Mr. Ted Thomson and Dr. Bill Finnis, accepted Mr. Garber's offer. However, the people in North Bay dug in their heels and put up a mighty fight to retain their club. Both Mr. Garber and I understood their position, but in the end they could not gather enough money to match Mr. Garber's offer. On February 12, 2002, the Board of Governors of the Ontario Hockey League approved the transfer of the franchise from North Bay to Saginaw.

Shortly after the franchise was awarded, I suggested to Mr. Garber that we should hire Mr. Costa Papista, the President of the North Bay operation, to become the President and General Manager of our club. Dick was concerned that I might be eliminating myself for that position unfairly, but I assured him that because of my age, it was a better fit for me to become a 'Senior' Consultant and let Costa assume the heavy burden of the day-to-day operations. We hired former Saginaw Gears star Dennis Desrosiers to coach the team. Dennis was the first player I signed to a contract to play with the Gears and the most popular player to ever don a Gears sweater. When his playing career ended, he had worked as a coach and manager.

Mr. Garber arranged a "Name The Team Contest" and about 10,000 fans submitted names over the Internet. The name of the team became "Saginaw Spirit" – a name submitted by over 45 fans. The club held a draw from the names of everyone who had submitted "Spirit" and Jessica Whitmill, a student of Saginaw's Handley Elementary School, was the winner. The club colours were selected as red, white, and blue and the uniform design was patterned after the U.S. Olympic Team sweaters from the Olympic Games in Salt Lake City. A team logo showing a patriotic bald eagle has also been very popular. The Saginaw Spirit was scheduled to open in Saginaw at the Saginaw County Event Center on Saturday, September 21, 2002, against the Sarnia Sting.

I believe that Dick Garber will be an outstanding Owner and Governor in the Ontario Hockey League. I am excited to work with the off ice team that he has put together. Costa Papista, our President and General Manager, Dennis Desrosiers our Coach, Jamey Hicks, our Assistant Coach, and Dan Halliburton, our new full time Director of Scouting. Some of the former North Bay scouts will remain with the Saginaw staff, probably a few really good ones who have yet to be named. Other good people on our staff are Cameron Knowles, our Director of Media & Community Relations, Craig Goslin, our Vice-President of Sales & Marketing, and Kae Pankow, whom I work with closely as she is our Director of Group Sales.

Yes, it is exciting to see this great on ice and off ice team that Dick Garber is assembling, and I look forward to being around for a while longer to watch this thrilling new franchise unfold. Dick's decision to build this franchise and to have me closely involved has really rekindled my hockey life.

AND SO . . . I'M BACK IN Saginaw again . . . back in the game I love . . . such a long way from that day in Olso, Norway as I watched the snow fall outside my hotel room, waiting to coach my Whitby Dunlops to the Word Championship . . .

As I write this epilogue, I am 76 years of age and feel greatly blessed still to be involved passionately in the game that I love, the greatest game in the world. I have now been active in hockey for over 53 years. As I reflect on those years, I remember, warmly, so many of my colleagues. I owe such a debt of gratitude to the more than 1100 players who have played for my various clubs over the years. Also to the many coaches who worked with me. Without good players and without competent coaches, one could ever have the success that I have enjoyed. I recall those early days scouting for the Boston Bruins and the other scouts I was associated with in that era — Lou Passadore with Montreal and the New York Rangers; Donnie Graham and Jimmy Skinner with the Detroit Red Wings; Scotty Bowman and Claude Ruel with the Montreal Canadiens;

Bob Wilson and Jack Davison with the Chicago Black Hawks; and Bob Davidson with the Toronto Maple Leafs, later assisted by my great friend Jim Gregory, who also doubled as the General Manager of the Toronto Marlboros and Toronto St. Mikes. Harold Cotton had been the Chief Scout of the Bruins for 25 years before I came along. I had the privilege to have signed the great Bobby Orr.

I recall vividly my exciting years in the IHL. Two or three of my better associates in that era were Ken Ullyot, the owner and General Manager of the Fort Wayne Komets, Morris Snider the General Manager and President of the Port Huron Flags, Bill Beagan, the Commissioner of the IHL in those days, and Frank Gallagher who owned the Flint Generals. Of course, my years in the expanded NHL were exciting and my colleagues were great men. Bill Torey, originally the General Manager of the Oakland Seals and then the GM of the New York Islanders, and I enjoyed many long conversations late into the night. Jack Riley, who ran the Pittsburgh Penguins remains a very good friend of mine, as does "Bud" Poile, the first General Manager of the Philadelphia Flyers . . . and so many others. My brother Gerald Blair scouted extensively in those years, as did the former great players Billy Taylor and "Red" Sullivan.

There are dozens of others I worked with who still mean a great deal to me . . . I have not forgotten them. I've been extremely blessed to be a part of the game of hockey for so many years.

Acknowledgements

THE AUTHOR WISHES TO acknowledge the following people for their help in many things involving the writing of this autobiography:

I wish to acknowledge my daughter Jill Blair for the untold hours she put into typing this manuscript and for her great help in editing.

I also wish to thank George Gross, Corporate Sports Editor of the *Toronto Sun* for writing the preface to this book; and Ron Brown, former Sports Editor of the *Kingston Whig Standard* for helping me find Quarry Press to publish this book originally and also for recording items that I recorded on tapes for the manuscript and for writing the introduction.

I also wish to thank my son-in law Peter Krahule for his technical help on the computer and also for helping to edit portions of the manuscript, and also my son Danny and his wife Libby for helping to edit this copy as well. I'd like to also thank our granddaughter Jennifer for helping edit portions of this book.

I would also like to thank Normie Defelice for locating pictures of the Clinton Comets the team.

I also wish to thank the close to 1100 players who played for me over more than 50 years in hockey and all the coaches and scouts who worked for me on various clubs over the years, including the late Ted O'Connor who was my Chief Scout in Minnesota years ago. Also the late Harold Cotton who was my Director of Player

Personnel in Minnesota and my brother Gerald Blair, who made many contributions over the years to my hockey career.

I also wish to thank Mr. Bob Hilderley, Publisher of Quarry Press, and Mr. Joe March, Director of Publishing at Stewart House Publishing, for their great assistance.